French Workbook

by Laura K. Lawless

for dummies®
A Wiley Brand

French Workbook For Dummies®

Published by: **John Wiley & Sons, Inc.**, 111 River Street, Hoboken, NJ 07030-5774, www.wiley.com

Copyright © 2023 by John Wiley & Sons, Inc., Hoboken, New Jersey

Published simultaneously in Canada

For general information on our other products and services, please contact our Customer Care Department within the U.S. at 877-762-2974, outside the U.S. at 317-572-3993, or fax 317-572-4002. For technical support, please visit www.wiley.com/techsupport.

Wiley publishes in a variety of print and electronic formats and by print-on-demand. Some material included with standard print versions of this book may not be included in e-books or in print-on-demand. If this book refers to media such as a CD or DVD that is not included in the version you purchased, you may download this material at http://booksupport.wiley.com. For more information about Wiley products, visit www.wiley.com.

Library of Congress Control Number: 2022946533

ISBN 978-1-119-98203-6 (pbk); ISBN 978-1-119-98205-0 (ebk); ISBN 978-1-119-98204-3 (ebk)

SKY10036979_101922

Contents at a Glance

Table of Contents

Introduction

French is one of the world's great languages. It's a native language on five continents, and it's one of the most common languages in the world. Millions of people in more than 30 countries speak it as a native language, and millions more like you want to learn it because of school, work, travel, or cultural understanding — or simply because they just love how it sounds.

The French take their language pretty seriously, and the **Académie française** (or *French Academy*) has assumed the role of protecting the language's purity for more than 350 years — although not everyone listens to the Académie. French is a working language of many major international organizations, so if you're looking for a job with the United Nations, the International Olympic Committee, the International Red Cross, or Interpol, for example, understanding and speaking French gives you an additional language to wow 'em with in the interview.

Regardless of whether you're planning to do business in France or Quebec, prepping for a trip to French-speaking Africa, trying to pass that next exam, or just looking for ways to impress the love of your life, this book can help you figure out how to speak, write, and understand French.

About This Book

French Workbook For Dummies is a combination reference book and workbook for people new to the French language. It's not a textbook, and you don't have to read it from cover to cover or in any particular order. Just take a look at the Table of Contents at the front of the book or Index at the rear to find the grammar point you want to understand or practice, and then flip to that page. The Appendixes offer quick-reference ways to look up unfamiliar French words, conjugate verbs, and remember details such as which verbs need **être** in the **passé composé**.

I divided the book into six parts, with each part broken into chapters on related topics. From using the present tense, to remembering the past, to looking forward to the future, I explain all about French verbs. I also talk about adjectives and adverbs, questions and negation, greetings and social niceties — everything you need to know to communicate effectively in French.

Not only do you read about French in this book, but you use it, as well. The self-contained chapters are divided into sections and include plenty of examples and practice exercises to make sure you understand what you've just read. The Answer Key at the end of each chapter lets you check yourself as you go.

Conventions Used in This Book

To make this book as easy to use as possible, I use certain conventions throughout:

>> I **bold** all the French words so that you can spot them immediately.

>> I provide English translations in *italics*. I also italicize English terms that I immediately follow with a definition.

>> Per French writing conventions, I precede question marks and all other two-part punctuation marks — exclamation points, *guillemets* (French quotation marks — **« Bonjour ! »**), colons, and semicolons — with a space.

>> Before each set of practice exercises, I provide an example in Q&A format to show you how to complete the task.

>> When a practice question has more than one correct answer, I provide the most common one.

>> The Answer Key at the end of each chapter provides the solutions to the practice exercises throughout that chapter.

Foolish Assumptions

I wrote this book with the following assumptions about you in mind, dear reader:

>> You're new to the French language.

>> You have little to no knowledge of French grammar.

>> You're looking for practice questions to test yourself and help cement your understanding, or to ensure that you score well on your next French quiz or exam.

>> You want to learn French in order to travel to French-speaking countries or communicate with French-speaking friends and family.

Icons Used in This Book

Like all *For Dummies* books, this one uses icons to indicate certain kinds of content. You can see them in the left-hand column throughout the book. Here's what they mean:

TIP

I use this icon to alert you to info that can save you time and frustration.

REMEMBER

This icon points out important concepts that you need to store in the back of your mind because you use them regularly.

WARNING

This icon highlights potential pitfalls to becoming truly familiar with the French language.

DIFFERENCES

This icon lets you know about key points of difference between French and English, or the varieties of French found in different countries.

PRACTICE

This icon pops up at the beginning of every practice exercise so that you know it's time to put your skills to the test.

Beyond the Book

In addition to the abundance of information and guidance related to embracing French that I provide in this book, you get access to even more help and information online at Dummies. com. Check out this book's online Cheat Sheet by going to www.dummies.com and searching for *French Workbook for Dummies Cheat Sheet*.

Where to Go from Here

French Workbook For Dummies is organized to let you read only what you want to read. Take a look at the Table of Contents (at the front of the book) or the Index (at the back), pick a topic, and go! Or you may want to start in Chapter 1 to figure out how to say *hello* (spoiler alert: the most important word you can know) and *good-bye*. Want to give orders or talk about the past? Then flip to Part 4. It's up to you!

No matter how you choose to read this book, I'm confident that it can help you get comfortable with French. Of course, don't let your practice end with the exercises here. Write to a French pen pal, visit French websites and social media, stream foreign flicks, attempt conversations with your French-speaking friends, or try to translate song lyrics into French while you're stuck in traffic. And when you have a grammar question, come back here and look it up. Pretty soon, the thoughts running through your head may take on a decidedly French flair.

Bon courage ! (*Good luck!*)

1

The Building Blocks of French

Get familiar with the most important word in French (**bonjour !** *hello!*).

Pick up some tips on working with the parts of speech and correctly using a bilingual dictionary.

Introduce yourself to nouns, gender, and number, which provide the foundation for grammatical agreement.

Use French possessives and demonstratives like a pro.

Express yourself with numbers, times, and dates so that you can get to where — and when — you need to go.

Chapter **1**

Getting to Know You

Bonjour ! (*Hello!*) and welcome to the most important chapter in this book and in your entire French language journey. Knowing how to greet people in French is more than just understanding that **bonjour** means *hello*; in fact, this simple word is vital to making sure that all of your interactions start off on the right foot.

In addition to sharing the different French greetings, I explain how to introduce yourself and others, offer tips on being polite, and describe the differences between subject pronouns.

French Greetings

As a kid, you might have been told that *please* is the magic word, but in French, it's definitely **bonjour** (*hello*) or an equivalent greeting (depending on the time of day and your relationship to the person you're talking to). In this section I cover the three primary French greetings that you need to be familiar with.

Hello

DIFFERENCES

In English, it's perfectly normal not to say "hello" in some situations. For example, when approaching a stranger for directions, English speakers are likely to say "excuse me" rather than "hello." In France, however, not using a greeting like **Bonjour** (*Hello*) to start a conversation is considered very rude. Any conversation — even a short one — simply can't begin without **bonjour** or another greeting. In a situation where you need to start with **Excusez-moi** (*Excuse me*), it's important to then add a greeting before anything else or you run the risk of being ignored or given a frosty look followed by a pointed, "Bonjour" in return.

Appropriate French greetings include

>> **bonjour** (*hello*): The greeting commonly used in the morning and afternoon, with anyone and everyone. The French language spoken in France doesn't have specific terms for *good morning* or *good afternoon* — **bonjour** is used for all of these. In comparison, Canadian French does have a different term for *good morning*: **bon matin**.

>> **bonsoir** (*good evening*): As opposed to **bonjour**, which means *hello*, *good morning*, and *good afternoon*, **bonsoir** means *good evening*. I can't give you a definite time when you should switch from **bonjour** to **bonsoir**, but a good rule of thumb is either 6 p.m. or when the sun starts to set, whichever is earlier. You can also take cues from the people around you. If you're in a room full of people all saying **bonsoir** to each other at 3 p.m., you can either be a rebel with **bonjour** or just go with the flow and say **bonsoir**.

>> **salut** (*hi*): Informal — you can and should use **salut** only with friends, family, and kids, at any time of day.

PRACTICE

Mind your manners! Decide which greeting is most appropriate with each person at the time given.

Q. Your cousin at 11 a.m.: _____

A. Salut (*Hi*)

1. The mail carrier at 8 a.m.: _____

2. A friend at 3 p.m.: _____

3. Your boss at 9 a.m.: _____

4. Your brand-new neighbor at 7 p.m.: _____

5. A waitress at 12:30 p.m.: _____

6. Your preschooler son's friend at 8 p.m.: _____

7. Your daughter at 1 p.m.: _____

8. A cashier at 6 p.m.: _____

9. Your spouse at 10 p.m.: _____

10. The plumber at 10 a.m.: _____

How are you?

Many English speakers say, "How are you?" to anyone and everyone, even when they don't expect an answer or assume it will be an automatic, "Fine." For the French, it's just the opposite: They ask the question only when they expect and care about the response. If you casually ask a French cashier or bank teller how they are, for example, you're likely to get a puzzled look in return.

Comment allez-vous ? means *How are you?* and is formal and/or plural, meaning you should use it when talking to either

>> A person with whom you use respectful language

>> More than one person

When talking to just one person with whom you use **tu** (see the section "Tu or vous: The second person," later in this chapter), you can use any of these more informal versions to ask *How are you?*

>> **Comment vas-tu ?**

>> **Comment tu vas ?**

>> **Comment ça va ?**

>> **Ça va ?**

All of these questions mean basically the same thing — *How are you?* — but grammatically, they're a bit different.

To answer any of the questions that begin with **Comment**, you can give a real response, such as **Super, bien sûr, je suis à Paris !** (*Great, of course, I'm in Paris!*), or you can say something non-committal, such as **Bien** (*Fine*) or **Très bien** (*Very good*). In addition, you can answer with **Ça va** (*Fine*).

In contrast, **Ça va ?** literally means *Is it going (well)?* So, in addition to any of the responses just mentioned, you can answer with a simple **Oui** (*Yes*) or **Non** (*No*).

You can also use **Ça va ?** when addressing more than one person with whom you use **tu**, such as your children or a group of friends.

TIP

You absolutely could have a conversation in French that consists of just two words repeated as questions and answers:

- **Ça va ?** (*How's it going?*)

- **Ça va, ça va. Ça va ?** (*Fine, fine. How's it going?*)

- **Ça va.** (*Fine.*)

However, you're more likely to have a few extra words thrown in:

- **Ça va ?** (*How's it going?*)

- **Ça va, merci. Et toi, ca va ?** (*Fine, thanks. And you, is it going well?*)

- **Oui, ça va bien.** (*Yes, fine.*)

Do you want to know how I am? Decide whether you should use **Ça va ?** with each of these people and circle your answer.

Q. A banker   Yes   No

A. No

11. Your daughter   Yes   No

12. Your new neighbors   Yes   No

13. A waitress   Yes   No

14. Your brother   Yes   No

15. A group of friends   Yes   No

16. A cashier   Yes   No

Won't you tell me your name?

When meeting someone for the first time, in addition to saying **Bonjour** (*Hello*), the two parties need to exchange names, or at least have someone else do it for them.

You can ask someone's name by saying either **Comment vous appelez-vous ?** or **Comment t'appelles-tu ?** (*What is your name?*). Your choice here depends on whether you're talking

>> Formally or to more than one person. (**Comment vous appelez-vous ?**)

>> To one person with whom you'll use **tu**. (**Comment t'appelles-tu ?**)

TIP

You may be tempted to think that you should always say **Comment vous appelez-vous ?** — after all, by definition, you're talking to someone you don't know, so **vous** would seem to make sense. But that's not the only criterion for using **vous**. See the section "Tu or vous: The second person," later in this chapter, for the full explanation.

You can answer the question *What is your name?* with any of the next four phrases. With the first two responses, you can provide your first name or your full name:

>> **Je m'appelle . . .** (*My name is . . .*)

>> **Je suis . . .** (*I am . . .*)

These next two phrases are more limited:

>> **Mon nom est . . .** (*My name is . . .*): Can only be used when you give your full name

>> **Mon prénom est . . .** (*My first name is . . .*): Can precede only your first name

You can introduce someone else with the following phrases (which both mean *I'd like to introduce you to . . .*):

» **Je vous présente . . .**

» **Je te présente . . .**

You can also say

» **Il s'appelle . . .** (*His name is . . .*)

» **Elle s'appelle . . .** (*Her name is . . .*)

» In an informal situation, simply **Voici . . .** (*This is . . .*).

If necessary, you can include a title in front of the name:

» **Monsieur/M.** (*Mr.*)

» **Madame/Mme** (*Mrs.*)

» **Mademoiselle/Mlle** (*Miss*)

PRACTICE

What's in a name? You're at a conference with your partner, Shay. You meet a woman whom you don't know and run into your friend Marc. Fill in the blanks with the correct introduction. (*Note:* You can use each phrase only once if at all. I marked out Je m'appelle because it's the answer to the example question.)

- Elle s'appelle

- Il s'appelle

- ~~Je m'appelle~~

- Je te présente

- Je vous présente

- Mon nom est

- Mon prénom est

Q. You: Bonsoir Madame. Comment vous appelez-vous ?

A. Woman: **Je m'appelle Agathe Anam.**

17 You: Bonsoir Mme Anam. _____ Laura.

18 _____ mon ami Shay, et

19 Shay, _____ Mme Anam.

20 Shay: Bonsoir Mme Anam. _____ Shay Lavee.

21 You: Ah, salut Marc ! Est-ce que tu connais cette dame ? _____
Mme Anam.

Using Other Social Niceties Appropriately

Although **bonjour** (*hello*) is the most important social nicety, it isn't the only one. You also need *please, thank you, you're welcome,* and *good-bye*.

Saying please, thank you, and you're welcome

You have two ways to say "please," based on — you guessed it! — whether you use **vous** or **tu** with the person:

>> **s'il vous plaît**

>> **s'il te plaît**

Merci means *thank you,* and you can make it stronger by adding **beaucoup** (*very much*).

You're welcome is **je vous en prie** or **je t'en prie**. You'll also hear **de rien** (*it was nothing*), but this response can seem ungracious.

Parting ways

There are quite a few different expressions you can use when leaving, such as

>> **au revoir** (*good-bye*)

>> **bonne journée** (*have a nice day*)

>> **bon/bonne après-midi** (*have a nice afternoon*)

   Note: The word **après-midi** can be either masculine or feminine with no difference in meaning

>> **bonne soirée** (*have a nice evening*)

>> **bonne nuit** (*good night*)

>> **à bientôt** (*see you soon*)

>> **à plus** (*see you later*)

>> **à la prochaine** (*until next time*)

Note that the last two farewells are slightly informal.

PRACTICE

Time to play matchmaker! Connect a social nicety on the left with the one on the right that you'd expect to hear in the same exchange. Each term can be matched only once. I get you started.

bonjour —————————— je vous en prie

bonjour ——————→ au revoir

bonsoir   bonne journée

salut   bonne soirée

s'il te plaît   á la prochaine

s'il vous plaît   je t'en prie

Understanding Subject Pronouns

The subject is the person, place, or thing that's doing something in a sentence. In "My dog has fleas," for example, *my dog* is the subject. A subject pronoun can replace a subject, so if you've already mentioned your dog, you can just say "he" or "she" when you refer to your dog again.

Subject pronouns exist in both French and English, but they're extra important in French because each one has its own conjugation, or verb form. In a verb conjugation table, each subject pronoun represents any noun that has the same number and grammatical person — the role the subject plays in the conversation. Subject pronouns may be singular or plural, and they may be first person (the speaker), second person (the listener/reader/recipient), or third person (everyone else). Table 1-1 breaks down the pronouns so that you can better understand them.

Table 1-1	French Subject Pronouns and Their English Cohorts	
Person	Singular	Plural
1st	**je** (*I*)	**nous** (*we*)
2nd	**tu** (*you*)	**vous** (*you*)
3rd (masculine)	**il** (*he, it*)	**ils** (*they*)
3rd (feminine)	**elle** (*she, it*)	**elles** (*they*)
3rd (indefinite)	**on** (*one, people, they, we*)	n/a

Note: In formal situations, **vous** can be singular — see the section "Tu or vous: The second person," later in this chapter, for details.

I explain the particularities and contradictions of the indefinite pronoun **on** in the section "Il, elle, or on: The third-person singular," later in this chapter.

French has a different conjugation for each grammatical person, whereas English usually has only two conjugations: one for third-person singular (*he walks*) and one for everything else (*I walk*, *you walk*, *we walk*, *they walk*). The following sections take a closer look at these pronouns to help you use them correctly.

DIFFERENCES

Je or nous: The first person

Je is the first-person singular pronoun. Unlike its English equivalent *I*, **je** is capitalized only when it begins a sentence.

> **Je suis écrivain.** (*I'm a writer.*)

> **Demain, je vais en France.** (*Tomorrow, I'm going to France.*)

Note that when **je** is followed by a word that begins with a vowel or mute **h** (see Chapter 3 for more about the mute **h**), it contracts to **j'**.

> **J'ai grandi en Floride.** (*I grew up in Florida.*)

> **Maintenant, j'habite en Californie.** (*Now I live in California.*)

Nous is the first-person plural, and it means *we*. You use it the same way in French and English.

> **Nous allons en France.** (*We're going to France.*)

> **Je pense que nous mangeons à midi.** (*I think we're eating at noon.*)

Here's a quick catch-up. You and your partner Dominique work different hours, so you often text to keep your schedules synced. Choose the correct first-person pronoun to match the translation.

PRACTICE

Q. You: Salut Dominique, _____ suis à la banque. (Hi Dominique, I'm at the bank.)

A. je

22 You: _____ vais rentrer dans une heure. (I'll be home in an hour.)

23 Dominique: Okay, _____ ai une chose à faire et puis (Okay, I have one thing to do, and then)

24 _____ avons des billets d'opéra. (We have opera tickets.)

25 You: Mais pourquoi ? _____ détestons l'opéra ! (But why ? We hate the opera !)

26 Dominique: Pas du tout — moi, _____ adore l'opéra. (Not at all — me, I love the opera.)

Tu or vous: The second person

Tu and **vous** both mean *you*, but French distinguishes between different kinds of *you*.

Tu is singular and informal, meaning that you use it only when you're talking to

>> One person whom you know well — such as a family member, friend, classmate, or colleague

>> A child or animal

For example, here I'm greeting a friend and then talking to a child:

Salut Aurélie, comment vas-tu ? (*Hi Aurélie, how are you?*)

Tu peux commencer maintenant. (*You can begin now.*)

Vous is plural and/or formal. You use it when you're talking to

>> One person whom you don't know or to whom you wish to show respect, such as a teacher, doctor, boss, or elderly person

>> More than one person, whether or not you know them

In the following examples I use **vous** in the first instance to show respect to my professor, while in the second example I need **vous** because I'm talking to more than one child:

Bonjour Professeur Degueldre, comment allez-vous ? (*Hello Professor Degueldre, how are you?*)

Allez les enfants, vous devez faire vos devoirs ! (*Come on kids, you have to do your homework!*)

TIP

If you're not sure whether to use **tu** or **vous**, err on the side of respect and opt for **vous**. Except when you're introduced to someone by a close friend, you normally start out using **vous** with any adults you meet. At some point, if you become friends, this new person may ask you to use **tu** by saying something like, "**On peut se tutoyer.**" ("*We can use tu with one another.*") English has no real equivalent to this — "Call me John" is the closest, but it doesn't indicate the same shift to intimacy as switching from **vous** to **tu** does. Using **tu** without this sort of invitation can be very offensive, but the French usually make allowances for non-native speakers.

PRACTICE

What do you know? Decide whether to use **tu** or **vous** with each of these people or groups of people and circle your answer.

Q. Your boss   tu   vous

A. vous

(27) Your spouse   tu   vous

(28) A cashier   tu   vous

29	Your two kids	tu	vous
30	Your doctor	tu	vous
31	A group of friends	tu	vous
32	The waiter	tu	vous
33	Your dentist	tu	vous
34	A kid at the park	tu	vous
35	Parents of kids at the park	tu	vous
36	The bartender	tu	vous

Il, elle, or on: The third-person singular

Il and **elle** mean *he* and *she*, respectively.

> **Il a deux sœurs.** (*He has two sisters.*)

> **Elle veut travailler ici.** (*She wants to work here.*)

In addition, when you want to say "it," you have to figure out the gender of the noun because you use **il** to refer to a masculine noun and **elle** to refer to a feminine noun (see Chapter 3 for details on noun gender).

> **Où est mon livre ? Il est sur la table.** (*Where is my book? It's on the table.*)

> **Je vois la voiture. Elle est dans la rue.** (*I see the car. It's in the street.*)

On is an indefinite pronoun that literally means *one*. But **on** can also mean *you*, *people* in general, or *we*, informally.

> **On ne doit pas dire cela.** (*One shouldn't say that.*)

> **On ne sait jamais.** (*You just never know.*)

> **On ne fait plus attention de nos jours.** (*People don't pay attention any more nowadays.*)

> **On va partir à midi.** (*We're going to leave at noon.*)

Judgment time. Your friends like to gossip and are always asking, **Qu'est-ce que tu penses de . . . ?** ("*What do you think about . . . ?*") Answer with the appropriate third-person singular pronoun.

Q. Qu'est-ce que tu penses de Laura ?

A. **Elle est géniale !** (*She's awesome!*).

37 Qu'est-ce que tu penses de Marc ? _____ est drôle.

38 Qu'est-ce que tu penses de Sandrine ? _____ est triste.

39 Qu'est-ce que tu penses d'Annette ? _____ est artistique.

40 Qu'est-ce que tu penses de Thomas ? _____ est acerbe.

41 Qu'est-ce que tu penses de David ? _____ est énigmatique.

42 Qu'est-ce que tu penses de Christelle ? _____ est honnête.

Ils or elles: The third-person plural

Ils and **elles** mean *they*.

Ils is used for

>> Groups of men or masculine nouns

>> Mixed groups of men and women

>> Masculine and feminine nouns together

Check out these examples of **ils** in action:

Paul et David (ils) habitent à Bruxelles. (*Paul and David [they] live in Brussels.*)

Où sont mes livres ? Ils sont dans ta chambre. (*Where are my books? They're in your room.*)

Lise, Marie-Laure, Robert et Anne (ils) partent ensemble. (*Lise, Marie-Laure, Robert, and Anne [they] are leaving together.*)

Elles is used only for

>> Groups of women

>> Feminine nouns

REMEMBER

Even if there's only one man in a group of a thousand women, you have to use **ils**:

Ma mère et ma sœur (elles) aiment danser. (*My mother and sister [they] like to dance.*)

Je vois tes clés. Elles sont sur mon bureau. (*I see your keys. They're on my desk.*)

PRACTICE

You work at an advertising firm, and you're writing to a colleague about an ad idea for a product called **la Sandwichière** (*the Sandwich Maker*). Choose the best pronoun-verb pair to fill in each blank.

Q. Marc, _____ (je suis, il est) prêt à commencer. (Marc, I'm ready to start.)

A. **je suis**

43 Michel, _____ (j'ai, il a) une idée pour une nouvelle publicité. (Michel, I have an idea for a new ad.)

44 _____ (Peux-tu, Pouvez-vous) m'aider ? (Can you help me?)

45 _____ (Nous pouvons, Vous pouvez) travailler ensemble. (We can work together.)

Voici mon idée. Il y a un père, une mère et un enfant dans la cuisine. (Here's my idea. A father, mother, and child are in the kitchen.)

46 Le père dit à sa femme, _____ (veux-tu, voulez-vous) quelque chose à manger ? (The father says to his wife, "Do you want something to eat?")

47 _____ (Il répond, Elle répond, On répond): (She responds:)

48 Oui, et _____ (je pense, tu penses, il pense, nous pensons) que David a faim aussi. ("Yes, and I think David is hungry, too.")

49 David dit à ses parents : Oui, moi aussi — _____ (peux-tu, pouvez-vous) me faire un sandwich ? (David says to his parents: "Yes, me too, can you make me a sandwich?")

50 _____ (Ils répondent, Elles répondent): (They respond:)

51 Non, _____ (tu peux, vous pouvez) le faire tout seul. ("No, you can do it yourself.)

52 _____ (J'ai, Nous avons) acheté une Sandwichière — ("We bought a sandwich maker —)

53 _____ (il est, elle est, on est) tellement simple à utiliser qu'un enfant peut faire son propre sandwich. ("It's so simple to use that a child can make his own sandwich.")

Answer Key to "Getting to Know You" Practice Questions

1. **Bonjour** (*Hello/Good morning*)
2. **Salut** (*Hi*)
3. **Bonjour** (*Hello/Good morning*)
4. **Bonsoir** (*Good evening*)
5. **Bonjour** (*Hello/Good afternoon*)
6. **Salut** (*Hi*)
7. **Salut** (*Hi*)
8. **Bonsoir** (*Good evening*)
9. **Salut** (*Hi*)
10. **Bonjour** (*Hello/Good morning*)
11. Yes
12. No
13. No
14. Yes
15. Yes
16. No
17. You: **Bonsoir Mme Anam. Mon prénom est Laura.** (*Good evening Mrs. Anam. My first name is Laura.*)
18. **Je vous présente mon ami Shay, et** (*I'd like to introduce you to my friend Shay, and*)
19. **Shay, je te présente Mme Anam.** (*Shay, I'd like to introduce you to Mrs. Anam.*)
20. Shay: **Bonsoir Mme Anam. Mon nom est Shay Lavee.** (*Good evening Mrs. Anam. My name is Shay Lavee.*)

21 You: **Ah, salut Marc ! Est-ce que tu connais cette dame ? Elle s'appelle Mme Anam.** (*Oh, hi Marc! Do you know this lady? Her name is Mrs. Anam.*)

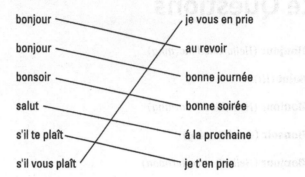

22 **je**

23 **j'**

24 **nous**

25 **nous**

26 **j'**

27 **tu**

28 **vous**

29 **vous**

30 **vous**

31 **vous**

32 **vous**

33 **vous**

34 **tu**

35 **vous**

36 **vous**

37 **Il est drôle.** (*He's funny.*)

38 **Elle est triste.** (*She's sad.*)

39 **Elle est artistique.** (*She's artistic.*)

40 **Il est acerbe.** (*He's acerbic.*)

41 **Il est énigmatique.** (*He's enigmatic.*)

(42) **Elle est honnête.** (*She's honest.*)

(43) **j'ai**

(44) **Peux-tu**

(45) **Nous pouvons**

(46) **veux-tu**

(47) **Elle répond**

(48) **je pense**

(49) **pouvez-vous**

(50) **Ils répondent**

(51) **tu peux**

(52) **Nous avons acheté**

(53) **elle est**

Chapter **2**

Understanding Parts of Speech and Bilingual Dictionaries

L anguage is made up of parts of speech — nouns, verbs, adjectives, and so on. Each of these building blocks has its own function and rules, and understanding them is key to using them correctly, particularly with a foreign language. If you don't know the difference between the parts of speech in English, you probably won't understand them in French either, which means you're likely to make a lot of mistakes when you write and speak.

Bilingual dictionaries are essential tools for speaking and understanding a new language, but misusing them is easy. You can't accept whatever the dictionary says as gospel — you need to know how to understand the symbols and abbreviations, how to make a choice when given several translations, and how much to trust the answers you get. This chapter explains the basic parts of speech, as well as how to get the most out of your bilingual dictionary.

Identifying the Parts of Speech

You're probably already familiar with at least some of the parts of speech, such as nouns and verbs, even though you don't necessarily think about them when speaking your native language. Because I use these terms throughout the book, I want to give you an overview of the parts of speech in the following sections.

To help illustrate the differences between parts of speech, I use an example sentence that has all eight essential parts of speech in both languages.

Je veux vraiment aller en France et visiter les musées célèbres.

(*I really want to go to France and visit the famous museums.*)

In the following sections, I bold the part of speech under consideration in my example French sentence and its English translation.

What's in a name? Nouns

Nouns are people, places, things, and ideas. They're the concrete and abstract things in your sentences, the who and the what that are doing something or having something done to them. Here, the example sentence from the preceding section has the nouns in bold (in both French and English).

Je veux vraiment aller en **France** et visiter les **musées** célèbres.

(*I really want to go to **France** and visit the famous **museums**.*)

France is a *proper noun* — a noun that refers to a specific person, place, or thing and that's always capitalized. Other proper nouns include Laura (that's me!) and the Louvre. *Museums* is a plural noun, which means it's also a *countable noun* because you can count it: one museum, two museums, three museums, and so on. *Collective nouns,* such as group and bunch, refer to a group of nouns considered a single unit: one group of students, a bunch of flowers. *Uncountable nouns,* such as beauty and fear, are things that you can't count.

DIFFERENCES In French, nouns are also masculine or feminine, which I explain in greater detail in Chapter 3. Nouns and verbs (see the section "Doing all the things with verbs," later in this chapter) provide the basic elements of any sentence. Nouns need verbs to tell them what they're doing, and verbs need nouns to explain who or what is acting or being acted upon. You can often replace nouns with pronouns — see the section "Pronouns: They're replacements," later in this chapter.

PRACTICE Doing double duty! Go to the beginning of this section and, starting with the first sentence, underline all the nouns from there to here. That's right, you should re-read this section and underline the nouns while you do it; the following example sentence and answer get you started. A cool thing about using the text itself as the basis for this exercise is that it gives you a chance to examine the very text that explains what you're doing. And it better familiarizes you with parts of speech in English, which is vital to understanding grammar essentials and developing your language skills.

Q. *Nouns are people, places, things, and ideas.*

A. <u>Nouns</u> are <u>people</u>, <u>places</u>, <u>things</u>, and <u>ideas</u>.

Articles (not the ones in magazines)

An article is a very particular part of speech. You can use it only with a noun in order to classify that noun in a particular way. English has two kinds of articles:

>> Definite article (*the*), as in *the book*

>> Indefinite article (*a/an*), as in *a book*

DIFFERENCES

Although English has just two kinds of articles, French has three kinds:

>> Definite articles: **le, la, les** (*the*)

Refers to something specific: **le livre** (*the book*), **la leçon** (*the lesson*), **les idées** (*the ideas*).

>> Indefinite articles: **un, une** (*a/an*), **des** (*some*)

Unspecific: **un homme** (*a man*), **une chaise** (*a chair*), **des mots** (*some words*).

>> Partitive articles: **du, de la, des** (*some*)

Partitive articles refer to a part or portion of something: **du pain** (*some bread*), **de la bière** (*some beer*). (**Note:** In English, *some* is technically considered an adjective, not an article.)

Chapter 3 has a lot more information about the French articles. While you're here, see if you can correctly identify the article in the example sentence (spoiler alert: The article's in bold).

Je veux vraiment aller en France et visiter **les** musées célèbres.

(*I really want to go to France and visit **the** famous museums.*)

PRACTICE

From the top! Return to the first sentence in this section and underline all the articles from there to here. The following example sentence and answer show you how it's done. While you review the text, take advantage of the opportunity to better familiarize yourself with how articles work both in English and French.

Q. An article is a very particular part of speech.

A. <u>An</u> article is <u>a</u> very particular part of speech.

Doing all the things with verbs

Verbs express actions and describe states of being. They tell you what's happening, what the situation is like, and whether any music is pounding in the background during it all. The verbs from the example sentence are in bold; you can discover why they don't always have the same number of words in both languages in Chapter 10.

Je **veux** vraiment **aller** en France et **visiter** les musées célèbres.

(*I really **want to go** to France and **visit** the famous museums.*)

Verbs are the most variable part of speech because they have all kinds of different forms, called conjugations, which help tell you who or what is doing something, when they're doing it, and how they feel about it. French verbs are classified by how they're conjugated:

>> Regular verbs
  • **-er** verbs
  • **-ir** verbs
  • **-re** verbs
>> Stem-changing verbs
>> Spelling-change verbs
>> Irregular verbs

In addition, verbs have many different forms that give you all kinds of information about their actions:

>> **Tense:** Tells you when the verb action takes place — in the present, past, or future — and whether it was completed (*perfect*) or incomplete (*imperfect*). See Chapters 6, 10, 15, and 16 for more info about verb tenses.

>> **Mood:** Shows how the speaker feels about the verb action — whether it's indicative, imperative, conditional, or subjunctive. You can flip to Chapter 14 to read more about the imperative; the other moods are more advanced topics for another day (and another book!)

>> **Voice:** Indicates the relationship between the subject and the verb — whether it's active, passive, or reflexive. Take a look at Chapter 7 for the reflexive voice and how it differs from active voice. The passive voice is a more advanced topic to be avoided for now.

PRACTICE

Do over! Find the first sentence in this section and underline all the verbs that you find, starting there and ending here. Use the following example sentence and answer to get the hang of it.

Q. *Verbs* express actions and describe states of being.

A. *Verbs* <u>express</u> actions and <u>describe</u> states of being.

Describing adjectives

Adjectives are flowery, helpful, and exciting words that describe nouns. Adjectives may tell you what color something is, whether it's new or old, or about its shape, size, or provenance. The example sentence has only one adjective.

Je veux vraiment aller en France et visiter les musées **célèbres**. (*I really want to go to France and visit the **famous** museums.*)

REMEMBER

Adjectives usually aren't essential, the way nouns and verbs are, because they just add some extra information to the basic facts. Compare *My brother has a car* to *My older brother has a red car* — the important information is that your brother has a car; the facts that he's older than you and that the car is red are just window dressing. Adjectives such as *older* and *red* are called descriptive adjectives, but adjectives come in many other useful varieties:

>> Demonstrative adjectives: **ce**, **cette**, **cet** (*this*, *that*), **ces** (*these*, *those*)

>> Indefinite adjectives: **quelques** (*some*), **certain** (*certain*), **plusieurs** (*several*)

>> Interrogative adjectives: **quel** (*which*)

>> Negative adjectives: **ne . . . aucun**, **ne . . . nul** (*no*, *not any*)

>> Possessive adjectives: **mon** (*my*), **ton** (*your*), **son** (*his/her*)

Unlike boring old English adjectives, French adjectives have masculine, feminine, singular, and plural forms so that they can agree with their nouns. (Chapter 11 tells you a lot of other interesting details about descriptive adjectives, and the Table of Contents at the front of this book or the Index at the rear tell you where to find more info about the other types of adjectives.)

PRACTICE

Find the first sentence in this section, and then underline all the adjectives that you see until you get to this point in the text. The following example question and answer take care of the first sentence for you. While you look for adjectives, also keep an eye out for any helpful rules about using adjectives that you missed on your first read-through.

Q. *Adjectives* are flowery, helpful, and exciting words that describe nouns.

A. *Adjectives* are <u>flowery</u>, <u>helpful</u>, and <u>exciting</u> words that describe nouns.

Using adverbs

Adverbs easily modify verbs, adjectives, and other adverbs. Like adjectives, adverbs aren't always essential, but rather, they add some extra information to the words that they're helpfully modifying. In the example sentence, *really* modifies the verb *want*.

Je veux **vraiment** aller en France et visiter les musées célèbres.

(*I **really** want to go to France and visit the famous museums.*)

English adverbs often end in −*ly* and indicate how the action of a verb is occurring: happily, quickly, rudely. Most of these words are *adverbs of manner*. The other kinds of adverbs are

>> Adverbs of frequency: **jamais** (*never*), **souvent** (*often*)

>> Adverbs of place: **ici** (*here*), **partout** (*everywhere*)

>> Adverbs of quantity: **très** (*very*), **beaucoup** (*a lot*)

>> Adverbs of time: **avant** (*before*), **demain** (*tomorrow*)

>> Interrogative adverbs: **quand** (*when*), **où** (*where*)

>> Negative adverbs: **ne . . . pas** (*not*), **ne . . . jamais** (*never*)

Check out Chapter 11 to understand more about French adverbs.

PRACTICE

Carefully underline the adverbs in this section. Starting with the first sentence (which I illustrate in the following example), underline all the adverbs from there to here. Take your time while you re-read this section, getting yourself comfortable with what adverbs are. (Knowing the parts of speech in English makes understanding a new language easier.)

Q. *Adverbs* easily modify verbs, adjectives, and other adverbs.

A. *Adverbs* <u>easily</u> modify verbs, adjectives, and other adverbs.

Pronouns: They're replacements

Pronouns are easy to understand; they replace nouns. That is, pronouns also refer to people, places, things, and ideas, but they let you avoid repeating the same words over and over.

For example, you could say, "Marc has a sister. His sister has a cat. The cat has fleas, and the fleas make the cat itch." But hearing those nouns repeated each time gets a little old. A much nicer way to say that would be, "Marc has a sister. She has a cat. It has fleas, and they make it itch." *She*, *it*, and *they* are personal pronouns because they have different forms for each grammatical person. (You can read about the concept of grammatical person in Chapter 1.) My trusty example sentence has one pronoun in it.

> **Je** veux vraiment aller en France et visiter les musées célèbres.
>
> (*I really want to go to France and visit the famous museums.*)

French has five types of personal pronouns. The following are all equivalent to *I/me*, *you*, or *he/him/it*:

>> Subject pronouns: **je**, **tu**, **il** (see Chapter 1)

>> Direct object pronouns: **me**, **te**, **le** (see Chapter 13)

>> Indirect object pronouns: **me**, **te**, **lui** (see Chapter 13)

>> Reflexive pronouns: **me**, **te**, **se** (see Chapter 7)

>> Stressed pronouns: **moi**, **toi**, **lui** (see Chapter 11)

French also has several kinds of impersonal pronouns — which doesn't mean they're unkind, just that they don't have different forms for each grammatical person. However, many of them do have different forms for masculine, feminine, singular, and plural. I give you some examples in this list (although I hold off on the translations for now):

>> Adverbial pronouns: **y**, **en**

>> Demonstrative pronouns: **celui**, **celle**

>> Indefinite pronouns: **autre**, **certain**

>> Interrogative pronouns: **quel**, **quelle**

>> Negative pronouns: **aucun, personne**

>> Possessive pronouns: **le mien, le tien**

>> Relative pronouns: **qui, que, dont**

I explain the different types of pronouns throughout this book: Chapter 13 covers adverbial pronouns, Chapter 4 explains demonstrative and possessive pronouns, Chapter 8 discusses interrogative pronouns, and Chapter 9 explains negative pronouns. Indefinite and relative pronouns are more advanced topics for your next French book adventure.

PRACTICE

Identify the pronouns in this section, starting at the top, and underline those pronouns. Take the lead from the following example question and answer, which help you locate the first sentence and the first pronoun in this section. Keep going until you find yourself back here.

Q. Pronouns are easy to understand; they replace nouns.

A. Pronouns are easy to understand; <u>they</u> replace nouns.

Prepositions: On top of it

A preposition is the part of speech that you put in front of a noun or pronoun to show the relationship between that word and another word or phrase. When you go *to* the store, return *from* vacation, or trip *over* the shoes you left sitting *under* a towel lying *on* the floor, the prepositions tell you how those verbs and nouns fit together. The shoes are *under* the towel, not *on*, *next to*, or wrapped *in* it. Prepositions may be one word (*to, at, about*) or part of a group of words (*next to, in front of, on top of*). The example sentence has one preposition.

> Je veux vraiment aller **en** France et visiter les musées célèbres.
>
> (*I really want to go **to** France and visit the famous museums.*)

Prepositions are difficult to translate, perhaps more so than any other part of speech. The French preposition **à**, for example, usually means *to, at,* or *in*, but also has other meanings in certain expressions:

>> Destination: **Je vais à Paris.** (*I'm going to Paris.*)

>> Current location: **Je suis à la banque. Il est à Londres.** (*I'm at the bank. He's in London.*)

>> Function: **un verre à vin** (*a wine glass/a glass for wine*)

>> Owner: **C'est à moi.** (*It's mine./It belongs to me.*)

You can't just memorize prepositions as a list of vocabulary words, but rather, you have to study and practice these grammatical terms along with their various functions. Chapter 12 explains all about prepositions.

PRACTICE

Underline the prepositions in this section. Lucky for you it's a short one — but this section is full of prepositions! So, sharpen your pencil, find the first sentence, and get underlining! (The following example question and answer help get you started.)

Q. A *preposition* is the part of speech that you put in front of a noun or pronoun to show the relationship between that word and another word or phrase.

A. A *preposition* is the part of speech that you put <u>in front of</u> a noun or pronoun to show the relationship <u>between</u> that word and another word or phrase.

Connecting with conjunctions

Conjunctions join two or more words or phrases, which can be either equal or unequal. My example sentence contains one conjunction.

Je veux vraiment aller en France **et** visiter les musées célèbres.

(*I really want to go to France **and** visit the famous museums.*)

They come in a couple of varieties:

>> **Coordinating conjunctions:** These words — such as *and, or, but* — bring together equals, as in *I like coffee and tea.* Other examples include *He can't read or write* and *We want to go, but we don't have time.*

You can tell that a conjunction is coordinating when you can reverse the joined items with little or no difference in meaning. Saying *I like coffee and tea* isn't any different from *I like tea and coffee.* Likewise, *We want to go, but we don't have time* means pretty much the same thing as *We don't have time, but we want to go.*

The most common coordinating conjunctions are

- **donc** (*so*)
- **et** (*and*)
- **mais** (*but*)
- **ni** (*nor*)
- **ou** (*or*)

>> **Subordinating conjunctions:** These conjunctions — such as *that, when, as soon as* — combine two *clauses,* meaningful groups of words that contain a subject and verb. The conjunction tells you that the clause after it is *subordinate,* meaning that clause is dependent on the main clause. For example:

- *He thinks that I'm smart* (I may or may not be smart, but he thinks I am)
- *I don't know when they'll arrive* (They're supposed to arrive, but I don't know when)
- *She left after the phone rang* (The phone rang, and then she left)

If you reverse the clauses while leaving the conjunction in the same place in these examples, you end up with either nonsense or a different meaning. *I am smart that he thinks* doesn't make any sense, and *The phone rang after she left* isn't the same thing as *She left after the phone rang* — in fact, it's just the opposite. This simple test lets you know that these conjunctions are subordinating rather than coordinating.

In English, subordinating conjunctions are often optional: we can say *He thinks that I'm smart* or *He thinks I'm smart* — both versions are grammatically correct and have the exact same meaning. In French, however, the subordinating conjunction is required: you must say **Il pense que je suis intelligent.**

The most common subordinating conjunctions are

- **après que** (*after*)
- **avant que** (*before*)
- **bien que** (*even though*)
- **parce que** (*because*)
- **puisque** (*since*)
- **quand** (*when*)
- **que** (*that*)
- **si** (*if*)

Did you get all that? Circle back to the first sentence in this section and locate and underline the conjunctions. Yes, re-read this section and underline the conjunctions while you do it; the following example question and answer get you started. I base this exercise on the text in this section to encourage you to take a closer look at the text and better familiarize yourself with this part of speech. The better your understanding of English parts of speech, the more effectively you can practice and understand French!

Q. Conjunctions join two or more words or phrases that are either equal or unequal.

A. Conjunctions join two or more words or phrases that are either equal or unequal.

Correctly Using a Bilingual Dictionary

A bilingual dictionary can be a wonderful tool or a terrible crutch. When you don't know what a word means or how to say something in another language, a bilingual dictionary can give you the answer. But it's not as simple as just looking something up and taking the first thing you see. You have to know what to look up, how to read the information provided, and how much you can depend on the answer you get. The following sections can help you make a bilingual dictionary a helpful tool and not a hindrance.

Figuring out what to look up

Although dictionaries have thousands of words, you can't find every single word you want just by looking it up. Dictionaries don't separately list different versions of words — including plurals, feminine versions, verb conjugations, comparatives, and superlatives — so you need to know where to find these words. You can find them only by looking for the default, singular, masculine, infinitive, unmodified word.

For example, suppose you see the word **mettez** for the first time and you want to know what it means. You grab your bilingual dictionary and discover that it has no entry for **mettez**. Instead of giving up, do a little grammatical analysis. **Mettez** ends in **–ez**, which is a common French verb ending (as you can read about in Chapter 6), so conjugate backwards — the infinitive is likely to be **metter**, **mettir**, or **mettre**. Look those up, and voilà ! You discover that **mettre** means *to put*.

Likewise, if you can't find **traductrice**, remove the feminine ending (which Chapter 3 explains) because the word in the dictionary is the default, masculine form **traducteur** (*translator*).

TIP

If you're trying to look up an expression, such as **Qui se ressemble s'assemble**, you can start by looking up the first word, **qui**, but you may not have any luck. The dictionary may include the expression under that entry, or it may list it under a different word that the dictionary editors thought was more of a key to the phrase, such as **ressembler**. Check there, and sure enough, you discover that it means *Those who resemble each other assemble*, so it's the French equivalent of the English proverb *Birds of a feather flock together*.

Note: Pronominal verbs, such as **se ressembler** and **se souvenir**, are listed in the dictionary under the verb, not the reflexive pronoun. So you look up **ressembler** and **souvenir**, not **se**. (You can read about pronominal verbs in Chapter 7.)

Considering context and part of speech

REMEMBER

Finding the word you want is only half the battle — you also need to think about what it means, which is why you have to understand *context* (the situation in which you're using the word). You may not have any idea what **un avocat** is (check out Figure 2-1), but when you look up **avocat**, you find two translations: *avocado* and *lawyer*. So you need to figure out from the context of the sentence you saw it in whether it's a food or a person. The context obviously makes a big difference as to which translation is correct (unless, perhaps, you're reading about a lawyer who dressed as guacamole for Halloween!)

FIGURE 2-1:
What the
French-English
Dictionary
entry for
avocat might
look like.

> **AVOCAT**
> [a vɔ ka] m subst
> (person) lawyer,
> (fruit) avocado

Likewise, if you want to know how to say "present" in French, you need to know whether you're looking for an adjective (Everyone is present), a noun (I bought you a present), or a verb (I want to present a petition). When you look up present in the dictionary, you see at least three translations: **présent**, **cadeau**, and **presenter**; see Figure 2-2. The dictionary doesn't know which one you want — the correct choice depends on context and on your knowing the difference between adjectives, nouns, and verbs. (If you're still not sure, head back up to the section "Identifying the Parts of Speech," earlier in this chapter, for some reminders.)

PRESENT
1) ['pre zənt] adj
   présent
2) ['pre zənt] m subst
   (grammar) présent,
   (gift) cadeau
3) [prɪ 'zent] verb
   présenter

TIP Some people like to keep a list of words to look up later, instead of putting the book or newspaper down every two minutes to look them up right away. If you're one of these folks, be sure to jot down the phrase or sentence, rather than just the word. Otherwise, when you get the dictionary out, you might discover that you can't figure out which translation makes the most sense because you just have a big list of words with no context to fit them into.

Understanding symbols and terminology

Dictionaries save space by using symbols and abbreviations, but not all dictionaries use the same ones. Check the first few pages of the dictionary — it should have a section that lists the abbreviations used throughout the book, the pronunciation notation, and symbols that indicate things such as word stress, formality or informality, archaic words, silent letters, and so on.

TIP The International Phonetic Alphabet, or IPA, is a standard system for showing how to pronounce words in any language. Unfortunately, many dictionaries either don't use it or adapt it with their own symbols, so you always need to check your dictionary to see which system it uses to explain pronunciation. The second line in Figure 2-1 shows the IPA spelling for the word **avocat** (*lawyer, avocado*).

The symbols and abbreviations aren't there just to look pretty! For example:

>> If a word is listed as *archaic,* you don't want to use it (unless you happen to be translating 14th-century poetry).

>> If a term is notated as *vulgar slang,* you definitely don't want to say that to your boss.

As I explain in the preceding section, think about how you're using a particular word before you make your selection from the translations offered.

Interpreting figurative language and idioms

When using a bilingual dictionary to determine a word's meaning, you also need to understand whether a term is being used literally or figuratively. French and English are both rich in figurative language, and translating can be tricky. Take the expression "Guy is hot." Literally, this means that Guy is very warm — he's wearing too many clothes, say, or he has a fever. Figuratively (and informally), it means that Guy is extremely good-looking. If you want to translate this sentence into French, you need to figure out which meaning you're after and then make sure to find the correct French translation for that meaning. When you look up the word — in this case, *hot* — the literal meaning(s) is normally listed first, followed by any figurative meaning(s). Figurative meanings have a notation such as *fig.* (short for figurative). (For the record, the literal translation of *Guy is hot* is **Guy a chaud**, and the figurative is **Guy est sexy**.)

You may run across figurative language when you translate into English, too. The French expression **connaître la musique** literally means *to know the music*, such as an actual song. Figuratively, it means *to know the routine*. You have to think about which of these English meanings is right for the context in which you saw or heard the French expression.

An idiom is an expression that can't be translated literally into another language because one or more words in it are used figuratively. *It's raining cats and dogs* doesn't really mean that household pets are falling from the sky; it just means that it's raining really hard. You absolutely can't look up the individual words to come up with **Il pleut des chats et des chiens** — that makes no sense at all to a French speaker. The French equivalent of *It's raining cats and dogs* is also an idiom: **Il pleut des cordes** (literally: *It's raining ropes*).

WARNING

Automated translators, such as online translation websites, translate very literally. Never use them to translate something that you plan to say to someone or write in a letter. Use automated translators only to help you get an idea of what something says by translating into a language you understand.

Verifying your findings

TIP

After you find your word or expression and have considered the context in which you plan to use it, verify what you've found. I suggest you use the following ideas to double-check that you're using the right meaning:

>> **Ask a native.** The best way to verify that you're using the right word is to ask a native speaker. Dictionaries are wonderful tools, but they're not infallible. Language changes — particularly informal language — and dictionaries change constantly. Even if they didn't, they still couldn't tell you that a certain expression or way of using a particular word "just doesn't sound right." Native speakers are the experts.

TIP

To find a native speaker, ask your professor whether they know anyone. If you have near you a local branch of the Alliance française (an international organization that promotes French language and francophone culture — `https://af-france.fr`), find out the time of the next meeting. Or you can try an online space such as the Progress with Lawless French Q&A Forum (`https://progress.lawlessfrench.com/questions`), part of the website created by yours truly, the humble author of this book.

>> **Do a reverse look-up.** One quick and easy way to check whether the word you found is the right one is to do a *reverse look-up,* which is when you look up the translation that the dictionary just gave you. For example, if you looked up *anger* in the English-French part of the dictionary and found that it means **colère** or **fureur**, you can then look up those two words in the French-English dictionary. This reverse look-up tells you that **colère** translates as *anger* and **fureur** translates as *fury*, indicating that **colère** is probably the better translation for *anger*.

Try monolingual dictionaries. If your French skills are up to it, another way to confirm a translation involves you looking up the English word in an English dictionary and the French translation in a French dictionary. For example, you could look up *anger* in an English dictionary and **colère** in a French dictionary, and then compare the definitions.

Answer Key to "Understanding Parts of Speech and Bilingual Dictionaries" Practice Questions

(1) **Underlining nouns in the section "What's in a name? Nouns":**

Nouns are <u>people</u>, <u>places</u>, <u>things</u>, and <u>ideas</u>. They're the concrete and abstract <u>things</u> in your <u>sentences</u>, the <u>who</u> and the <u>what</u> that are doing something or having something done to them. Here, the example <u>sentence</u> from the preceding <u>section</u> has the <u>nouns</u> in bold (in both <u>French</u> and <u>English</u>):

Je veux vraiment aller en <u>France</u> et visiter les <u>musées</u> célèbres.

(I really want to go to <u>France</u> and visit the famous <u>museums</u>.)

<u>France</u> is a proper <u>noun</u> — a <u>noun</u> that refers to a specific <u>person</u>, <u>place</u>, or <u>thing</u> and that's always capitalized. Other proper <u>nouns</u> include <u>Laura</u> (that's me!) and the <u>Louvre</u>. <u>Museums</u> is a plural <u>noun</u>, which means it's also a countable <u>noun</u> because you can count it: one <u>museum</u>, two <u>museums</u>, three <u>museums</u>, and so on. Collective <u>nouns</u>, such as <u>group</u> and <u>bunch</u>, refer to a <u>group</u> of <u>nouns</u> considered a single <u>unit</u>: one <u>group</u> of <u>students</u>, a <u>bunch</u> of <u>flowers</u>. Uncountable <u>nouns</u>, such as <u>beauty</u> and <u>fear</u>, are <u>things</u> that you can't count.

In <u>French</u>, <u>nouns</u> are also masculine or feminine, which I explain in greater <u>detail</u> in <u>Chapter</u> 3. <u>Nouns</u> and <u>verbs</u> (see the <u>section</u> "Doing all the things with verbs," later in this chapter) provide the basic <u>elements</u> of any <u>sentence</u>. <u>Nouns</u> need <u>verbs</u> to tell them what they're doing, and <u>verbs</u> need <u>nouns</u> to explain who or what is acting or being acted upon. You can often replace <u>nouns</u> with <u>pronouns</u> — see the <u>section</u> "<u>Pronouns</u>: They're <u>replacements</u>," later in this <u>chapter</u>.

(2) **Finding articles in the section "Articles (not the ones in magazines)":**

<u>An</u> article is <u>a</u> very particular part of speech. You can use it only with <u>a</u> noun in order to classify that noun in <u>a</u> particular way. English has two kinds of articles:

Definite article (<u>the</u>), as in "<u>the</u> book"

Indefinite article (<u>a/an</u>), as in "<u>a</u> book"

Although English has just two kinds of articles, French has three kinds:

Definite articles: <u>le</u>, <u>la</u>, <u>les</u> (<u>the</u>)

Refers to something specific: <u>le</u> livre (<u>the</u> book), <u>la</u> leçon (<u>the</u> lesson), <u>les</u> idées (<u>the</u> ideas).

Indefinite articles: <u>un</u>, <u>une</u> (<u>a/an</u>), <u>des</u> (some)

Unspecific: <u>un</u> homme (<u>a</u> man), <u>une</u> chaise (<u>a</u> chair), <u>des</u> mots (some words).

Partitive articles: <u>du</u>, <u>de la</u>, <u>des</u> (some)

Partitive articles refer to <u>a</u> part or portion of something: <u>du</u> pain (some bread), <u>de la</u> bière (some beer). (Note: In English, some is technically considered <u>an</u> adjective, not <u>an</u> article.)

Chapter 3 has <u>a</u> lot more information about <u>the</u> French articles. While you're here, see if you can correctly identify <u>the</u> article in <u>the</u> example sentence (spoiler alert: <u>The</u> article's in bold).

Je veux vraiment aller en France et visiter <u>les</u> musées célèbres.

(I really want to go to France and visit <u>the</u> famous museums.)

(3) **Identifying verbs in the section "Doing all the things with verbs":**

Verbs express actions and describe states of being. They tell you what's happening, what the situation is like, and whether any music is pounding in the background during it all. The verbs from the example sentence are in bold; you can discover why they don't always have the same number of words in both languages in Chapter 10.

Je **veux** vraiment **aller** en France et **visiter** les musées célèbres.

(I really want to go to France and visit the famous museums.)

Verbs are the most variable part of speech because they have all kinds of different forms, called conjugations, which help tell you who or what is doing something, when they're doing it, and how they feel about it. French verbs are classified by how they're conjugated:

Regular verbs

–er verbs

–ir verbs

–re verbs

Stem-changing verbs

Spelling-change verbs

Irregular verbs

In addition, verbs have many different forms that give you all kinds of information about their actions:

Tense: Tells you when the verb action takes place — in the present, past, or future — and whether it was completed (perfect) or incomplete (imperfect). See Chapters 6, 10, 15, and 16 to learn about verb tenses.

Mood: Shows how the speaker feels about the verb action — whether it's indicative, imperative, conditional, or subjunctive. You can flip to Chapter 14 to learn about the imperative; the other moods are more advanced topics for another day (and another book!)

Voice: Indicates the relationship between the subject and the verb — whether it's active, passive, or reflexive. Take a look at Chapter 7 to learn about the reflexive voice and how it differs from active voice. The passive voice is a more advanced topic to be avoided for now.

(4) **Spotting adjectives in the section "Describing adjectives":**

Adjectives are flowery, helpful, and exciting words that describe nouns. Adjectives may tell you what color something is, whether it's new or old, or about its shape, size, or provenance. The example sentence has only one adjective.

Je veux vraiment aller en France et visiter les musées célèbres.

(I really want to go to France and visit the famous museums.)

Adjectives usually aren't essential, the way nouns and verbs are, because they just add some extra information to the basic facts. Compare My brother has a car to My older brother has a red car — the important information is that your brother has a car; the facts that he's older than you and that the car is red are just window dressing. Adjectives such as older and red are called descriptive adjectives, but adjectives come in many other useful varieties:

Demonstrative adjectives: ce, cette, cet (this, that), ces (these, those)

Indefinite adjectives: quelques (some), certain (certain), plusieurs (several)

Interrogative adjectives: quel (which)

Negative adjectives: ne ... aucun, ne ... nul (no, not any)

Possessive adjectives: mon (my), ton (your), son (his/her)

Unlike boring old English adjectives, French adjectives have masculine, feminine, singular, and plural forms so that they can agree with their nouns. (Chapter 11 tells you a lot of other interesting details about descriptive adjectives, and the Table of Contents at the front of this book or the Index at the rear tell you where to find more info about the other types of adjectives.)

(5) **Underlining adverbs in the section "Using adverbs":**

Adverbs easily modify verbs, adjectives, and other adverbs. Like adjectives, adverbs aren't always essential, but rather, they add some extra information to the words that they're helpfully modifying. In the example sentence, really modifies the verb want.

Je veux vraiment aller en France et visiter les musées célèbres.

(I really want to go to France and visit the famous museums.)

English adverbs often end in –ly and indicate how the action of a verb is occurring: happily, quickly, rudely. Most of these words are adverbs of manner. The other kinds of adverbs are

Adverbs of frequency: jamais (never), souvent (often)

Adverbs of place: ici (here), partout (everywhere)

Adverbs of quantity: très (very), beaucoup (a lot)

Adverbs of time: avant (before), demain (tomorrow)

Interrogative adverbs: quand (when), où (where)

Negative adverbs: ne ... pas (not), ne ... jamais (never)

Read Chapter 11 thoroughly to understand more about French adverbs.

(6) **Picking out pronouns in the section "Pronouns: They're replacements":**

Pronouns are easy to understand; they replace nouns. That is, pronouns also refer to people, places, things, and ideas, but they let you avoid repeating the same words over and over.

For example, you could say, "Marc has a sister. His sister has a cat. The cat has fleas, and the fleas make the cat itch." But hearing those nouns repeated each time gets a little old. A much nicer way to say that would be, "Marc has a sister. She has a cat. It has fleas, and they make it itch." She, it, and they are personal pronouns because they have different forms for each grammatical person. (You can read about the concept of grammatical person in Chapter 1.) My trusty example sentence has one pronoun in it.

Je veux vraiment aller en France et visiter les musées célèbres.

(I really want to go to France and visit the famous museums.)

French has five types of personal pronouns. The following are all equivalent to I/me, you, or he/him/it:

Subject pronouns: je, tu, il (see Chapter 2)

Direct object pronouns: me, te, le (see Chapter 13)

Indirect object pronouns: me, te, lui (see Chapter 13)

Reflexive pronouns: me, te, se (see Chapter 7)

Stressed pronouns: moi, toi, lui (see Chapter 11)

French also has several kinds of impersonal pronouns — which doesn't mean they're unkind, just that they don't have different forms for each grammatical person. However, many of them do have different forms for masculine, feminine, singular, and plural. I give you some examples in this list although I hold off on the translations for now:

Adverbial pronouns: y, en

Demonstrative pronouns: celui, celle

Indefinite pronouns: autre, certain

Interrogative pronouns: quel, quelle

Negative pronouns: aucun, personne

Possessive pronouns: le mien, le tien

Relative pronouns: qui, que, dont

I explain the different types of pronouns throughout this book: Chapter 13 covers adverbial pronouns, Chapter 4 explains demonstrative and possessive pronouns, Chapter 8 discusses interrogative pronouns, and Chapter 9 explains negative pronouns. Indefinite and relative pronouns are more advanced topics for your next French book adventure.

7) **Finding the prepositions in the section "Prepositions: On top of it":**

A preposition is the part of speech that you put in front of a noun or pronoun to show the relationship between that word and another word or phrase. When you go to the store, return from vacation, or trip over the shoes you left sitting under a towel lying on the floor, the prepositions tell you how those verbs and nouns fit together. The shoes are under the towel, not on, next to, or wrapped in it. Prepositions may be one word (to, at, about) or part of a group of words (next to, in front of, on top of). The example sentence has one preposition.

Je veux vraiment aller en France et visiter les musées célèbres.

(I really want to go to France and visit the famous museums.)

Prepositions are difficult to translate, perhaps more so than any other part of speech. The French preposition à, for example, usually means to, at, or in, but also has other meanings in certain expressions:

Destination: Je vais à Paris. (I'm going to Paris.)

Current location: Je suis à la banque. Il est à Londres. (I'm at the bank. He's in London.)

Function: un verre à vin (a wine glass/a glass for wine)

Owner: C'est à moi. (It's mine./It belongs to me.)

You can't just memorize prepositions as a list of vocabulary words, but rather, you have to study and practice these grammatical terms along with their various functions. Chapter 12 explains all about prepositions.

8. **Uncovering conjunctions in the section "Connecting with conjunctions":**

Conjunctions join two or more words or phrases, which can be either equal or unequal. My example sentence contains one conjunction.

Je veux vraiment aller en France et visiter les musées célèbres.

(I really want to go to France and visit the famous museums.)

They come in a couple of varieties:

Coordinating conjunctions: These words — such as and, or, but — bring together equals, as in I like coffee and tea. Other examples include He can't read or write and We want to go, but we don't have time.

You can tell that a conjunction is coordinating when you can reverse the joined items with little or no difference in meaning. Saying I like coffee and tea isn't any different from I like tea and coffee. Likewise, We want to go, but we don't have time means pretty much the same thing as We don't have time, but we want to go.

The most common coordinating conjunctions are

donc (so)

et (and)

mais (but)

ni (nor)

ou (or)

Subordinating conjunctions: These conjunctions — such as that, when, and as soon as — combine two clauses, meaningful groups of words that contain a subject and verb. The conjunction tells you that the clause after it is subordinate, meaning that clause is dependent on the main clause. For example:

He thinks that I'm smart (I may or may not be smart, but he thinks I am)

I don't know when they'll arrive (They're supposed to arrive, but I don't know when)

She left after the phone rang (The phone rang, and then she left).

If you reverse the clauses while leaving the conjunction in the same place in these examples, you end up with either nonsense or a different meaning. I am smart that he thinks doesn't make any sense, and The phone rang after she left isn't the same thing as She left after the phone rang — in fact, it's just the opposite. This simple test lets you know that these conjunctions are subordinating rather than coordinating.

In English, subordinating conjunctions are often optional: We can say He thinks that I'm smart or He thinks I'm smart — both versions are grammatically correct and have the exact same meaning. In French, however, the subordinating conjunction is required: you must say Il pense que je suis intelligent.

The most common subordinating conjunctions are

après que (after)

avant que (before)

bien que (even though)

parce que (because)

puisque (since)

quand (when)

que (that)

si (if)

Chapter **3**

Figuring Out Nouns and Articles

Nouns are the people, places, and things in your sentences, the who and what that are doing whatever it is that needs to be done — or that are having something done to them — and where all this excitement is taking place. You're surrounded by nouns — this book, these words, my writing, your location.

Nouns can be specific, general, owned, unowned, nearby, or far away. Nouns are either singular or plural, and in French, every noun is masculine or feminine — even tables and chairs! This chapter explains the number and gender of French nouns, as well as the articles that often need to be used with them.

Genre Bending: Writing with Masculine and Feminine Nouns

A basic, singular noun refers to just one of something: a book, the cheese, my house. In English, that's about all there is to know about singular nouns. French, however, adds a little more to it: Every noun has a *gender* (**genre**), either masculine or feminine. The following sections spell out the need-to-know details about gender.

Determining the gender of nouns

In English, only nouns referring to people, certain animals, and some boats and cars have gender. But in French, all nouns have a gender, which matters not only for the noun itself, but also affects several other French parts of speech. A noun's gender determines which form of articles, adjectives, pronouns, and sometimes past participles you have to use, so knowing the gender is vital to speaking and writing in French. Some words even have different meanings depending on their gender, such as **le mari** (*husband*) and **la mari** (*marijuana*). So if you're talking to a police officer, be sure to use the masculine article when telling him that your husband is at home; otherwise, you may just find a search warrant waiting for you when you get there!

Most nouns that refer to people have a logical gender. **Homme** (*man*), **garçon** (*boy*), and **serveur** (*waiter*) are masculine, and **femme** (*woman*), **fille** (*girl*), and **serveuse** (*waitress*) are feminine. Animals and inanimate objects, however, are another *kettle* (**poissonnière** — feminine) of *fish* (**poisson** — masculine) altogether. The gender of objects and many animals is arbitrary — or at least, it seems that way to English speakers. In most cases, you can't just look at a word and know what gender it is — you have to memorize the gender of each word when you learn it.

TIP

The best way to remember the gender of nouns is to make vocabulary lists that include an article for each noun (see "Understanding Article Types, Gender, and Number," later in this chapter, for details). If possible, use indefinite articles because they don't change in front of vowels. Then, when you look at your list, the gender of the article tells you the gender of the noun: You can see that **un ordinateur** (*computer*) is masculine, due to the masculine article, and that **une télévision** (*television*) is feminine.

REMEMBER

A few word endings tend to indicate whether a noun is masculine or feminine. Words that end in –**age**, as in **message** and **mirage**, and –**eau**, such as **manteau** (*coat*) and **chapeau** (*hat*), are usually masculine. On the other hand, most words that end in –**ion**, like **nation** and **possession**, and –**té**, such as **liberté** (*freedom*) and **égalité** (*equality*), are feminine. But there are exceptions to all of these, and thousands of nouns don't end with these letters, so your best bet is to include articles for the words in your vocabulary lists and just memorize the articles and nouns together.

Making nouns feminine

Nouns that refer to people often have a masculine default form that can be made feminine (see Table 3-1 for examples). Here's how to make the gender switch:

>> To make most nouns feminine, just add –**e** to the end. For example, **un étudiant** (*male student*) becomes **une étudiante** (*female student*).

>> If a masculine noun ends in –**en** or –**on**, add –**ne** for the feminine form: **Un pharmacien** (*male pharmacist*) becomes **une pharmacienne** (*female pharmacist*).

>> Nouns that end in –**er** change to –**ère** for the feminine.

>> Nouns that end in –**eur** may become feminine with –**euse** or –**rice**.

>> Nouns that end in –**e** in the masculine form have no change for the feminine (other than in the article, which changes from **un**, **le**, or **du** to **une**, **la**, or **de la**).

Table 3-1   Examples of Nouns in Masculine and Feminine Forms

English	Masculine	Feminine
lawyer	un avocat	une avocate
electrician	un électricien	une électricienne
boss	un patron	une patronne
cashier	un caissier	une caissière
seller	un vendeur	une vendeuse
translator	un traducteur	une traductrice
tourist	un touriste	une touriste

TIP

If you're talking about one person whose gender you don't know, such as "one tourist" — if you don't know whether it's a man or woman, you always default to the masculine: **un touriste.**

Nouns that are always masculine or feminine

A number of French nouns have only a masculine or a feminine form, regardless of the gender of the person they refer to. Many of the masculine nouns refer to professions that are stereotypically considered "for men" — and the feminist police haven't entirely caught up with the language police, at least in France. In Canada and some other French-speaking countries, most nouns that refer to professions have both masculine and feminine forms. Some French feminists are working to use these in France, as well, and some feminized nouns are now more widely accepted. However, the **Académie française**, which regulates what it describes as the purity of the French language, doesn't move quickly to recognize the changing French language, and thus this institution doesn't consider feminized titles as correct French.

Traditionally, the following nouns are always masculine:

- » **un charpentier** (*carpenter*)
- » **un gouverneur** (*governor*)
- » **un médecin** (*doctor*)
- » **un ministre** (*minister*)
- » **un peintre** (*painter*)
- » **un plombier** (*plumber*)
- » **un poète** (*poet*)
- » **un pompier** (*firefighter*)
- » **un sculpteur** (*sculptor*)
- » **un témoin** (*witness*)

And these nouns are always feminine:

>> **une brute** (*boor, lout*)

>> **une connaissance** (*acquaintance*)

>> **une dupe** (*dupe, sucker*)

>> **une idole** (*idol*)

>> **une personne** (*person*)

>> **une star** (*movie star*)

>> **une vedette** (*movie star*)

>> **une victime** (*victim*)

PRACTICE

Time to switch things up. Make each of the masculine nouns feminine and the feminine nouns masculine, but watch out for nouns that can be only one or the other!

Q. un avocat

A. **une avocate** (*female lawyer*)

1. une boulangère _____

2. un pompier _____

3. une employée _____

4. un étudiant _____

5. une pharmacienne _____

6. un infirmier _____

7. une idole _____

8. un médecin _____

9. une vedette _____

10. un acteur _____

Part Deux: Making Nouns Plural

In addition to masculine and feminine forms, most nouns also have singular and plural forms. Making a noun plural in French is very similar to making a noun plural in English. You usually just add an **–s**, as with changing **un homme** (*a man*) to **deux hommes** (*two men*) and **la femme** (*the woman*) to **les femmes** (*the women*). The final **s** is silent, which means that the singular and plural forms of these nouns are pronounced the same way. But you can tell that the noun is plural because the article or number changes.

As I explain in the section "Determining the gender of nouns," earlier in this chapter, French often has masculine and feminine words for nouns referring to people, such as **un ami** (*male friend*) and **une amie** (*female friend*). However, French is a tad sexist when referring to groups of people. If you have a group of mixed masculine and feminine nouns, you always default to the masculine plural: **des amis**. The only time you can say **des amies** is when you're talking about a group of just girl friends, with not a single male in the bunch. However, if you have 65 girls and just 1 boy, you use **des amis**. (Not very fair, I know.)

The following sections explain how to form a plural when you can't simply add an –s.

Remembering your x's: Other plural patterns

Although most French nouns just add an –s for plurals, a few take an –x, with or without some other letter changes/additions. The singular form of these nouns always ends in one of the following letter combinations, which let you know that –x marks the (plural) spot. See Table 3-2 for some examples.

Table 3-2   Plural Patterns

English	French Singular	Singular Ending	French Plural	Plural Ending
work	**le travail**	–ail	**les travaux**	–aux
newspaper	**le journal**	–al	**les journaux**	–aux
jewel	**le joyau**	–au	**les joyaux**	–aux
coat	**le manteau**	–eau	**les manteaux**	–eaux
game	**le jeu**	–eu	**les jeux**	–eux

Irregular plurals

Some French nouns don't have distinct plural forms. When a noun ends in **–s**, **–x**, or **–z**, you don't add anything to make the word plural; the singular and plural forms are identical. To tell the difference between the singular and plural, you have to pay special attention to the article (for more on articles, see the following section):

>> **le mois** (*the month*) becomes **les mois**

>> **le prix** (*the price*) becomes **les prix**

>> **le nez** (*the nose*) becomes **les nez**

A few French nouns have irregular plurals — see Table 3-3 to memorize the most common ones.

Table 3-3   Common French Nouns that Have Irregular Plurals

English	French Singular	French Plural
eye	un œil	des yeux
ma'am/Mrs.	madame	mesdames
miss	mademoiselle	mesdemoiselles
sir/Mr.	monsieur	messieurs
sky	le ciel	les cieux

REMEMBER The plurals of **madame**, **mademoiselle**, and **monsieur** add an **–s** at the end of the word, which is normal, but the first part of the word also changes from the singular possessive adjective (**mon–** or **ma–**, which means *my*) to the plural possessive adjective **mes–**. See Chapter 4 for more info about possessives.

PRACTICE Plural practice: Make each of these singular nouns plural.

Q. couteau

A. **couteaux** (*knives*)

11 garçon _____

12 fille _____

13 feu _____

14 pois _____

15 cheval _____

16 monsieur _____

17 ciel _____

18 madame _____

19 gaz _____

20 œil _____

Understanding Article Types, Gender, and Number

Articles are small words that you can use only with nouns, and they have two purposes:

>> Presenting (or introducing) a noun

>> Indicating the gender and number of a noun

There are three kinds of French articles: definite, indefinite, and partitive. The following sections describe these three types of articles and identifies when and how you should use them in your French writing and speech.

Defining the definite articles

Definite articles indicate that the noun they're presenting is specific. In English, the definite article is *the*. French has three different definite articles, which tell you whether the noun is masculine, feminine, or plural. If the noun is singular, the article is **le** or **la**, depending on the noun's gender:

>> **le** is for a masculine noun: **le père** (*the father*)

>> **la** is for a feminine noun: **la mère** (*the mother*)

If the noun is plural, the definite article is always **les**, no matter what gender the nouns are: **les parents** (*the parents*), **les pères** (*the fathers*), **les mères** (*the mothers*).

REMEMBER

If a singular noun begins with a vowel or mute **h** (see following Tip), the definite article **le** or **la** contracts to l':

>> **l'ami** (*the male friend*)

>> **l'avocate** (*the female lawyer*)

>> **l'homme** (*the man*)

For plural nouns, the article is still **les**:

>> **les amis** (*the male or mixed gender friends*)

>> **les avocates** (*the female lawyers*)

>> **les hommes** (*the men*)

TIP

You'll see the terms *mute h* and its antonym *aspirated h* throughout this book. Although the letter **h** is always silent in French, it has two varieties that act in very different ways.

When a word starts with a mute **h**, the word acts as if it begins with a vowel, meaning that it uses contractions, such as l' for **le** and **la**, and j' for **je** (see Chapter 1 for more on using **je**).

In comparison, words that start with an aspirated **h** act as though they begin with a consonant, so **le** and **la** don't contract to l', and **je** doesn't contract to j'.

Here are some common words beginning with a mute **h**:

>> **habiller, j'habille** (*to dress, I dress*)

>> **habiter, j'habite** (*to live, I live*)

>> **l'habitude** (f) (*habit*)

>> **l'hébreu** (m) (*Hebrew*)

>> **l'herbe** (f) (*grass*)

>> **hésiter, j'hésite** (*to hesitate, I hesitate*)

>> **l'homme** (m) (*man*)

>> **l'hôtel** (m) (*helium*)

>> **l'huître** (f) (*oyster*)

>> **l'humeur** (f) (*mood*)

The following are some examples of words that begin with an aspirated h:

>> **haleter, je halète** (*to pant, I'm panting*)

>> **le haricot** (*bean*)

>> **le hasard** (*luck, chance*)

>> **la hauteur** (*height*)

>> **le héros** (*hero*)

>> **le hibou** (*owl*)

>> **le hockey** (*hockey*)

>> **le homard** (*lobster*)

>> **hoqueter, je hoquette** (*to hiccup, I'm hiccupping*)

>> **le hublot** (*porthole*)

 It's definitely time to practice! Choose the correct definite article for each of these nouns. The gender (m/f) is provided in parentheses.

PRACTICE

Q. garçon (m)

A. le garçon (*the boy*)

21 _____ stylo (m)

22 _____ herbe (f)

23 _____ été (m)

24 _____ livres (m)

(25) _____ dame (f)

(26) _____ hommes (m)

(27) _____ eau (f)

(28) _____ maisons (f)

(29) _____ hibou (m)

(30) _____ œil (m)

The French definite article is much more common than its English counterpart. In both languages, you use it when referring to a specific noun, as in **le livre que j'ai acheté** (*the book [that] I bought*).

DIFFERENCES

In French, the definite article is also repeated in front of each noun in a list; for example, **Parfois on voit le soleil et la lune en même temps** (*Sometimes we see the sun and moon at the same time*).

In addition, you use the French definite article to talk about the general sense of a noun (that is, to refer to the concept of the noun rather than a specific portion or instance of it) as in **J'aime le chocolat** (*I like chocolate*) and **Elle ne regarde pas la télé** (*She doesn't watch TV*).

PRACTICE

An adamant shopper! You know exactly what you want, so make your shopping list by using definite articles. The gender (m/f) is provided in parentheses.

Q. À _____ boulangerie (f)

A. À la boulangerie (*At the bakery*)

(31) _____ baguette (f)

(32) _____ croissant (m)

(33) _____ quiches (f)

(34) À _____ épicerie (f)

(35) _____ sel (m)

(36) _____ œufs (m) et

(37) _____ huile d'olive (f)

(38) À _____ crémerie (f)

(39) _____ fromage (m) et

(40) _____ yaourt (m)

Sorting out indefinite articles

Indefinite articles refer to an unspecific noun, "a" noun (any old noun) rather than "the" noun (the specific one you just used in your sentence). The English indefinite articles are *a* and *an*, and the one you use depends on whether the noun that follows begins with a consonant sound (*a*) or a vowel sound (*an*). However, in French, which indefinite article you use doesn't depend on the letter that starts the noun, but rather the gender and number (singular versus plural) of the noun.

Here are French's three indefinite articles:

>> **un** (for a masculine noun): **un livre** (*a book*), **un ananas** (*a pineapple*)

>> **une** (for a feminine noun): **une fraise** (*a strawberry*), **une idée** (*an idea*)

>> **des** (for all plural nouns): **des livres** (*some books*), **des idées** (*some ideas*), **des ananas** (*some pineapples*)

You use the indefinite article basically the same way in French and English — to refer to an unspecific noun, as in **J'ai une voiture** (*I have a car*) or **Je veux voir un film** (*I want to see a movie*).

TIP

Note that **un** and **une** can also mean *one*.

J'ai un frère et une sœur (*I have one brother and one sister*).

See Chapter 5 for more about numbers.

Des is the plural indefinite article, which you use for two or more masculine and/or feminine nouns.

Nous voyons des chats. (*We see some cats.*)

Je cherche des idées. (*I'm looking for some ideas.*)

PRACTICE

Choose the correct article for each of these nouns. The gender (m/f) is provided in parentheses.

Q. maison (f)

A. **une maison** (*a house*)

(41) jardin (m)

(42) tables (f)

(43) amie (f)

(44) livres (m)

(45) orange (f)

(46) hommes (m)

47 boisson (f)

48 café (m)

49 enfants (m)

50 anorak (m)

When you make a sentence that contains any indefinite article negative, the article changes to **de**, meaning *not a* or *not any*.

> **Je n'ai pas de voiture.** (*I don't have a car.*)

In front of a vowel or mute **h**, **de** contracts to **d'**.

> **Je ne cherche pas d'idées.** (*I'm not looking for any ideas.*)

See Chapter 9 for more information about negation.

PRACTICE

No, not that! Your friend always gets it wrong. Fill in the blanks with the correct indefinite article. The gender (m/f) is provided in parentheses.

Q. Tu as une sœur.

A. Non, je n'ai pas _____ sœur, j'ai un frère. (*No, I don't have a sister, I have a brother.*)

51 Non, je n'achète pas _____ chat.

52 Non, je ne veux pas _____ bière.

53 Non, je ne mange pas _____ cerises.

54 Non, je ne cherche pas _____ appartement.

55 Non, je ne regarde pas _____ série.

Looking at some partitive articles

Partitive articles are used with things that you take or use only a part of. They don't exist in English, so the best translation is the word *some*. Like French definite articles, there are three partitive articles:

>> **du** for a masculine noun: **du pain** (*some bread*)

>> **de la** for a feminine noun: **de la salade** (*some salad*)

>> **des** for plural nouns: **des épinards** (*some spinach*)

French has a number of plural nouns that have singular English equivalents, including

>> **des asperges** (*asparagus*)

>> **des brocolis** (*broccoli*)

>> **des cheveux** (*hair*)

>> **des conseils** (*advice*)

>> **des crevettes** (*shrimp*)

>> **des devoirs** (*homework*)

>> **des échecs** (*chess*)

>> **des épinards** (*spinach*)

>> **des meubles** (*furniture*)

>> **des pâtes** (*pasta*)

>> **des progrès** (*progress*)

>> **des vacances** (*vacation*)

You use the partitive article with food, drink, and other things that you usually take or use only a part (some) of, such as air and money. You also need the partitive article for abstract things, such as intelligence and patience. If you do eat or use all of something, and if it's countable, then you need the definite or indefinite article. Compare the following:

>> **J'achète du chocolat.** (*I'm buying some chocolate* — 1 pound.)

J'achète le chocolat. (*I'm buying the chocolate* — that kind that you like so much, or the one that Jacques told me about.)

>> **Je veux du gâteau.** (*I want some cake* — such as one piece, or the part that's in the bakery display case.)

Je veux un gâteau. (*I want a cake* — a whole one from the bakery, or one that Annette bakes for me.)

The partitive article is either two words or a contraction of two words:

>> The feminine partitive article **de la** is made up **de** and the feminine definite article **la**.

>> The masculine partitive article **du** is a contraction of **de** plus the masculine article **le**.

>> The plural partitive article **des** is a contraction of **de** plus the plural definite article **les**.

You can see more about these contractions in Chapter 12.

When a singular noun begins with a vowel or mute **h**, the singular partitive articles **du** and **de la** have to contract to **de l'**:

>> **de l'oignon** (*some onion*)

>> **de l'eau** (*some water*)

>> **de l'hélium** (*some helium*)

When you make a sentence that contains a partitive article negative, the article contracts down to **de**, meaning *not . . . any*.

Je n'achète pas de chocolat. (*I'm not buying any chocolate.*)

In front of a vowel or mute **h**, **de** contracts to **d':**

Je ne veux pas d'oignon. (*I don't want any onion.*)

See Chapter 9 for more information about negation.

Now for the quizzy part: Choose the correct article for each of these nouns. The gender (m/f) is provided in parentheses.

PRACTICE

Q. thé (m)

A. **du thé** (*some tea*)

56 pain (m)

57 moutarde (f)

58 eau (f)

59 asperges (m)

60 frites (f)

61 argent (m)

62 glace (f)

63 pâtes (f)

64 café (m)

65 progrès (m)

The sum of all articles

This section offers a quick recap of the different meanings and uses of the three kinds of articles discussed in the preceding sections:

>> **Definite articles:** With specific nouns, as well as the general sense (or concept) of a noun

>> **Indefinite articles:** With unspecific nouns

>> **Partitive articles:** When discussing a portion or some of a noun

PRACTICE

Now, see whether you know how to use these different kinds of articles together in this combo exercise!

You and Jules are going to a new restaurant for dinner. Fill in the blanks with the correct article — note that you must use each of the following articles at least once:

d' — de — de l' — de la — des — du — l' — la — le — les — un — une

Q. Jules: Comment s'appelle _____ restaurant (m) ?

A. le (*What is the name of the restaurant?*)

66 You: Il s'appelle Chez Laura. J'ai _____ amie (f) qui habite à côté. Elle dit que tous _____ plats (m) sont délicieux !

67 Jules: Il fait froid, est-ce que tu vas porter _____ anorak (m) ?

68 You: Non, je ne porte pas d'anorak (m), seulement _____ écharpe (f).

69 Jules: Je vais porter _____ gants (m) mais pas _____ chapeau (m).

70 You: OK, on y va ! _____ voiture (f) est dans _____ garage (m).

71 Jules: Est-ce que tu vas prendre _____ vin (m) ?

72 You: Non, pas _____ vin (m) pour moi. Je vais boire _____ eau (f). J'aime bien _____ eau (f) au citron.

73 Jules: Je veux _____ frites (f) avec _____ moutarde (f).

74 You: Oh non, _____ moutarde (f) est trop épicée ! Je préfère _____ (f) mayonnaise.

75 Jules: Ma salade est délicieuse, _____ ananas (m) dessus, c'est intéressant !

Answer Key to "Figuring Out Nouns and Articles" Practice Questions

1. **un boulanger** (*male baker*)
2. **un pompier** (*firefighter* — always masculine)
3. **un employé** (*male employee*)
4. **une étudiante** (*female student*)
5. **un pharmacien** (*male pharmacist*)
6. **une infirmière** (*female nurse*)
7. **une idole** (*idol* — always feminine)
8. **un médecin** (*doctor* — always masculine)
9. **une vedette** (*movie star* — always feminine)
10. **une actrice** (*actress*)
11. **garçons** (*boys*)
12. **filles** (*girls*)
13. **feux** (*fires*)
14. **pois** (*peas*)
15. **chevaux** (*horses*)
16. **messieurs** (*sirs*)
17. **cieux** (*skies*)
18. **mesdames** (*ladies*)
19. **gaz** (*gases*)
20. **yeux** (*eyes*)
21. **le stylo** (*the pen*)
22. **les herbes** (*the herbs*)
23. **l'été** (*the summer*)
24. **les livres** (*the books*)
25. **la dame** (*the woman*)
26. **les hommes** (*the men*)

(27) **l'eau** (*the water*)

(28) **les maisons** (*the houses*)

(29) **le hibou** (*the owl*)

(30) **l'œil** (*the eye*)

(31) **la baguette** (*the baguette*)

(32) **le croissant** (*the croissant*)

(33) **les quiches** (*the quiches*)

(34) **À l'épicerie** (*At the grocery store*)

(35) **le sel** (*the salt*)

(36) **les œufs** (*the eggs*)

(37) **l'huile d'olive** (*the olive oil*)

(38) **À la crémerie** (*At the dairy*)

(39) **le fromage** (*the cheese*)

(40) **le yaourt** (*the yogurt*)

(41) **un jardin** (*a garden*)

(42) **des tables** (*some tables*)

(43) **une amie** (*a friend*)

(44) **des livres** (*some books*)

(45) **une orange** (*an orange*)

(46) **des hommes** (*some men*)

(47) **une boisson** (*a drink*)

(48) **un café** (*a coffee*)

(49) **des enfants** (*some kids*)

(50) **un anorak** (*a jacket*)

(51) **Non, je n'achète pas de chat.** (*No, I'm not buying a cat.*)

(52) **Non, je ne veux pas de bière.** (*No, I don't want a beer.*)

(53) **Non, je ne mange pas de cerises.** (*No, I'm not eating cherries.*)

(54) **Non, je ne cherche pas d'appartement.** (*No, I'm not looking for an apartment.*)

(55) **Non, je ne regarde pas de série.** (*No, I'm not watching a TV series.*)

(56) **du pain** (*some bread*)

(57) **de la moutarde** (*some mustard*)

(58) **de l'eau** (*some water*)

(59) **des asperges** (*some asparagus*)

(60) **des frites** (*some fries*)

(61) **de l'argent** (*some money*)

(62) **de la glace** (*some ice cream*)

(63) **des pâtes** (*some pasta*)

(64) **du café** (*some coffee*)

(65) **des progrès** (*some progress*)

(66) You: **Il s'appelle Chez Laura. J'ai une amie qui habite à côté. Elle dit que tous les plats sont délicieux !** (*It's called Chez Laura. I have a friend who lives next door. She says that all of the dishes are delicious!*)

(67) Jules: **Il fait froid, est-ce que tu vas porter un anorak ?** (*It's cold out, are you going to wear a jacket?*)

(68) You: **No, je ne porte pas d'anorak.** (*No, I'm not wearing a jacket.*)

(69) Jules: **Je vais porter des gants mais pas de chapeau.** (*I'm going to wear [some] gloves but not a hat.*)

(70) You: **OK, on y va ! La voiture est dans le garage.** (*Okay, let's go! The car is in the garage.*)

(71) Jules: **Est-ce que tu vas prendre du vin ?** (*Are you going to have some wine?*)

(72) You: **Non, pas de vin pour moi. Je vais boire de l'eau. J'aime bien l'eau au citron.** (*No, no wine for me. I'm going to drink [some] water. I really like water with lemon.*)

(73) Jules: **Je veux des frites avec de la moutarde.** (*I want some fries with [some] mustard.*)

(74) You: **Oh non, la moutarde est trop épicée ! Je préfère la mayonnaise.** (*Oh no, mustard is too spicy! I prefer mayonnaise.*)

(75) Jules: **Ma salade est délicieuse, l'ananas dessus, c'est intéressant !** (*My salad is delicious, the pineapple on top is interesting!*)

Chapter **4**

Showing Up and Owning Up: Demonstratives and Possessives

A lthough French articles (which I talk about in Chapter 3) tell you whether a noun is definite, indefinite, or partial, other types of determiners identify a specific noun (*demonstratives*) or the owner of a noun (*possessives*).

Like articles and the nouns that they modify, demonstratives and possessives can have many different forms: singular, plural, masculine, and feminine. In addition, they can be adjectives or pronouns, depending on whether they modify a noun or replace it. This chapter demonstrates everything you need to know to make these demonstratives and possessives yours for keeps.

A Little of This and That: Using Demonstratives

You use demonstrative adjectives and pronouns when you want to talk about something specific, such as *this, that, these,* or *those. Demonstrative adjectives* are used with nouns; *demonstrative pronouns* are used in place of nouns. The following sections explain all about both of these demonstratives.

Demonstrative adjectives

The demonstrative adjective goes in front of a noun to indicate that you're referring to this or that particular noun. For example, if you say, "This book is more interesting than that book," the demonstrative adjectives *this* and *that* make it clear that the book you're holding or looking at — *this book* — is more interesting than *that book* — the one over on the other table or that someone else is holding.

Like other French adjectives (see Chapter 11), demonstrative adjectives have different forms depending on the gender and number of the noun they're used with. In addition, you use a special form of demonstrative adjective to modify a masculine noun that begins with a vowel or mute **h** — see Table 4-1.

Table 4-1   Demonstrative Adjectives

Gender	Singular (This/That)	Plural (These/Those)
masculine	ce	ces
masculine + vowel or mute **h**	cet	ces
feminine	cette	ces

Check out these examples:

>> Masculine: **Ce livre est intéressant.** (*This/That book is interesting.*)

>> Masculine + vowel: **Je veux lire cet article.** (*I want to read this/that article.*)

>> Masculine + mute **h**: **Cet homme est grand.** (*This/That man is tall.*)

>> Feminine: **Je vais acheter cette robe.** (*I'm going to buy this/that dress.*)

TIP The plural demonstrative adjective is always **ces** — "cettes" and "cets" don't exist. As you can see in the following examples, where I use exactly the same nouns as in the previous examples, **ce, cette,** and **cet** all become **ces** in the plural.

>> **Ces livres sont intéressants.** (*These/Those books are interesting.*)

>> **Je veux lire ces articles.** (*I want to read these/those articles.*)

>> **Ces hommes sont grands.** (*These/Those men are tall.*)

>> **Je vais acheter ces robes.** (*I'm going to buy these/those dresses.*)

Demo time! Show you understand by filling in the blanks with the correct form of the demonstrative adjective. The gender (m/f) is provided in parentheses.

Q. _____ livre (m)

A. **ce livre** (*this/that book*)

1. _____ table (f)

2. _____ arbre (m)

3. _____ chiens (m)

4. _____ eau (f)

5. _____ maisons (f)

6. _____ hélium (m)

7. _____ étudiants (m)

8. _____ étudiantes (f)

9. _____ habitude (f)

10. _____ artichauts (m)

Ce, cet, and **cette** can all mean *this* or *that* — French doesn't have separate words to make this distinction. You can usually tell by context, but if not, you can add the suffixes **–ci** (*here*) and **–là** (*there*) to the end of the noun.

> **Ce livre est drôle.** (*This/That book is funny.*)
>
> **Ce livre-ci est intéressant.** (*This book [here] is interesting.*)
>
> **Ce livre-là est stupide.** (*That book [there] is stupid.*)

The plural demonstrative adjective **ces** can mean *these* or *those*; again, you can use **–ci** and **–là** to clarify, if necessary.

> **Ces maisons sont vertes.** (*These/Those houses are green.*)
>
> **Ces maisons-ci sont grises.** (*These houses [here] are gray.*)
>
> **Ces maisons-là sont jaunes.** (*Those houses [there] are yellow.*)

Decision time! Your friend can never make up their mind about anything — help them out by providing the correct form of the demonstrative article, as well as the appropriate suffix. **Quel** means *which*, and the different forms let you know the gender and number of the noun (see Chapter 8 to learn about the interrogative adjective quel).

Q. Quel livre ?

A. Ce livre-ci. (*This book*)

11 Quelle peinture ? _____ (This painting)

12 Quels abricots ? _____ (Those apricots)

13 Quel ordinateur ? _____ (That computer)

14 Quelles aubergines ? _____ (These eggplants)

15 Quel restaurant ? _____ (This restaurant)

16 Quelle boulangerie ? _____ (That bakery)

17 Quelles chaussures ? _____ (These shoes)

18 Quels écouteurs ? _____ (Those earbuds)

19 Quel hébergement ? _____ (This lodging)

20 Quelle école ? _____ (That school)

Demonstrative pronouns

French demonstrative pronouns are very similar to demonstrative adjectives, except that they're not used with nouns; rather, they're used instead of nouns. The English demonstrative pronouns are *this one, that one, the one(s), these,* and *those.* French has four demonstrative pronouns because it needs different forms for masculine, feminine, singular, and plural — see Table 4-2.

Table 4-2   **Demonstrative Pronouns**

Gender	Singular	Plural
masculine	celui	ceux
feminine	celle	celles

REMEMBER A demonstrative pronoun basically replaces a demonstrative adjective + noun combination, and in the same way as a demonstrative adjective, it can indicate something that's close or far. To use a demonstrative pronoun, you need to remove both the demonstrative adjective and noun, and then replace them with the demonstrative pronoun.

See how the adjectives and pronouns are related in Table 4-3.

Table 4-3   Demonstrative Adjectives Become Demonstrative Pronouns

Gender and Number	Demonstrative Adjective + Noun	Demonstrative Pronoun
masculine singular	**cet homme** (*this/that man*)	**celui** (*this one/that one*)
feminine singular	**cette femme** (*this/that woman*)	**celle** (*this one/that one*)
masculine plural	**ces hommes** (*these/those men*)	**ceux** (*these/those*)
feminine plural	**ces femmes** (*these/those women*)	**celles** (*these/those*)

Celui and **celle** can both mean *this one* or *that one*, and **ceux** and **celles** can both mean *these (ones)* or *those (ones)*. In the same way that you can with demonstrative adjectives (see the preceding section), you can use the suffixes **–ci** or **–là** to specify whether you're talking about *this* or *that one* and *these* or *those*.

> **Quel livre veux-tu, celui-ci ou celui-là ?** (*Which book do you want, this one [here] or that one [there]?*)

> **J'aime cette lampe-là mieux que celles-ci.** (*I like that lamp [there] better than these [here].*)

Note that the preceding sentence uses both a demonstrative adjective (in the phrase **cette lampe-là**) and a demonstrative pronoun (**celles–ci**).

PRACTICE

Your indecisive friend needs help selecting all kinds of things. Provide them with the correct form of the demonstrative pronoun and the appropriate suffix.

Q. Quel livre ?

A. Celui-ci. (*This one*)

21 Quelles chaussettes ? _____ (Those ones)

22 Quelle université ? _____ (That one)

23 Quel clavier ? _____ (This one)

24 Quelles valises ? _____ (These ones)

25 Quel avion ? _____ (That one)

26 Quelle émission ? _____ (This one)

27 Quelles voitures ? _____ (These ones)

28 Quels oiseaux ? _____ (Those ones)

29 Quel appartement ? _____ (This one)

30 Quelle banane ? _____ (That one)

You can also use demonstrative pronouns with the preposition **de** + a word or phrase to indicate whom something belongs to or where it's from. (You can find out more about this possessive structure in the following section.)

> **Je veux acheter des vêtements aussi jolis que ceux de Pauline.** (*I want to buy some clothes as pretty as Pauline's. Literally: I want to buy some clothes as pretty as those of Pauline.*)

Demonstrate your understanding of demonstratives by filling in the blanks with the correct demonstrative adjective or demonstrative pronoun.

Q. J'aime _____ manteau.

A. **J'aime ce manteau.** (*I like this coat.*)

31 Je pense que cette maison-ci est plus jolie que _____-là. (I think this house is prettier than that one.)

32 Je veux _____ chien. (I want this/that dog.)

33 Préfères-tu le fromage du Vermont ou bien _____ du Wisconsin ? (Do you prefer cheese from Vermont or Wisconsin?)

34 Je connais _____ homme. (I know this/that man.)

35 Je cherche un film — _____ que nous avons regardé ensemble. (I'm looking for a movie — the one we watched together.)

36 J'ai acheté _____ vêtements. (I bought these/those clothes.)

37 Tes idées sont plus viables que _____ de Marc. (Your ideas are more workable than Marc's.)

38 Je n'aime pas _____ idée. (I don't like this/that idea.)

39 Tu peux utiliser mon ordinateur ; — c'est _____-ci. (You can use my computer — it's this one.)

40 Je ne connais pas _____ femmes. (I don't know these/those women.)

Possession: Channeling the Spirit of Ownership

No, possession has nothing to do with ghosts — at least, not in this book. I'm talking about the grammatical structures you use to express who owns something. When you want to make it clear that what's mine is mine and what's yours is mine, you need to know about possession.

French has three different ways to express ownership: the possessive **de**, possessive adjectives, and possessive pronouns. These are equivalent in English to the possessive *'s*, possessive adjectives, and possessive pronouns, respectively. The following sections explain all of these different means of possession so that you can make sure that everyone knows whose is whose.

Possession using de

DIFFERENCES

In English, when you want to say that something belongs to someone or something, you commonly use an apostrophe: either *'s* or *s'*. French is completely different. You have to reverse the order of the nouns and join them with the preposition **de** (*of*). In other words, start with the definite article and the thing that's owned, then add **de** and the owner.

la maison de Michel (*Michel's house*; literally: *the house of Michel*)

les chaussures d'André (*André's shoes*; literally: *the shoes of André*)

l'idée de l'étudiant (*the student's idea*; literally: *the idea of the student*)

la chambre de mes sœurs (*my sisters' room*; literally: *the room of my sisters*)

When **de** precedes the definite articles **le** or **les**, they contract to make **du** and **des**, respectively (find out more about these contractions in Chapter 12).

le lit [de + le] du chien (*the dog's bed*; literally, *the bed of the dog*)

la chambre [de + les] des enfants (*the kids' room*; literally, *the room of the kids*)

All jumbled up! You made a packing list for the upcoming family trip — and then accidentally put it through the shredder. See if you can piece it back together.

PRACTICE

Q. Denise — portable (m)

A. **le portable de Denise** (*Denise's laptop*)

41 Pierre — livres (m) _____

42 les enfants — tente (f) _____

43 le bébé — doudou (m) _____

44 Simon — oreiller (m) _____

45 les garçons — bicyclettes (f) _____

Working with possessive adjectives

Possessive adjectives go in front of nouns to tell you whom or what those nouns belong to. You use them pretty much the same way in French and English, but French has a lot more of them: different forms for masculine, feminine, singular, and plural. In order to use the correct French possessive adjective, you need to consider the person who owns the noun, as well as the gender and number of the noun. To say *my house*, you need to remember that **maison** (*house*) is feminine and singular, so you want to use the feminine singular form of the adjective: **ma maison**. See Table 4-4 for the different forms of French possessive adjectives.

Table 4-4 **Possessive Adjectives**

English	Masculine	Feminine	Plural
my	**mon**	**ma**	**mes**
your (**tu** form)	**ton**	**ta**	**tes**
his/her/its	**son**	**sa**	**ses**
our	**notre**	**notre**	**nos**
your (**vous** form)	**votre**	**votre**	**vos**
their	**leur**	**leur**	**leurs**

Singular subjects

French possessive adjectives for first-, second-, and third-person singular subjects (the owners of the nouns) have three forms, depending on the gender, number, and first letter of the noun they precede (the possession) — see Table 4-5.

Table 4-5 **Singular-Owner Possessive Adjectives**

	Masculine (Before Any Letter)	Feminine	Feminine Before a Vowel	Plural
1st person	**mon frère**	**ma sœur**	**mon idole**	**mes frères, mes sœurs**
	(*my brother*)	(*my sister*)	(*my idol*)	(*my brothers, my sisters*)
2nd person	**ton frère**	**ta sœur**	**ton idole**	**tes frères, tes sœurs**
	(*your brother*)	(*your sister*)	(*your idol*)	(*your brothers, your sisters*)
3rd person	**son frère**	**sa sœur**	**son idole**	**ses frères, ses sœurs**
	(*his/her brother*)	(*his/her sister*)	(*his/her idol*)	(*his/her brothers, his/her sisters*)

DIFFERENCES

In English, the choice of *his* or *her* depends on the gender of the owner (the person/thing that possesses the object): *Tom's sister* becomes his *sister*, and *Jane's sister* becomes her *sister*. In French, it's just the opposite: the gender of the *thing possessed* determines whether to say **son** or **sa**:

>> *His sister* and *her sister* are both translated as **sa sœur** because **sœur** is feminine.

>> *His brother* and *her brother* are both translated as **son frère** because **frère** is masculine.

If you really need to be clear about whether you mean *his* or *her*, you can add **à lui** (literally, "of him") or **à elle** ("of her"):

>> **C'est son frère à lui.** (*It's his brother, brother "of him."*)

>> **C'est son frère à elle.** (*It's her brother, brother "of her."*)

You can use **ma**, **ta**, and **sa** only with a feminine noun that begins with a consonant or an aspirated **h**. When a feminine noun begins with a vowel or mute **h**, you use the masculine adjective (**mon**, **ton**, or **son**).

When the thing owned is plural, the possessive adjective is always **mes**, **tes**, or **ses**, regardless of the gender or first letter.

PRACTICE

Whose is whose? Fill in the blanks with the correct form of the possessive adjective. The gender (m/f) is provided in parentheses.

Q. _____ livre (m)

A. **mon livre** (my book)

46 your dress: _____ robe (f)

47 her jacket: _____ anorak (m)

48 my cats: _____ chats (m)

49 his water: _____ eau (f)

50 your kids: _____ enfants (m)

51 my sock: _____ chaussette (f)

52 his mother: _____ mère (f)

53 your apartment: _____ appartement (m)

54 his stories: _____ histoires (f)

55 her father: _____ père (m)

Plural owners

First-, second-, and third-person *plural owners* have only two forms of the possessive adjective: singular and plural. Whether the noun being possessed is masculine or feminine — and whether it starts with a consonant or vowel — doesn't matter for plural owners. The only thing that counts is whether the owned item is singular or plural. (See what I did there?) See Table 4-6.

Table 4-6   Plural-Owner Possessive Adjectives

	Singular	Plural
1st person plural	**notre frère, notre sœur**	**nos frères, nos sœurs**
	(our brother, our sister)	(our brothers, our sisters)
2nd person plural	**votre frère, votre sœur**	**vos frères, vos sœurs**
	(your brother, your sister)	(your brothers, your sisters)
3rd person plural	**leur frère, leur sœur**	**leurs frères, leurs sœurs**
	(their brother, their sister)	(their brothers, their sisters)

PRACTICE

Prove you own all of this possessive information by translating the following into French, using the possessive **de** or a possessive adjective, as appropriate.

Q. Jean's pen

A. le stylo de Jean

56 my house _____

57 Louise's book _____

58 your computer (**tu** form) _____

59 Benoît's school _____

60 our friends _____

61 your car (**vous** form) _____

62 their bedroom _____

63 the victim's accident _____

64 your sister's kids (**tu** form) _____

65 her dad's apartment _____

Yours, mine, and ours: Understanding possessive pronouns

Possessive pronouns are a lot like possessive adjectives (see the section "Working with possessive adjectives," earlier in this chapter), except that you use possessive pronouns in place of nouns, rather than with them. The English possessive pronouns are *mine, yours, his, hers, its, ours,* and *theirs*. And if you think that's a lot, just wait until you see all the different French forms!

French has different possessive pronouns depending on the gender and number of the possessed nouns. As opposed to possessive adjectives, which have just three forms (masculine, feminine, plural) for singular owners, when it comes to possessive pronouns, there are four different forms: masculine and feminine singular and masculine and feminine plural — see Table 4-7.

Table 4-7 Singular-Owner Possessive Pronouns

English	Masculine Singular	Feminine Singular	Masculine Plural	Feminine Plural
mine	**le mien**	**la mienne**	**les miens**	**les miennes**
yours (**tu** form)	**le tien**	**la tienne**	**les tiens**	**les tiennes**
his/hers/its	**le sien**	**la sienne**	**les siens**	**les siennes**

WARNING

Note that the forms change according to the gender and number of the thing owned, not the owner.

For example:

> **Je vois ton livre, où est le mien ?** (*I see your book, where is mine?*)
>
> **La sœur de Nicolas est sympa, et la tienne aussi.** (*Nicolas's sister is nice, and yours [is] too.*)

REMEMBER

Just like possessive adjectives, which you can read about in the section "Working with possessive adjectives," earlier in this chapter, the third-person singular possessive pronoun's form is based on the gender of the noun being replaced, not the gender of the subject. **Le sien**, **la sienne**, **les siens**, and **les siennes** can all mean *his*, *hers*, or *its*:

> **Ma voiture est ici, la sienne est là-bas.** (*My car is here, his/hers is over there.*)

In comparison to the singular owners, which have four different possessive adjectives (see Table 4-7), the plural owners (**nous**, **vous**, and **ils/elles**) have only three forms because the plural possessive pronouns are the same, regardless of gender. And the only difference between masculine and feminine is the definite article that precedes the pronoun — see Table 4-8.

Table 4-8 Plural-Owner Possessive Pronouns

English	Masculine Singular	Feminine Singular	Plural
ours	**le nôtre**	**la nôtre**	**les nôtres**
yours (**vous** form)	**le vôtre**	**la vôtre**	**les vôtres**
theirs	**le leur**	**la leur**	**les leurs**

Note these particulars:

>> Each possessive pronoun has to start with a definite article

>> Although the **nous** and **vous** forms of the possessive pronoun have a *circumflex* (note the ô in **le nôtre** and **le vôtre**), the possessive adjectives don't (**notre**, **votre**).

Here are some sentences that use possessive pronouns:

> **J'ai trouvé un stylo. C'est le vôtre ?** (*I found a pen. Is it yours?*)
>
> **As-tu tes clés ? Je ne peux pas trouver les nôtres.** (*Do you have your keys? I can't find ours.*)
>
> **Notre maison est jolie, mais je préfère la leur.** (*Our house is pretty, but I prefer theirs.*)

This house is possessed! Test yourself on all the different possessive possibilities with this visit to a haunted house.

PRACTICE

Q. I think Fatoma's house is haunted!

Je pense que _____ est hantée !

A. la maison de Fatoma

66 Her house is very old,

_____ est très vieille,

67 and her garden is a mess of twisted trees. (**jardin**, m)

et _____ est un fouillis d'arbres tordus.

68 All of her windows are broken. (**fenêtre**, f)

Toutes _____ sont cassées . . .

69 And her cats!

Et _____ !

70 I like cats, but hers are mean.

J'aime bien les chats, mais _____ sont méchants,

71 And their fur is entirely black, of course. (pelage, m)

Et _____ pelage est tout noir, bien sûr.

72 So no, I don't want to visit your friend's house,

Alors non, je ne veux pas visiter _____,

73 I prefer mine!

je préfère _____ !

Answer Key to "Demonstratives and Possessives" Practice Questions

1. **cette table** (*this/that table*)
2. **cet arbre** (*this/that tree*)
3. **ces chiens** (*these/those dogs*)
4. **cette eau** (*this/that water*)
5. **ces maisons** (*these/those houses*)
6. **cet hélium** (*this/that helium*)
7. **ces étudiants** (*these/those students*)
8. **ces étudiantes** (*these/those female students*)
9. **cette habitude** (*this/that habit*)
10. **ces artichauts** (*these/those artichokes*)
11. **Cette peinture-ci**
12. **Ces abricots-là**
13. **Cet ordinateur-là**
14. **Ces aubergines-ci**
15. **Ce restaurant-ci ?**
16. **Cette boulangerie-là**
17. **Ces chaussures-ci ?**
18. **Ces écouteurs-là**
19. **Cet hébergement-ci**
20. **Cette école-la ?**
21. **Celles-là**
22. **Celle-là**
23. **Celui-ci**
24. **Celles-ci**
25. **Celui-là**
26. **Celle-ci**

(27) **Celles-ci**

(28) **Ceux-là**

(29) **Celui-ci**

(30) **Celle-là**

(31) **Je pense que cette maison-ci est plus jolie que celle-là.** (*I think this house is prettier than that one.*)

(32) **Je veux ce chien.** (*I want this/that dog.*)

(33) **Préfères-tu le fromage du Vermont ou bien celui du Wisconsin ?** (*Do you prefer cheese from Vermont or Wisconsin?*)

(34) **Je connais cet homme.** (*I know this/that man.*)

(35) **Je cherche un film — celui que nous avons regardé ensemble.** (*I'm looking for a movie — the one we watched together.*)

(36) **J'ai acheté ces vêtements.** (*I bought these/those clothes.*)

(37) **Tes idées sont plus viables que celles de Marc.** (*Your ideas are more workable than Marc's.*)

(38) **Je n'aime pas cette idée.** (*I don't like this/that idea.*)

(39) **Tu peux utiliser mon ordinateur — c'est celui-ci.** (*You can use my computer — it's this one.*)

(40) **Je ne connais pas ces femmes.** (*I don't know these/those women.*)

(41) **les livres de Pierre** (*Pierre's books*)

(42) **la tente des enfants** (*the kids' tent*)

(43) **le doudou du bébé** (*the baby's blankie*)

(44) **l'oreiller de Simon** (*Simon's pillow*)

(45) **les bicyclettes des garçons** (*the boys' bikes*)

(46) **ta robe**

(47) **son anorak**

(48) **mes chats**

(49) **son eau**

(50) **tes enfants**

(51) **ma chaussette**

(52) **sa mère**

(53) **ton appartement**

(54) **ses histoires**

(55) **son père**

(56) **ma maison** (*my house*)

(57) **le livre de Louise** (*Louise's book*)

(58) **ton ordinateur** (*your computer*)

(59) **l'école de Benoît** (*Benoît's school*)

(60) **nos amis/nos amies** (*our friends*)

(61) **votre voiture** (*your car*)

(62) **leur chambre** (*their bedroom*)

(63) **l'accident de la victime** (*the victim's accident*)

(64) **les enfants de ta sœur** (*your sister's kids*)

(65) **l'appartement de son père** (*her dad's apartment*)

(66) **Sa maison est très vieille,**

(67) **et son jardin est un fouillis d'arbres tordus.**

(68) **Toutes ses fenêtres sont cassées.**

(69) **Et ses chats !**

(70) **J'aime bien les chats, mais les siens sont méchants.**

(71) **Et leur pelage est tout noir, bien sûr.**

(72) **Alors non, je ne veux pas visiter la maison de ton amie,**

(73) **je préfère la mienne !**

Chapter **5**

The 4-1-1 on Numbers, Dates, and Time

Numbers are one of the most basic and useful parts of language. In addition to simple counting, you need numbers for talking about dates, time, prices, phone numbers, addresses, and so much more. Before you can make appointments, find out how much something costs, shop in bulk, or give that cute barista your digits, you have to know your numbers. But being able to say and understand numbers is only half the battle — writing them is another matter because you need to know how to spell and abbreviate them, as well. This chapter explains French cardinal and ordinal numbers and calendar words, as well as how to put everything together for talking about dates and time.

Using Numbers

Before you can do anything with numbers, you need to know what they are. French numbers have a few special characteristics that make them a little tricky for English speakers. Plus, reciting numbers and writing them are two different tasks. The following sections highlight a few important points about cardinal and ordinal numbers so that you don't make any faux pas in your writing.

Counting on cardinal numbers: 1, 2, 3

Cardinal numbers are for counting. Cardinals are the most common numbers; you could even call them the normal numbers. You use cardinal numbers for talking about things like how many times you've seen your favorite movie and how much time you spent at the beach today.

Starting with numbers 0 to 19

The low numbers are easy. You may already know them backwards and forwards, but if not, all you need to do is memorize them like any other vocab list.

Check out the following list of numbers from 0 to 19:

>> **zéro** (*zero*)

>> **un, une** (*one*)

>> **deux** (*two*)

>> **trois** (*three*)

>> **quatre** (*four*)

>> **cinq** (*five*)

>> **six** (*six*)

>> **sept** (*seven*)

>> **huit** (*eight*)

>> **neuf** (*nine*)

>> **dix** (*ten*)

>> **onze** (*eleven*)

>> **douze** (*twelve*)

>> **treize** (*thirteen*)

>> **quatorze** (*fourteen*)

>> **quinze** (*fifteen*)

>> **seize** (*sixteen*)

>> **dix-sept** (*seventeen*)

>> **dix-huit** (*eighteen*)

>> **dix-neuf** (*nineteen*)

REMEMBER

One is the only cardinal number that has a masculine form (**un**) and a feminine form (**une**), which you use in front of nouns. Note that these are identical to the singular indefinite articles (see Chapter 3).

PRACTICE

Counting on fingers and toes: Practice French numbers (and a few new terms) with some simple math. The other vocabulary you need is **plus** (*plus*), **moins** (*minus*), and **égal** (*equals*). Be sure to maximize your practice by spelling out the number, rather than using digits.

Q. un plus un égal _____

A. deux

1 six moins trois égal _____

2 dix plus cinq égal _____

3 treize moins neuf égal _____

4 dix-sept plus deux égal _____

5 treize moins douze égal _____

(6) neuf plus neuf égal _____

(7) cinq moins trois égal _____

(8) onze plus six égal _____

(9) huit moins huit égal _____

(10) douze plus deux égal _____

Adding on with numbers 20 to 69

TIP

When you get to numbers in the 20s, you have to start doing some addition, just like in English: Take the tens number and add the ones number. For example, *twenty-two* is *twenty* (**vingt**) followed by *two* (**deux**) and joined by a hyphen: *twenty-two* — **vingt-deux**. *Twenty-three* is **vingt-trois**.

The process is the same for all the numbers up to 69, except for 21, 31, 41, 51, and 61. For those, you need the word **et** (*and*) between the two numbers, with or without hyphens connecting each word. (With hyphens is the accepted spelling since the far-reaching 1990 spelling reform; without hyphens is the traditional spelling.)

See the following mini-table for some examples, which you can use as the pattern for the rest of the numbers.

vingt (20)	**trente** (30)	**quarante** (40)	**cinquante** (50)	**soixante** (60)
vingt-et-un (21)	**trente-et-un** (31)	**quarante-et-un** (41)	**cinquante-et-un** (51)	**soixante-et-un** (61)
vingt et un	**trente et un**	**quarante et un**	**cinquante et un**	**soixante et un**
vingt-deux (22)	**trente-deux** (32)	**quarante-deux** (42)	**cinquante-deux** (52)	**soixante-deux** (62)
vingt-trois (23)	**trente-trois** (33)	**quarante-trois** (43)	**cinquante-trois** (53)	**soixante-trois** (63)

PRACTICE

The power of tens! Find out if you've mastered these French numbers by adding or subtracting 10. You'll need some additional vocabulary: **plus** (*plus*), **moins** (*minus*), and **égal** (*equals*). Be sure to maximize your practice by spelling out the number, rather than using digits.

Q. vingt plus dix égal _____

A. trente

(11) cinquante et un moins dix égal _____

(12) vingt-trois plus dix égal _____

(13) soixante-neuf moins dix égal _____

(14) trente-sept plus dix égal _____

15 quarante et un moins dix égal _____

16 cinquante-cinq plus dix égal _____

17 soixante-six moins dix égal _____

18 vingt-neuf plus dix égal _____

19 trente-huit moins dix égal _____

20 quarante-quatre plus dix égal _____

Getting weird with numbers 70-99

DIFFERENCES

When you get past 69, you have to start doing some real math. To say 70 in French, you say **soixante-dix**, which literally means *"sixty-ten."* Seventy-one is *"sixty and eleven"* (**soixante-et-onze**), 72 is *"sixty-twelve"* (**soixante-douze**), and so on up to 79 — *"sixty-nineteen"* (**soixante-dix-neuf**).

The numbers 80 to 99 are even stranger — you have to do multiplication, too. The French term for 80 is **quatre-vingts** — *"four twenties."* And then, 81 is **quatre-vingt-un**, 82 is **quatre-vingt-deux** — yada, yada, yada — 89 is **quatre-vingt-neuf**, and 90 is **quatre-vingt-dix**.

The 90s then continue like the 70s, adding on the tens number: 91 is **quatre-vingt-onze**, 92 is **quatre-vingt-douze**, and so on. Notice that 80 is the only number that has an **s** on the word **vingts**. You can see these numbers in all their strange glory in this mini-table.

soixante-dix (70)	**quatre-vingts** (80)	**quatre-vingt-dix** (90)
soixante-et-onze (71)	**quatre-vingt-un** (81)	**quatre-vingt-onze** (91)
soixante-douze (72)	**quatre-vingt-deux** (82)	**quatre-vingt-douze** (92)
soixante-treize (73)	**quatre-vingt-trois** (83)	**quatre-vingt-treize** (93)
soixante-quatorze (74)	**quatre-vingt-quatre** (84)	**quatre-vingt-quatorze** (94)
soixante-quinze (75)	**quatre-vingt-cinq** (85)	**quatre-vingt-quinze** (95)
soixante-seize (76)	**quatre-vingt-six** (86)	**quatre-vingt-seize** (96)
soixante-dix-sept (77)	**quatre-vingt-sept** (87)	**quatre-vingt-dix-sept** (97)
soixante-dix-huit (78)	**quatre-vingt-huit** (88)	**quatre-vingt-dix-huit** (98)
soixante-dix-neuf (79)	**quatre-vingt-neuf** (89)	**quatre-vingt-dix-neuf** (99)

PRACTICE

Five-and-dime time! Test yourself on these tricky French numbers by adding or subtracting 5 or 10. The other vocabulary you need is **plus** (*plus*), **moins** (*minus*), and **égal** (*equals*). Be sure to maximize your practice by spelling out the number, rather than using digits.

Q. soixante-dix plus cinq égal _____

A. **soixante-quinze**

21 quatre-vingt-neuf moins dix égal _____

22 soixante-dix-huit plus dix égal _____

23 soixante-seize moins cinq égal _____

24 quatre-vingt-quatre plus cinq égal _____

25 quatre-vingt-dix-huit moins dix égal _____

26 quatre-vingt-un plus dix égal _____

27 soixante-dix-neuf moins cinq égal _____

28 quatre-vingt-cinq plus cinq égal _____

29 quatre-vingt-dix moins dix égal _____

30 soixante-douze plus cinq égal _____

DIFFERENCES

The French spoken in France doesn't have unique words for 70, 80, and 90, but other French-speaking countries do. In Switzerland, *seventy* is **septante**, *eighty* is **huitante**, and *ninety* is **nonante**. In Belgium, they say **septante**, **quatre-vingts**, and **nonante**.

PRACTICE

Take a swing at the French numbers and do some counting. For each number provided, spell out the number that comes before and after it.

Q. un

A. **zéro, deux** (*zero, two*)

31 six _____

32 dix _____

33 treize _____

34 dix-neuf _____

35 trente _____

36 quarante-et-un _____

37 cinquante-neuf _____

38 soixante-dix _____

39 quatre-vingt-un _____

40 quatre-vingt-dix-huit _____

Going big with numbers 100 and up

If you've survived the numbers 0 to 99, including the tricky calculations of the 70s through 90s, **félicitations !** (*congratulations!*) The rest of the French numbers are pretty straightforward. Here are just two things to watch out for:

>> **Plurals:** All the big number words — except for **mille** (*thousand*) — end in **s** when referring to more than one of that amount.

>> **Billion:** The word *billion* is a false friend (a word that looks similar in French and English but has different meanings). In English, a *billion* is a *thousand millions* (1,000,000,000), but in French, **un billion** means *a million millions*, which equals a *trillion* (1,000,000,000,000).

The following mini-table shows you the singular and plural forms of the big numbers. Follow the plural pattern for numbers three (hundred/thousand/and so on) and up.

cent (*hundred*/100)	**deux cents** (*two hundred*/200)
mille (*thousand*/1,000)	**deux mille** (*two thousand*/2,000)
un million (*million*/1,000,000)	**deux millions** (*two million*/2,000,000)
un milliard (*billion*/1,000,000,000)	**deux milliards** (*two billion*/2,000,000,000)
un billion (*trillion*/1,000,000,000,000)	**deux billions** (*two trillion*/2,000,000,000,000)

TIP Cent and **mille** aren't preceded by articles; **j'ai cent dollars** means *I have a hundred dollars.*

Assigning rank with ordinal numbers

Suppose you want to tell people that you work on the 17th floor or that you plan to come in first in next year's Tour de France (hey, you've been training). In that case, you need ordinal numbers, which allow you to rank things.

You form most French ordinal numbers by taking the cardinal number and adding the suffix **–ième** (see the section "Counting on cardinal numbers: 1, 2, 3," earlier in this chapter, for details on cardinal numbers). *Third*, for instance, is **troisième**. Ordinal numbers can be abbreviated with a superscript e, so you can write 3rd as 3e.

TIP When you convert cardinals to ordinals, you may need to make a few spelling changes before you can add the suffix:

>> For numbers such as **quatre** and **onze**, you have to lose the **e: quatrième** (*fourth*), **onzième** (*eleventh*).

>> At the end of **cinq**, you have to add **u: cinquième** (*fifth*).

>> As for **neuf**, the **f** changes to **v: neuvième** (*ninth*).

The only ordinal number that doesn't end in **–ième** is *first*. It's nothing like the cardinal number **un** (*one*), and it's the only ordinal number that has two forms: The masculine form is **premier**, abbreviated 1er, and the feminine is **première** (1re or 1ère). See Chapter 3 for details on gender.

Table 5-1 breaks down the numbers and shows the ordinal and corresponding cardinal numbers for one through ten.

Table 5-1 Ordinal Numbers

English Ordinal Number	English Abbreviation	French Cardinal Number	French Ordinal Number	Abréviation
first	1st	**un, une**	**premier, première**	1er, 1re
second	2nd	**deux**	**deuxième**	2^e
third	3rd	**trois**	**troisième**	3^e
fourth	4th	**quatre**	**quatrième**	4^e
fifth	5th	**cinq**	**cinquième**	5^e
sixth	6th	**six**	**sixième**	6^e
seventh	7th	**sept**	**septième**	7^e
eighth	8th	**huit**	**huitième**	8^e
ninth	9th	**neuf**	**neuvième**	9^e
tenth	10th	**dix**	**dixième**	10^e

The rest of the ordinal numbers follow the same pattern; the only ones to watch out for are 21st, 31st, and so on, which are in the format [tens number] + **et** + **unième**: **vingt-et-unième** (*21st*), **trente-et-unième** (*31st*), and so on.

Make sure you have your ordinals in order. Convert each cardinal number into an ordinal and provide the abbreviation.

PRACTICE

Q. trois

A. **troisième**, 3e (*third*, 3rd)

41 dix _____

42 sept _____

43 un _____

44 trente _____

45 quarante-quatre _____

46 cinquante-et-un _____

47 soixante-douze _____

48 quatre-vingt-onze _____

49 quatre-vingt-dix-neuf _____

50 cent _____

Mark Your Calendar: Expressing Days, Months, and Dates

Got plans? Knowing French calendar words and how to say what day it is makes it easier for you to make appointments, break dates, plan outings, and make sure you don't "accidentally" end up working all weekend when you're supposed to be visiting the in-laws. If you want to be sure everyone knows when to meet, you need to know how to talk about dates in French. The following sections give you the lowdown on the days of the week, the months of the year, and all the dates on the calendar. (After reading this chapter, you can make sure your French-speaking friends never forget your birthday again!)

Knowing the days of the week

Most of the days of the week end in –**di**, except for Sunday, which begins with those two letters.

Here are the **jours de la semaine** (*days of the week*):

» **lundi** (*Monday*)

» **mardi** (*Tuesday*)

» **mercredi** (*Wednesday*)

» **jeudi** (*Thursday*)

» **vendredi** (*Friday*)

» **samedi** (*Saturday*)

» **dimanche** (*Sunday*)

 In French, the week starts on Monday, not Sunday, and you don't capitalize the days.

DIFFERENCES If you want to know what day of the week it is, you first need to know how to ask. (Check out Chapter 8 for more information about asking and answering questions in French.) You can phrase this question a couple different ways in French: **Quel jour sommes-nous ?** (*What day is it?*) or **C'est quel jour aujourd'hui ?** (*What day is today?*) You can answer such a question with either of the following phrases followed by the day of the week: **Nous sommes** or **On est**.

Nous sommes dimanche. (*It's Sunday.*)

On est mardi. (*It's Tuesday.*)

To say that something happened or is going to happen on a certain day, you just use that day with no preposition or article: **Je vais aller à la banque vendredi** means *I will go to the bank on Friday.*

To say that something happens every week on a certain day, you use the definite article: **Je vais à la banque le vendredi** means *I go to the bank on Fridays.*

Here are some other useful words related to days and weeks:

>> **avant-hier** (*the day before yesterday*)

>> **hier** (*yesterday*)

>> **aujourd'hui** (*today*)

>> **demain** (*tomorrow*)

>> **après-demain** (*the day after tomorrow*)

>> **la semaine dernière** (*last week*)

>> **cette semaine** (*this week*)

>> **la semaine prochaine** (*next week*)

In France, *the weekend* is called **le weekend**, while in Canada, it's called **la fin de semaine**.

DIFFERENCES

Your friend is in such a hurry, they're always one day ahead! Set them straight with the correct day of the week or related word.

PRACTICE

Q. C'est lundi.

A. Non, c'est dimanche.

51 On est jeudi. Non, _____.

52 Nous sommes samedi. Non, _____.

53 Nous sommes mercredi. Non, _____.

54 On est dimanche. Non, _____.

55 Nous sommes mardi. Non, _____.

56 On est vendredi. Non, _____.

57 On est lundi. Non, _____.

58 Nous sommes allés au parc hier. Non, _____.

59 Nous allons partir après-demain. Non, _____.

60 La fête est demain. Non, _____.

An even dozen: Identifying the months

The French words for months are fairly similar to their English counterparts, but you definitely need to watch out for some spelling differences. Whenever you're writing a letter to your pen pal in Senegal or an e-mail to that business associate in Switzerland, you want to ensure that you use and spell the month correctly. This list shows you the months of the year (which, like the days of the week, aren't capitalized in French):

>> **janvier** (*January*)

>> **février** (*February*)

>> **mars** (*March*)

>> **avril** (*April*)

>> **mai** (*May*)

>> **juin** (*June*)

>> **juillet** (*July*)

>> **août** (*August*)

>> **septembre** (*September*)

>> **octobre** (*October*)

>> **novembre** (*November*)

>> **décembre** (*December*)

To say that something happened or will happen in a given month, use the preposition **en** (*in*) or the phrase **au mois de** (*in the month of*):

J'ai acheté ma voiture en juin. (*I bought my car in June.*)

Nous allons déménager au mois de novembre. (We're going to move in [the month of] November.)

'Tis the season

The French words for the seasons don't much resemble their English translations, but they are equal in number (four):

>> **le printemps** (*spring*)

>> **l'été** (*summer*)

>> **l'automne** (*fall*)

>> **l'hiver** (*winter*)

Although you can't tell by the definite articles that I've included, all four seasons are masculine.

PRACTICE

A good year: Fill in this calendar with the missing months (from the preceding section) and seasons.

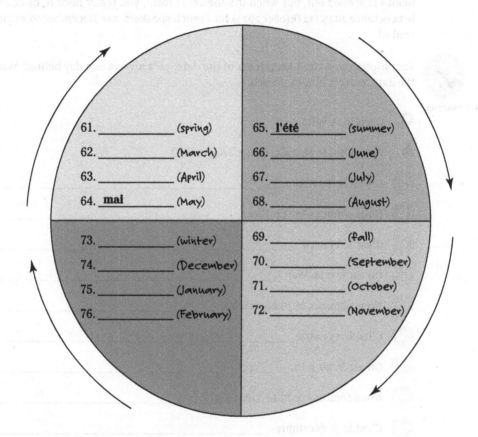

61. _____ (spring)

62. _____ (March)

63. _____ (April)

64. __mai__ (May)

65. __l'été__ (summer)

66. _____ (June)

67. _____ (July)

68. _____ (August)

73. _____ (winter)

74. _____ (December)

75. _____ (January)

76. _____ (February)

69. _____ (fall)

70. _____ (September)

71. _____ (October)

72. _____ (November)

Day, month, and year: Scoping out the dating scene

From meetings, to parties, to jetting off to the Côte d'Azur for the weekend, every event takes place on a particular date. So if you want to invite and be invited, you need to know how to talk about dates. The first thing to know (besides the days of the week and months of the year — see the sections "Knowing the days of the week" and "An even dozen: Identifying the months," earlier in this chapter) is the question **Quelle est la date ?** (*What's the date?*).

To answer, you can say **C'est, On est,** or **Nous sommes,** followed by the definite article **le** + cardinal number + month + year (the year is optional). *Note:* The day comes before the month and has to be preceded by **le.** For example, you can say **C'est le 3 [trois] mai** (*It's May 3*) or **On est le 22 [vingt-deux] février 2023 [deux mille vingt-trois]** (*It's February 22, 2023*).

DIFFERENCES

You always use the cardinal (counting) number to say the date in French except when you're talking about the first day of the month; for that, you use the ordinal: **C'est le 1ᵉʳ [premier] décembre** (*It's December 1st*).

The short form of the date also goes day/month/year, so **le 25 novembre 2021** is shortened to 25/11/21. The day always comes before the month, which isn't such a big deal when the month is spelled out, but when it's the short form, you really need to be careful — 12/10/25 is **le 12 octobre 2025** (*12 October 2025*) for French speakers, not December 10 as an American would read it!

PRACTICE

Your brother just can't keep track of the date; he's always one day behind. When he announces the date, correct him in French.

Q. C'est le 15 août.

A. **Non, c'est le 16 août.** (*No, it's August 16.*)

77 On est le 5 octobre. _____

78 Nous sommes le 13 juillet. _____

79 C'est le 19 avril. _____

80 On est le 9 janvier. _____

81 Nous sommes le 30 septembre. _____

82 C'est le 15 mars. _____

83 On est le 1er juin. _____

84 Nous sommes le 27 février. _____

85 C'est le 31 décembre. _____

86 On est le 8 mai. _____

Understanding Time Differences

When writing and speaking French, knowing and telling the time is an important concept to master. Otherwise, you may show up half a day early for meetings, mix up the train schedules, or miss that lunch date you made. How do you prevent such catastrophes? Well, the first thing you need to know is how to ask what time it is: **Quelle heure est-il ?**

DIFFERENCES

In French, people tell time on the 24-hour clock, like military time (but without the uniforms). So the morning hours are 1 to 12, and the afternoon and evening hours are 13 to 24. To convert back to a 12-hour clock, subtract 12 from any time greater than 12.

TIP

To give the time, you say **Il est** followed by the number, the word **heure(s)**, and any modifiers that describe the minutes. For example, if it's 7 a.m., you say **Il est sept heures**. If it's 2 p.m., **Il est quatorze heures**. And if it's 1 a.m., **Il est une heure** — au lit ! (*It's 1 a.m. — go to bed!*)

Now you just need the modifiers. To modify with minutes, use cardinal numbers (see the section "Counting on cardinal numbers: 1, 2, 3," earlier in this chapter). You can add these numbers by just tacking them on after **heure(s)**. For instance, 1:20 a.m. is **une heure vingt**. After you get past 30 minutes, you have a choice of either adding the minutes onto the current hour or subtracting them from the next hour with **moins** (*minus*). So 2:40 a.m. is either **deux heures quarante** (*two-forty*) or **trois heures moins vingt** (*twenty minutes to three*).

Just like you can say *half past* or *quarter to* in English, you can use similar phrases when telling the time in French.

>> To say _____-*thirty*, add **et demie** (literally, *and a half*).

>> To say *quarter after* the hour, use **et quart** (literally, *and a quarter*).

>> To say *quarter to*, tack on **moins le quart** (literally, *minus the quarter*).

Here are a few examples to consider.

Il est une heure moins le quart. (*It's quarter to one [12:45 a.m.].*)

Il est une heure et quart or **Il est une heure quinze** (*It's quarter after one* or *It's one-fifteen [1:15 a.m.]*)

Il est une heure et demie or **Il est une heure trente**. (*It's half past one* or *It's one-thirty [1:30 a.m.].*)

Note: **Moins le quart** requires the article **le**, but **et quart** doesn't.

And just like English, French has special words for the 12 o'clocks:

>> **midi** (*noon*)

>> **minuit** (*midnight*)

You can use **et quart** and **et demi** with these words as well. Note that the adjective **demi** is in the masculine because **midi** and **minuit** are masculine, as opposed to **heure** (*hour*), which is feminine and therefore takes the feminine form **demie**. See Chapter 11 for more info about adjective agreement.

The short version of French times has an **h** (short for **heures**) where English speakers use a colon or period.

14 h 00 (*2:00 p.m./2.00 p.m.*)

8 h 30 (*8:30 a.m./8.30 a.m.*)

Take a look at Table 5-2 to see all this timely information spelled out.

If you want to talk about when something (say, a conference call) is happening, rather than what time it is right now, say **À quelle heure est la téléconférence ?** (*What time is the conference call?*). To answer, you just start with that event and add **est à** and the time: **La téléconférence est à midi.** (*The conference call is at noon.*)

Table 5-2   French Times

Time	Heure (Hour)	Abréviation (Abreviation)
12 a.m. (midnight)	minuit	0 h 00
1 a.m.	une heure	1 h 00
2 a.m.	deux heures	2 h 00
3 a.m.	trois heures	3 h 00
4:15 a.m.	quatre heures et quart quatre heures quinze	4 h 15
5:30 a.m.	cinq heures et demie cinq heures trente	5 h 30
6:45 a.m	sept heures moins le quart	6 h 45
12 p.m. (noon)	midi	12 h 00
1 p.m.	treize heures	13 h 00
2 p.m.	quatorze heures	14 h 00
3 p.m.	quinze heures	15 h 00
4:05 p.m.	seize heures cinq	16 h 05
5:17 p.m.	dix-sept heures dix-sept	17 h 17
6:55 p.m	dix-neuf heures moins cinq	18 h 55

PRACTICE

As the department administrative assistant, your job is to keep track of everyone's schedules and provide people with a copy of the weekly planner. But Christiane lost hers, and she remembers the day everything is happening but not the time. For each question that follows, answer with a complete sentence, spelling out the time shown on the weekly planner.

lundi	mardi	mercredi	jeudi	vendredi
	8h30 — rendez-vous avec Martin			8h45 — conférence de presse
9h10 — téléconférence			9h50 — réunion syndicale	
11h50 — déjeuner avec Mme LeBlanc		12h00 — déjeuner avec Paul et Claire		12h40 — déjeuner avec Sophie
	16h00 — Étienne arrive			16h55 — vol pour Genève
		18h20 — Le Mariage de Figaro		18h00 — Dîner à La Lune

Q. À quelle heure est le rendez-vous avec Martin ?

A. **Le rendez-vous avec Martin est à huit heures et demie.** (*The appointment with Martin is at 8:30 a.m.*)

(87) À quelle heure est le dîner à La Lune ?

(88) À quelle heure est le déjeuner avec Paul et Claire ?

(89) À quelle heure est le vol pour Genève ?

(90) À quelle heure est la réunion syndicale ?

(91) À quelle heure est Le Mariage de Figaro ?

(92) À quelle heure est l'arrivée d'Étienne ?

(93) À quelle heure est la conférence de presse ?

(94) À quelle heure est le déjeuner avec Mme LeBlanc ?

(95) À quelle heure est la téléconférence ?

(96) À quelle heure est le déjeuner avec Sophie ?

Answer Key to "The 4-1-1 on Numbers, Dates, and Time" Practice Questions

(1) **six moins trois égal trois** (*six minus three equals three*)

(2) **dix plus cinq égal quinze** (*ten plus five equals fifteen*)

(3) **treize moins neuf égal quatre** (*thirteen minus nine equals four*)

(4) **dix-sept plus deux égal dix-neuf** (*seventeen plus two equals nineteen*)

(5) **treize moins douze égal un** (*thirteen minus twelve equals one*)

(6) **neuf plus neuf égal dix-huit** (*nine plus nine equals eighteen*)

(7) **cinq moins trois égal deux** (*five minus three equals two*)

(8) **onze plus six égal dix-sept** (*eleven plus six equals seventeen*)

(9) **huit moins huit égal zéro** (*eight minus eight equals zero*)

(10) **douze plus deux égal quatorze** (*twelve plus two equals fourteen*)

(11) **cinquante-et-un moins dix égal quarante-et-un** (*fifty-one minus ten equals forty-one*)

(12) **vingt-trois plus dix égal trente-trois** (*twenty-three plus ten equals thirty-three*)

(13) **soixante-neuf moins dix égal cinquante-neuf** (*sixty-nine minus ten equals fifty-nine*)

(14) **trente-sept plus dix égal quarante-sept** (*thirty-seven plus ten equals forty-seven*)

(15) **quarante-et-un moins dix égal trente-et-un** (*forty-one minus ten equals thirty-one*)

(16) **cinquante-cinq plus dix égal soixante-cinq** (*fifty-five plus ten equals sixty-five*)

(17) **soixante-six moins dix égal cinquante-six** (*sixty-six minus ten equals fifty-six*)

(18) **vingt-neuf plus dix égal trente-neuf** (*twenty-nine plus ten equals thirty-nine*)

(19) **trente-huit moins dix égal vingt-huit** (*thirty-eight minus ten equals twenty-eight*)

(20) **quarante-quatre plus dix égal cinquante-quatre** (*forty-four plus ten equals fifty-four*)

(21) **quatre-vingt-neuf moins dix égal soixante-dix-neuf** (*eighty-nine minus ten equals seventy-nine*)

(22) **soixante-dix-huit plus dix égal quatre-vingt-huit** (*seventy-eight plus ten equals eighty-eight*)

(23) **soixante-seize moins cinq égal soixante-et-onze** (*seventy-six minus five equals seventy-one*)

(24) **quatre-vingt-quatre plus cinq égal quatre-vingt-neuf** (*eighty-four plus five equals eighty-nine*)

(25) **quatre-vingt-dix-huit moins dix égal quatre-vingt-huit** (*ninety-eight minus ten equals eighty-eight*)

(26) **quatre-vingt-un plus dix égal quatre-vingt-onze** (*eighty-one plus ten equals ninety-one*)

(27) **soixante-dix-neuf moins cinq égal soixante-quatorze** (*seventy-nine minus five equals seventy-four*)

(28) **quatre-vingt-cinq plus cinq égal quatre-vingt- dix** (*eighty-five plus five equals ninety*)

(29) **quatre-vingt-dix moins dix égal quatre-vingts** (*ninety minus ten equals eighty*)

(30) **soixante-douze plus cinq égal soixante-dix-sept** (*seventy-two plus five equals seventy-seven*)

(31) **cinq, sept** (*five, seven*)

(32) **neuf, onze** (*nine, eleven*)

(33) **douze, quatorze** (*twelve, fourteen*)

(34) **dix-huit, vingt** (*eighteen, twenty*)

(35) **vingt-neuf, trente-et-un** (*twenty-nine, thirty-one*)

(36) **quarante, quarante-deux** (*forty, forty-two*)

(37) **cinquante-huit, soixante** (*fifty-eight, sixty*)

(38) **soixante-neuf, soixante-et-onze** (*sixty-nine, seventy-one*)

(39) **quatre-vingts, quatre-vingt-deux** (*eighty, eighty-two*)

(40) **quatre-vingt-dix-sept, quatre-vingt-dix-neuf** (*ninety-seven, ninety-nine*)

(41) **dixième**, 10e (*tenth, 10th*)

(42) **septième**, 7e (*seventh, 7th*)

(43) **premier**, 1er (*first, 1st*)

(44) **trentième**, 30e (*thirtieth, 30th*)

(45) **quarante-quatrième**, 44e (*forty-fourth, 44th*)

(46) **cinquante-et-unième**, 51e (*fifty-first, 51st*)

(47) **soixante-douzième**, 72e (*seventy-second, 72nd*)

(48) **quatre-vingt-onzième**, 91e (*ninety-first, 91st*)

(49) **quatre-vingt-dix-neuvième**, 99e (*ninety-ninth, 99th*)

(50) **centième**, 100e (*hundredth, 100th*)

(51) **on est mercredi** (*it's Wednesday*)

(52) **nous sommes vendredi** (*it's Friday*)

(53) **nous sommes mardi** (*it's Tuesday*)

(54) **on est samedi** (*it's Saturday*)

(55) **nous sommes lundi** (*it's Monday*)

(56) **on est jeudi** (*it's Thursday*)

(57) **on est dimanche** (*it's Sunday*)

(58) **nous sommes allés au parc avant-hier** (*we went to the park the day before yesterday*)

(59) **nous allons partir demain** (*we are going to leave tomorrow*)

(60) **la fête est aujourd'hui** (*the party is today*)

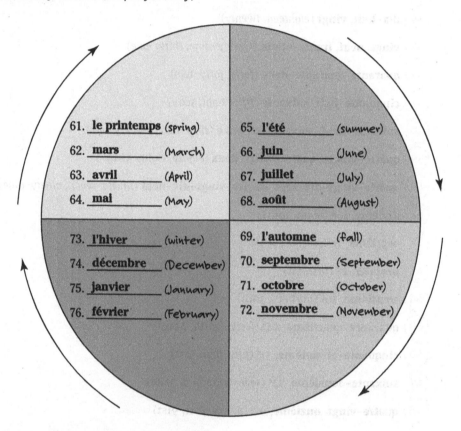

61. le printemps (spring)
62. mars (March)
63. avril (April)
64. mai (May)

65. l'été (summer)
66. juin (June)
67. juillet (July)
68. août (August)

73. l'hiver (winter)
74. décembre (December)
75. janvier (January)
76. février (February)

69. l'automne (fall)
70. septembre (September)
71. octobre (October)
72. novembre (November)

(77) **Non, on est le 6 octobre.** (*No, it's October 6.*)

(78) **Non, nous sommes le 14 juillet.** (*No, it's July 14.*)

(79) **Non, c'est le 20 avril.** (*No, it's April 20.*)

(80) **Non, on est le 10 janvier.** (*No, it's January 10.*)

(81) **Non, nous sommes le 1er octobre.** (*No, it's October 1.*)

(82) **Non, c'est le 16 mars.** (*No, it's March 16.*)

(83) **Non, on est le 2 juin.** (*No, it's June 2.*)

(84) **Non, nous sommes le 28 février.** (*No, it's February 28.*)

(85) **Non, c'est le 1er janvier.** (*No, it's January 1.*)

(86) **Non, on est le 9 mai.** (*No, it's May 9.*)

(87) **Le dîner à La Lune est à dix-huit heures.** (*Dinner at La Lune is at 6 p.m.*)

(88) **Le déjeuner avec Paul et Claire est à midi.** (*Lunch with Paul and Claire is at noon.*)

(89) **Le vol pour Genève est à dix-sept heures moins cinq [seize heures cinquante-cinq].** (*The flight to Geneva is at five to 5 p.m. [4:55 p.m.].*)

(90) **La réunion syndicale est à dix heures moins dix [neuf heures cinquante].** (*The union meeting is at ten to 10 a.m. [9:50 a.m.]*)

(91) **Le Mariage de Figaro est à dix-huit heures vingt.** (*The Marriage of Figaro is at 6:20 p.m.*)

(92) **L'arrivée d'Étienne est à seize heures.** (*Étienne's arrival is at 4 p.m.*)

(93) **La conférence de presse est à neuf heures moins le quart [huit heures quarante-cinq].** (*The press conference is at quarter to nine a.m. [8:45 a.m.]*)

(94) **Le déjeuner avec Mme LeBlanc est à midi moins dix [onze heures cinquante].** (*Lunch with Mrs. LeBlanc is at ten to noon [11:50 a.m.]*)

(95) **La téléconférence est à neuf heures dix.** (*The conference call is at 9:10 a.m.*)

(96) **Le déjeuner avec Sophie est à midi quarante [treize heures moins vingt].** (*Lunch with Sophie is at 12:40 [twenty to 1:00 p.m.]*)

2

The Here and Now: Writing in the Present

Speak in the moment by using the present tense.

Conjugate different kinds of verbs and use them so that you can talk about what you're doing right now.

Ask some questions and give some answers.

Tackle negation.

Sort out infinitives and present participles, two verb forms that exist in both French and English but act very differently in the two languages.

Chapter **6**

Right Here, Right Now: The Present Tense

Here's your chance to get a handle on the present tense, your link to talking about what's going on and the way things are. This most common French verb tense — which is also one of the most complicated tenses — describes what's happening, what people's routines are, what a current situation is like, and all about that present you're opening right now. The English simple present tense (*I sing*) and present progressive tense (*I am singing*) are both generally translated with the French present tense: **je chante**.

TIP

In order to stress that something is happening right now, the way *I'm singing* does, use the construction **être en train de**: Je suis en train de chanter — *I am (in the process of) singing (right now)*. But don't overdo it; most of the time, the plain old present tense does the job just fine.

Using the French present tense is easy; the hard part is choosing the right verb form because the conjugations are different for regular, stem-changing, spelling-change, and irregular verbs. This chapter covers the types of verbs and present-tense verb conjugations.

The Mainstream: Conjugating Regular Verbs

Regular verbs are groups of verbs that are all conjugated the same way, so when you know how to conjugate one, you can conjugate them all — kind of a package deal. Verbs that aren't yet conjugated appear in their infinitive form (the one you find in the dictionary, as discussed in

Chapter 2), and the three groups of regular verbs are classified by their infinitive endings: −er, −ir, and −re. The following sections show you how to get them in shape.

The most common regular verbs: −er

The verbs that end in −er are by far the largest category of French verbs. To conjugate −er verbs, remove −er from the infinitive to find the stem, and then add the appropriate ending: −e, −es, −e, −ons, −ez, or −ent.

REMEMBER Verb conjugations and endings are always listed in the same order: first-, second-, and third-person singular, followed by first-, second-, third-person plural. In this book, verb tables have the singular pronouns and conjugations on the left, and the plural pronouns and conjugations on the right. Elsewhere, you might also see verb tables that stack all six conjugations top to bottom, from **je** to **ils.**

The following table conjugates **parler** (*to speak*).

parler (to speak)

je parle	nous parlons
tu parles	vous parlez
il/elle/on parle	ils/elles parlent

Je parle français. (*I speak French.*)

Thousands of regular French verbs end in −er. Here are several of the more common ones:

- **aimer** (*to like, to love*)
- **chercher** (*to look for*)
- **danser** (*to dance*)
- **détester** (*to hate*)
- **donner** (*to give*)

- **jouer** (*to play*)
- **penser** (*to think*)
- **regarder** (*to watch, to look at*)
- **travailler** (*to work*)
- **trouver** (*to find*)

PRACTICE Test yourself on regular −er French verbs by conjugating the verb in parentheses for the grammatical person provided.

Q. je _____ (jouer)

A. **je joue** (*I play*)

1. j'_____ (aimer)

2. tu _____ (détester)

3. il _____ (trouver)

4. nous _____ (penser)

5 vous _____ (travailler)

6 elles _____ (donner)

7 je _____ (chercher)

8 tu _____ (parler)

9 elle _____ (danser)

10 nous _____ (regarder)

Another common regular verb ending: –ir

The –**ir** verbs fill the No. 2 slot on the charts of the most common verb types. To conjugate regular –**ir** verbs, remove –**ir** from the infinitive and add the endings: –**is**, –**is**, –**it**, –**issons**, –**issez**, and –**issent**. Here's how you conjugate **finir** (*to finish*).

finir (to finish)

je finis	nous finissons
tu finis	vous finissez
il/elle/on finit	ils/elles finissent

Il finit le dessin. (*He's finishing the drawing.*)

You can find hundreds of regular –**ir** French verbs. Check out some of the more common ones:

>> **avertir** (*to warn*)

>> **bâtir** (*to build*)

>> **choisir** (*to choose*)

>> **établir** (*to establish*)

>> **grandir** (*to grow*)

>> **réagir** (*to react*)

>> **remplir** (*to fill*)

>> **réunir** (*to meet*)

>> **réussir** (*to succeed*)

>> **vieillir** (*to grow old*)

PRACTICE

Test yourself on regular –**ir** French verbs by conjugating the verb in parentheses for the grammatical person provided.

Q. j' _____ (avertir)

A. **j'avertis** (*I warn*)

11 je _____ (vieillir)

12 tu _____ (réagir)

13 il _____ (bâtir)

14 nous _____ (grandir)

15 vous _____ (réussir)

16 elles _____ (établir)

17 je _____ (remplir)

18 tu _____ (choisir)

19 elle _____ (réunir)

20 nous _____ (finir)

The third type of regular verbs: –re

The regular –re verbs round out the list of regular French verbs. To conjugate regular –re verbs, remove –re from the infinitive, which gives you the stem, and then add the endings: –s, –s, (add nothing for 3rd person singular), –ons, –ez, and –ent. Here's how you conjugate **perdre** (*to lose*).

perdre (to lose)

je perds	nous perdons
tu perds	vous perdez
il/elle/on perd	ils/elles perdent

Nous perdons du poids. (*We're losing weight.*)

French has dozens of regular –re verbs, including the following:

>> **attendre** (*to wait [for]*)

>> **défendre** (*to defend*)

>> **descendre** (*to descend, go down*)

>> **entendre** (*to hear*)

>> **étendre** (*to stretch, to spread*)

>> **fondre** (*to melt*)

>> **prétendre** (*to claim*)

>> **rendre** (*to give back, return something*)

>> **répondre** (*to answer*)

>> **vendre** (*to sell*)

PRACTICE

Test yourself on regular –re verbs by conjugating the verb in parentheses for the grammatical person provided.

Q. je_____ (perdre)

A. **je perds** (*I lose*)

21 je_____ (défendre)

22 tu_____ (répondre)

(23) elle _____ (entendre)

(24) nous _____ (prétendre)

(25) vous _____ (fondre)

(26) ils _____ (étendre)

(27) je _____ (rendre)

(28) tu _____ (descendre)

(29) il _____ (vendre)

(30) nous _____ (attendre)

Rounding up regular French verbs

PRACTICE

Let's get regular! Test yourself on the three different kinds of regular French verbs all mixed together by conjugating the verb in parentheses for the grammatical person provided.

Q. elle _____ (donner)

A. **elle donne** (*she gives*)

(31) il _____ (descendre)

(32) je _____ (travailler)

(33) vous _____ (remplir)

(34) nous _____ (rendre)

(35) tu _____ (chercher)

(36) j' _____ (attendre)

(37) elle _____ (jouer)

(38) ils _____ (vieillir)

(39) nous _____ (réagir)

(40) tu _____ (penser)

Preserving Pronunciation with Spelling-Change Verbs

Spelling-change verbs have the same endings as regular –er verbs (see the section "The Mainstream: Conjugating Regular Verbs," earlier in this chapter), but for pronunciation reasons, they have a slight spelling change in certain conjugations. French has two types of spelling-change verbs: those that end in –**cer** and those that end in –**ger**. The following sections can help you conjugate them.

Working with –cer verbs

In French, the letter **c** has two sounds: hard, like the *c* in *coal*, and soft, like the *c* in *celery*. The French **c** is

>> Hard when it precedes the vowels **a**, **o**, or **u**

>> Soft when it precedes **e**, **i**, or **y**

REMEMBER

The **c** at the end of –**cer** verbs is soft because it precedes **e**, which means it needs to be soft in all conjugations. For example, take the verb **prononcer** (*to pronounce*), which is conjugated like a regular –er verb with one exception. In the **nous** form, if you follow the normal rules, you get the conjugation "**prononcons**," which would mean the **c** has a hard pronunciation. To avoid that, the **c** changes to **ç**. Now, you have **nous prononçons**, and the **c** is soft, just like in the infinitive and all the other conjugations. Take a look at the verb table.

prononcer (to pronounce)

je prononce	nous prononçons
tu prononces	vous prononcez
il/elle/on prononce	ils/elles prononcent

Tu prononces bien. (*Your pronunciation is good.* Literally: *You pronounce well.*)

French has dozens of –**cer** verbs, including the following:

>> **annoncer** (*to announce*)

>> **avancer** (*to advance*)

>> **balancer** (*to sway*)

>> **commencer** (*to begin*)

>> **dénoncer** (*to denounce*)

>> **divorcer** (*to divorce*)

>> **effacer** (*to erase*)

>> **influencer** (*to influence*)

>> **lancer** (*to throw*)

>> **remplacer** (*to replace*)

Managing –ger verbs

Like **c**, the letter **g** also has two sounds in French: hard, like the *g* in *goal*, and soft, like the *g* in *massage*. The French **g** is

» Hard when it precedes **a**, **o**, or **u**

» Soft when it precedes **e**, **i**, or **y**

The **g** at the end of –**ger** verbs is soft, so it has to be soft in all its conjugations. For example, take the verb **bouger** (*to move*). You conjugate it like a regular –**er** verb, except for the **nous** form. To avoid "**bougons**" with a hard g, you add an **e**: **bougeons**. This change makes the **g** soft, like in the infinitive and all the other conjugations.

bouger (to move)

je bouge	nous bougeons
tu bouges	vous bougez
il/elle/on bouge	ils/elles bougent

Ils bougent beaucoup. (*They're moving a lot.*)

French has dozens of –**ger** verbs, including these:

» **arranger** (*to arrange*)

» **changer** (*to change*)

» **corriger** (*to correct*)

» **déménager** (*to move house*)

» **déranger** (*to disturb*)

» **diriger** (*to direct*)

» **exiger** (*to demand, insist*)

» **loger** (*to lodge*)

» **manger** (*to eat*)

» **voyager** (*to travel*)

Practicing with spelling-change verbs

PRACTICE

Cast a spell! Test yourself on spelling-change verbs by conjugating the verb in parentheses for the grammatical person provided.

Q. il _____ (bouger)

A. **il bouge** (*he moves*)

41 nous _____ (commencer)

42 je _____ (manger)

43 tu _____ (effacer)

44 vous _____ (corriger)

45 elles _____ (remplacer)

46 nous _____ (exiger)

Dissecting Stem-Changing Verbs

Stem-changing verbs take the same endings as regular –er verbs, but they have two different *stems* (the infinitive minus –er). There are five types of stem-changing verbs, but the patterns in their conjugations are the same: The **nous** and **vous** forms of the verb take the regular stem, and the singular forms and third-person plural have a stem change. The following sections take a closer look at the five types.

Tackling –yer verbs

Verbs that end in –**yer** have two stems:

>> A regular stem that keeps **y** for the **nous** and **vous** conjugations

>> An irregular stem with **i** in place of **y** for the other conjugations

Here I conjugate **employer** (*to employ*).

employer (to employ, make use of)

j'emploie	nous employons
tu emploies	vous employez
il/elle/on emploie	ils/elles emploient

Tu emploies bien ton temps. (*You make good use of your time.*)

There are dozens of –**yer** verbs, such as

>> **balayer** (*to sweep*)

>> **effrayer** (*to frighten*)

>> **ennuyer** (*to bore, to annoy*)

>> **envoyer** (*to send*)

>> **essayer** (*to try*)

>> **essuyer** (*to wipe*)

>> **nettoyer** (*to clean*)

>> **payer** (*to pay*)

>> **tutoyer** (*to use* [**tu**])

>> **vouvoyer** (*to use* [**vous**])

TIP

This stem change, although required for verbs that end in –**oyer** and –**uyer**, is optional for verbs that end in –**ayer**. Verbs such as **payer** can be conjugated with or without the stem-change: **Je paie** and **je paye** are equally correct.

PRACTICE

Test yourself on –**yer** verbs by conjugating the verb in parentheses for the grammatical person provided.

Q. tu _____ (ennuyer)

A. **tu ennuies** (*you annoy*)

(47) nous _____ (nettoyer)

(48) j'_____ (essayer)

(49) elle _____ (envoyer)

(50) vous _____ (payer)

(51) ils _____ (tutoyer)

(52) tu _____ (essuyer)

Figuring out –eler verbs

A few verbs that end in **–eler** have a regular stem with a single l in the **nous** and **vous** conjugations and an irregular **ll** for the other conjugations. This example conjugates **épeler** (*to spell [out]*).

épeler (to spell [out])

j'épelle	nous épelons
tu épelles	vous épelez
il/elle/on épelle	ils/elles épellent

Vous épelez trop lentement. (*You spell too slowly.*)

There are only a few other **–eler** verbs:

» **appeler** (*to call*)

» **rappeler** (*to call back, recall*)

» **renouveler** (*to renew*)

The verbs **geler** (*to freeze*) and **peler** (*to peel*) don't follow this pattern of doubling the l. You conjugate them like **–e*er** verbs (see the section "Looking at –e*er verbs," later in this chapter, for more info).

PRACTICE

Test yourself on **–eler** verbs by conjugating the verb in parentheses for the grammatical person provided.

Q. je _____ (rappeler)

A. **je rappelle** (*I recall*)

(53) vous _____ (renouveler)

(54) elles _____ (appeler)

(55) tu _____ (épeler)

56 nous _____ (rappeler)

57 je _____ (renouveler)

58 il _____ (appeler)

Focusing on –eter verbs

Most verbs that end in **–eter** have a regular stem that contains a single **t** in the **nous** and **vous** conjugations and an irregular **tt** for the other conjugations. See how you conjugate **jeter** (*to throw*).

jeter (to throw)

je jette	nous jetons
tu jettes	vous jetez
il/elle/on jette	ils/elles jettent

Elle jette Marc à l'eau. (*She's throwing Marc in the water.*)

The most common **–eter** verbs are

» **feuilleter** (*to leaf through*)

» **hoqueter** (*to hiccup*)

» **projeter** (*to project*)

» **rejeter** (*to reject*)

WARNING

The verb **acheter** (*to buy*) is an exception; it's conjugated like **–e*er** verbs. See the following section for the details on those conjugations.

PRACTICE

Test yourself on **–eter** verbs by conjugating the verb in parentheses for the grammatical person provided.

Q. il _____ (rejeter)

A. **il rejette** (*he rejects*)

59 tu _____ (hoqueter)

60 nous _____ (feuilleter)

61 vous _____ (projeter)

62 ils _____ (jeter)

63 je _____ (rejeter)

64 elle _____ (feuilleter)

Looking at –e*er verbs

Verbs that end in –e*er have an unstressed e in the infinitive followed by a consonant such as n or v. Conjugated, these verbs have a regular stem with an unaccented e and an irregular stem with a *grave accent* è. Consider the following example of **mener** (*to lead*).

mener (to lead)

je mène	nous menons
tu mènes	vous menez
il/elle/on mène	ils/elles mènent

Ils mènent les débats. (*They're leading the debates.*)

French has many common –e*er verbs (including the exceptions to the –eler and –eter verbs I mention in the sections "Figuring out –eler verbs" and "Focusing on –eter verbs," earlier in this chapter). Some of these verbs include the following:

>> **acheter** (*to buy*)

>> **amener** (*to bring*)

>> **élever** (*to bring up, to raise*)

>> **emmener** (*to take*)

>> **enlever** (*to remove*)

>> **geler** (*to freeze*)

>> **lever** (*to lift, raise*)

>> **peler** (*to peel*)

>> **peser** (*to weigh*)

>> **promener** (*to walk, lead*)

PRACTICE

Test yourself on –e*er verbs by conjugating the verb in parentheses for the grammatical person provided.

Q. nous _____ (peser)

A. **nous pesons** (*we weigh*)

65 tu _____ (lever)

66 j'_____ (emmener)

67 vous _____ (promener)

68 ils _____ (peler)

69 elle _____ (élever)

70 nous _____ (geler)

Dealing with –é*er verbs

Verbs that end in –é*er have a regular stem that keeps the *acute accent* é for **nous** and **vous** and an irregular stem that changes to the grave accent è. The following example conjugates **gérer** (*to manage*).

gérer (to manage)

je gère	nous gérons
tu gères	vous gérez
il/elle/on gère	ils/elles gèrent

Nous gérons le projet. (We're managing the project.)

Some –é*er verbs include

- **célébrer** (*to celebrate*)
- **compléter** (*to complete*)
- **considérer** (*to consider*)
- **espérer** (*to hope*)
- **modérer** (*to moderate*)

- **posséder** (*to possess*)
- **préférer** (*to prefer*)
- **répéter** (*to repeat*)
- **suggérer** (*to suggest*)
- **tolérer** (*to tolerate*)

PRACTICE

Test yourself on –é*er verbs by conjugating the verb in parentheses for the grammatical person provided.

Q. ils _____ (espérer)

A. **ils espèrent** (*they hope*)

71 je_____ (célébrer)

72 vous _____ (modérer)

73 il _____ (suggérer)

74 elles _____ (préférer)

75 tu _____ (tolérer)

76 nous _____ (considérer)

TIP

These boots were made for walkin'! Stem-changing verbs are also known as *boot verbs*, thanks to a little trick you can do to remember which four forms have stem changes: draw a line encircling them — it makes the shape of a boot! See Figure 6-1.

FIGURE 6-1:
Help for
remembering
the four forms
that have stem
changes.

je promène	nous promenons
tu promènes	vous promenez
il promène	ils promènent

Cleaning up conjugations

PRACTICE

While writing cautionary memos to several employees, your computer crashed, and all the conjugated verbs turned into infinitives! Fill in the blanks with the correct conjugation for the spelling-change and stem-changing verbs provided.

Q. vous _____ (tolérer)

A. tolérez

Attention
Memo à David et Philippe :

Je m' **(77)**_____ (appeler) Anne et je **(78)**_____
(gérer) la section B7. Les autres gérants et moi
(79)_____ (changer) notre politique de courriel.
Vous **(80)**_____ (envoyer) souvent des messages
personnels, et nous **(81)**_____ (considérer) que
c'est une infraction à vos contrats. Nous **(82)**_____
(commencer) à surveiller vos ordinateurs ; si vous
(83)_____ (répéter) cette activité, nous ne
(84)_____ (renouveler) pas vos contrats.
J' **(85)**_____ (espérer) que vous **(86)**_____
(essayer) de ne plus écrire à vos amis quand vous
travaillez.

Attention
Memo à Sylvie :

Nous (87)_____ (rejeter) ta note de frais. Quand tu
(88)_____ (voyager), tu (89)_____ (payer) trop pour
des hôtels trois étoiles. Nous (90)_____ (exiger) que nos
employés se (91)_____ (loger) dans des hôtels deux
étoiles. Même si tu (92)_____ (préférer) les hôtels de
luxe, nous (93)_____ (suggérer) que tu (94)_____
(considérer) les frais et que tu te (95)_____ (modérer).

Attention
Memo à Georges :

Il y a deux problèmes. D'abord, tu ne (96)_____
(compléter) pas ton travail — tu n' (97)_____ (épeler)
rien correctement et tu ne (98)_____ (corriger) pas tes
erreurs. Nous (99)_____ (diriger) un programme de relecture
systématique pour améliorer l'image que tu (100)_____
(projeter) dans les meetings. De surcroît, te (101)_____
(rappeler) — tu que nous n' (102)_____ (employer) pas de
femme de service ? Nous (103)_____ (enlever) les tableaux
blancs parce que tu les (104)_____ (effacer) mais tu ne
les (105)_____ (nettoyer) pas.

The Rebels: Conjugating Irregular Verbs

As if all the different regular verb patterns weren't enough to remember (flip back to the section "The Mainstream: Conjugating Regular Verbs," earlier in this chapter, for more on the regular stuff), French also has numerous irregular verbs, which have either unique conjugations or patterns limited to just a few verbs. Unfortunately, I don't know of any shortcut for memorizing them — but irregular verbs don't have to be the bane of your existence. You just have to practice conjugations until they feel natural.

To get better at conjugating verbs, try this quick exercise. Choose a verb and practice writing and reciting the conjugations for each subject pronoun. Take 10 minutes to do this exercise every day, and the conjugations should become second nature in no time. Once you've mastered one verb, choose another, rinse, and repeat!

TIP

The following sections look at several types of irregular French verbs and help you keep track of them all.

Coming right up: Verbs conjugated like venir

Venir (*to come*), **tenir** (*to hold*), and all their derivatives (verbs that end in -venir or -tenir) are conjugated with a stem change, as well as irregular endings. In the singular conjugations and the third-person plural, the **e** in the stem changes to **ie**; the **nous** and **vous** forms don't have a stem change. (As for stem-changing verbs, you can remember which persons get stem changes by drawing a line around the singular forms and the third-person plural of **venir** and **tenir** to make a boot shape. Check out figure 6-1 in this chapter.) Then add the endings **–s**, **–s**, **–t**, **–ons**, **–ez**, and **–nent**. The best way to understand these verbs is to take a look at the following table, memorize the pattern, and apply it to other verbs that end in -venir or -tenir.

venir (to come)

je viens	nous venons
tu viens	vous venez
il/elle/on vient	ils viennent

Il vient dans deux heures. (*He's coming in two hours.*)

Other verbs that follow this conjugation include **contenir** (*to contain*), **maintenir** (*to maintain*), and **revenir** (*to come back*).

Going out — and out like a light: Verbs conjugated like sortir and dormir

Dormir (*to sleep*) and most verbs that end in **–tir**, like **sortir** (*to go out*), are conjugated with the endings of regular **–re** verbs, except in the third-person singular. In the singular conjugations, the consonant plus **–ir** ending is dropped before adding the endings **–s**, **–s**, and (here's the irregular ending) **–t**. In the plurals, just **–ir** is dropped and the endings are **–ons**, **–ez**, and **–ent**.

sortir (to go out)

je sors	nous sortons
tu sors	vous sortez
il/elle/on sort	ils/elles sortent

Nous sortons ce soir. (*We're going out tonight.*)

Other verbs that follow this same conjugation include **mentir** (*to lie*), **sentir** (*to smell, to feel*), and **partir** (*to leave*).

Offering and opening: Verbs conjugated like offrir and ouvrir

Verbs that end in –**frir** and –**vrir**, such as **offrir** (*to offer*) and **ouvrir** (*to open*), are irregular –**ir** verbs that are conjugated with the same endings as regular –**er** verbs. So you basically drop the –**ir** ending to find the stem and add the following endings: –**e**, –**es**, –**e**, –**ons**, –**ez**, and –**ent**.

Check out the following example.

ouvrir (to open)

j'ouvre	nous ouvrons
tu ouvres	vous ouvrez
il/elle/on ouvre	ils/elles ouvrent

Elles ouvrent la porte. (*They're opening the door.*)

Other similarly conjugated verbs include **découvrir** (*to discover*), **couvrir** (*to cover*), and **souffrir** (*to suffer*).

Taking: Verbs conjugated like prendre

Prendre (*to take*) and all its derivatives are conjugated with regular –**re** endings in the singular conjugations (–**s**, –**s**, add nothing). The plural forms, however, drop the **d**, and the third-person plural also takes on an extra **n**; these forms then take the regular –**re** verb endings –**ons**, –**ez**, and –**ent**.

prendre (to take)

je prends	nous prenons
tu prends	vous prenez
il/elle/on prend	ils/elles prennent

Tu prends beaucoup de photos. (*You take a lot of pictures.*)

Similarly conjugated verbs include **apprendre** (*to learn*), **comprendre** (*to understand*), and **surprendre** (*to surprise*).

Beating and putting: Verbs conjugated like battre and mettre

Verbs that end in -**ttre**, like **battre** (*to beat*) and **mettre** (*to put*), as well as all their derivatives, have just one **t** in the singular conjugations, while the plurals keep **tt**. Then all the conjugations use the regular –**re** verb endings –**s**, –**s**, add nothing, –**ons**, –**ez**, and –**ent**.

battre (to beat)

je bats	nous battons
tu bats	vous battez
il/elle/on bat	ils/elles battent

Ils battent toujours l'autre équipe. (*They always beat the other team.*)

Examples of similarly conjugated verbs include **admettre** (*to admit*), **promettre** (*to promise*), and **transmettre** (*to transmit, to convey*).

Abilities and wants: Pouvoir and vouloir

The conjugations for **pouvoir** (*can, to be able to*) and **vouloir** (*to want*) are very similar. They have stem changes as well as irregular endings. Check out the tables that follow.

pouvoir (can, to be able to)

je peux	nous pouvons
tu peux	vous pouvez
il/elle/on peut	ils/elles peuvent

Tu peux partir. (*You may leave.*)

vouloir (to want)

je veux	nous voulons
tu veux	vous voulez
il/elle/on veut	ils/elles veulent

Elles veulent danser. (*They want to dance.*)

Making do: Verbs conjugated like faire

Faire (*to make, to do*) and all its derivatives share a conjugation pattern, although I can't offer you an easy way to explain what happens here — you just need to memorize these forms and apply them to other verbs that end in -faire.

faire (to make, do)

je fais	nous faisons
tu fais	vous faites
il/elle/on fait	ils/elles font

Il fait le lit. (*He's making the bed.*)

Similarly conjugated verbs include **défaire** (*to undo*), **refaire** (*to redo*), and **satisfaire** (*to satisfy*).

Seeing is believing: Voir, c'est croire

Voir (*to see*) and **croire** (*to believe*) are conjugated the same way. Take a look.

voir (to see)

je vois	nous voyons
tu vois	vous voyez
il/elle/on voit	ils/elles voient

Nous voyons le volcan. (*We see the volcano.*)

croire (to believe)

je crois	nous croyons
tu crois	vous croyez
il/elle/on croit	ils/elles croient

Il croit au Père Noël. (*He believes in Santa Claus.*)

PRACTICE

Provide the correct conjugation for the verb in parentheses.

Q. Je _____ (partir) à midi.

A. **Je pars à midi.** (*I'm leaving at noon.*)

106 Je ne _____ (comprendre) pas.

107 Il _____ (vouloir) manger.

108 Vous _____ (pouvoir) venir.

109 Je _____ (dormir) en classe.

110 Qu'est-ce que tu _____ (faire) ce soir ?

111 Ils _____ (ouvrir) la fenêtre même quand il fait froid.

112 Nous _____ (prendre) beaucoup de notes.

113 Elle _____ (mettre) les livres sur la table.

114 Si tu _____ (croire) que c'est juste, d'accord.

115 _____-vous (voir) l'hôtel ?

Tackling unique irregular verbs

Some of the most important French verbs have completely unique conjugations. They have nothing in common, other than the fact that they're some of the most commonly used French verbs. To master them, you just need to write out the conjugations and practice saying them. (While you expand your vocab, use these verbs to discuss the cool things you have, talk about where your neighbor is going, or tell other people what they absolutely have to know.) Use these words regularly, and the conjugations will be rolling off your tongue and out of your pen in no time.

avoir (to have)

j'ai	nous avons
tu as	vous avez
il/elle/on a	ils/elles ont

J'ai une idée. (*I have an idea.*)

être (to be)

je suis	nous sommes
tu es	vous êtes
il/elle/on est	ils/elles sont

Tu es très intelligent. (*You are very smart.*)

aller (to go)

je vais	nous allons
tu vas	vous allez
il/elle/on va	ils/elles vont

Nous allons en France. (*We're going to France.*)

devoir (must, to have to)

je dois	nous devons
tu dois	vous devez
il/elle/on doit	ils/elles doivent

Vous devez essayer. (*You have to try.*)

savoir (to know)

je sais	nous savons
tu sais	vous savez
il/elle/on sait	ils/elles savent

Elles savent nager. (*They know how to swim.*)

dire (to say, tell)

je dis	nous disons
tu dis	vous dites
il/elle/on dit	ils/elles disent

Tu dis des mensonges. (*You're telling lies.*)

boire (to drink)

je bois	nous buvons
tu bois	vous buvez
il/elle/on boit	ils/elles boivent

Elle boit trop. (*She drinks too much.*)

vivre (to live)

je vis	nous vivons
tu vis	vous vivez
il/elle/on vit	ils/elles vivent

Nous vivons ensemble. (*We live together.*)

Translate these sentences with unique verbs into French.

Q. We are here.

A. Nous sommes ici.

116 You (plural) have some questions. _____

117 We are drinking wine. _____

118 I have to open the door. _____

119 You (a friend) are going to Belgium. _____

120 They (f) know why you're early. _____

121 She has a problem. _____

122 You (plural) live in France. _____

123 We have to leave. _____

124 I am telling the truth. _____

125 They (m) are ready. _____

Answer Key to "Right Here, Right Now: The Present Tense" Practice Questions

1. **j'aime** (*I like*)

2. **tu détestes** (*you hate*)

3. **il trouve** (*he finds*)

4. **nous pensons** (*we think*)

5. **vous travaillez** (*you work*)

6. **elles donnent** (*they give*)

7. **je cherche** (*I'm looking for*)

8. **tu parles** (*you talk*)

9. **elle danse** (*she dances*)

10. **nous regardons** (*we watch*)

11. **je vieillis** (*I get old*)

12. **tu réagis** (*you react*)

13. **il bâtit** (*he builds*)

14. **nous grandissons** (*we're growing up*)

15. **vous réussissez** (*you succeed*)

16. **elles établissent** (*they establish*)

17. **je remplis** (*I fill*)

18. **tu choisis** (*you choose*)

19. **elle réunit** (*they meet*)

20. **nous finissons** (*we finish*)

21. **je défends** (*I defend*)

22. **tu réponds** (*you answer*)

23. **elle entend** (*she hears*)

24. **nous prétendons** (*we claim*)

(25) **vous fondez** (*you melt*)

(26) **ils étendent** (*they stretch*)

(27) **je rends** (*I return*)

(28) **tu descends** (*you go down*)

(29) **il vend** (*he sells*)

(30) **nous attendons** (*we wait*)

(31) **il descend** (*he goes down*)

(32) **je travaille** (*I work*)

(33) **vous remplissez** (*you fill*)

(34) **nous rendons** (*we return*)

(35) **tu cherches** (*you're looking for*)

(36) **j'attends** (*I wait*)

(37) **elle joue** (*she plays*)

(38) **ils vieillissent** (*they're getting old*)

(39) **nous réagissons** (*we react*)

(40) **tu penses** (*you think*)

(41) **nous commençons** (we begin)

(42) **je mange** (*I eat*)

(43) **tu effaces** (*you erase*)

(44) **vous corrigez** (*you correct*)

(45) **elles remplacent** (*they replace*)

(46) **nous exigeons** (*we demand*)

(47) **nous nettoyons** (*we clean*)

(48) **j'essaie/essaye** (*I try*)

(49) **elle envoie** (*she sends*)

(50) **vous payez** (*you pay*)

51) **ils tutoient** (*they use* **tu**)

52) **tu essuies** (*you wipe*)

53) **vous renouvelez** (*you renew*)

54) **elles appellent** (*they call*)

55) **tu épelles** (*you spell*)

56) **nous rappelons** (*we recall*)

57) **je renouvelle** (*I renew*)

58) **il appelle** (*he calls*)

59) **tu hoquettes** (*you hiccup*)

60) **nous feuilletons** (*we leaf through*)

61) **vous projetez** (*you project*)

62) **ils jettent** (*they throw*)

63) **je rejette** (*I reject*)

64) **elle feuillette** (*she leafs through*)

65) **tu lèves** (*you lift*)

66) **j'emmène** (*I take*)

67) **vous promenez** (*you walk*)

68) **ils pèlent** (*they peel*)

69) **elle élève** (*she raises*)

70) **nous gelons** (*we freeze*)

71) **je célèbre** (*I celebrate*)

72) **vous modérez** (*you moderate*)

73) **il suggère** (*he suggests*)

74) **elles préfèrent** (*they prefer*)

75) **tu tolères** (*you tolerate*)

76) **nous considérons** (*we consider*)

Attention
Memo à David et Philippe :

Je m'(77) **appelle** Anne et je (78) **gère** la section B7.
Les autres gérants et moi (79) **changeons** notre politique
de courriel. Vous (80) **envoyez** souvent des messages
personnels, et nous (81) **considérons** que c'est une
infraction à vos contrats. Nous (82) **commençons** à
surveiller vos ordinateurs ; si vous (83) **répétez**
cette activité, nous ne (84) **renouvelons** pas vos
contrats. J'(85) **espère** que vous (86) **essayez** maintenant
de ne plus écrire à vos amis quand vous travaillez.

*(My name is Anne, and I manage section B7. The other managers and I are
changing our e-mail policy. You often send personal messages, and we consider
that a breach of your contracts. We are starting to watch your computers; if
you repeat this activity, we are not renewing your contracts. I hope that you now
try not to write to your friends anymore when you work.)*

Attention
Memo à Sylvie :

Nous (87) **rejetons** ta note de frais. Quand tu
(88) **voyages**, tu (89) **paies** (or **payes**) trop pour des
hôtels trois étoiles. Nous (90) **exigeons** que nos
employés se (91) **logent** dans des hôtels deux étoiles.
Même si tu (92) **préfères** les hôtels de luxe, nous
(93) **suggérons** que tu (94) **considères** les frais et que tu
te (95) **modères**.

*(We are rejecting your expense report. When you travel, you pay too much for
three-star hotels. We insist that our employees stay in two-star hotels. Even if
you prefer luxury hotels, we suggest that you consider the costs and
moderate yourself.)*

	Attention
	Memo à Georges :
	Il y a deux problèmes. D'abord, tu ne (96) **complètes** pas
	ton travail — tu n'(97) **épelles** rien correctement et tu ne
	(98) **corriges** pas tes erreurs. Nous (99) **dirigeons** un
	programme de relecture systématique pour améliorer l'image
	que tu (100) **projettes** dans les meetings. De surcroît, te
	(101) **rappelles**-tu que nous n'(102) **employons** pas de femme
	de service ? Nous (103) **enlevons** les tableaux blancs
	parce que tu les (104) **effaces** mais tu ne les
	(105) **nettoies** pas.
	(There are two problems. First of all, you do not complete your work — you don't
	spell anything correctly, and you don't correct your mistakes. We direct you to
	systematically proofread in order to improve the image you project in meetings.
	In addition, do you remember that we don't employ cleaners? We are removing the
	whiteboards because you erase them but you don't clean them.)

(106) **Je ne comprends pas.** (*I don't understand.*)

(107) **Il veut manger.** (*He wants to eat.*)

(108) **Vous pouvez venir.** (*You can come.*)

(109) **Je dors en classe.** (*I sleep in class.*)

(110) **Qu'est-ce que tu fais ce soir ?** (*What are you doing this evening?*)

(111) **Ils ouvrent la fenêtre même quand il fait froid.** (*They open the window even when it's cold.*)

(112) **Nous prenons beaucoup de notes.** (*We take a lot of notes.*)

(113) **Elle met les livres sur la table.** (*She's putting the books on the table.*)

(114) **Si tu crois que c'est juste, d'accord.** (*If you believe it's fair, okay.*)

(115) **Voyez-vous l'hôtel ?** (*Do you see the hotel?*)

(116) **Vous avez des questions.**

(117) **Nous buvons du vin.**

(118) **Je dois ouvrir la porte.**

119. **Tu vas en Belgique.**

120. **Elles savent pourquoi tu es/vous êtes en avance.**

121. **Elle a un problème.**

122. **Vous vivez en France.**

123. **Nous devons partir.**

124. **Je dis la vérité.**

125. **Ils sont prêts.**

Chapter 7

Sorting Out Pronominal Verbs: Idioms, Oneself, and Each Other

Pronominal verbs may sound like something out of a grammatical horror story, but *pronominal* is just a fancy word that means *with a pronoun*. The pronoun in question is the *reflexive pronoun*, and its only job is to tell you that the verb you're using has a special meaning. You can also use most pronominal verbs without the reflexive pronoun, but then the meaning of that verb changes — sometimes slightly, sometimes significantly. Pronominal verbs are often mistakenly called reflexive verbs when, in fact, reflexive verbs are just one type of pronominal verb.

Pronominal verbs are different from other verbs in that they need a reflexive pronoun to tell you one of three things:

>> The subject is performing the action of the verb on itself.

>> Two or more subjects are performing the action on one another.

>> The verb has a special meaning, unrelated to the one it has without the pronoun.

This chapter explains how to correctly use reflexive pronouns, the types of pronominal verbs, and how to use pronominal verbs effectively.

Examining the Relationship between Reflexive Pronouns and Pronominal Verbs

Pronominal verbs are just like other verbs in that they describe actions and have to be conjugated for different tenses and moods. The difference is that pronominal verbs, in addition to subject pronouns (see Chapter 1), also need reflexive pronouns. This section explains what reflexive pronouns are and how to use them correctly.

Reflexive pronouns are the pronouns that you have to use with pronominal verbs. There are three key things you need to know about them. They're

>> Personal, meaning that you use a different one for each grammatical person (Chapter 1 explains grammatical person in detail)

>> Required when using pronominal verbs

>> Used only with pronominal verbs, nowhere else

See Table 7-1 for the French reflexive pronouns in all their forms.

Table 7-1 Reflexive Pronouns

Subject Pronoun	Reflexive Pronoun	Before a Vowel or Mute h	In the Imperative
je	me	m'	
tu	te	t'	toi
il, elle, on	se	s'	
nous	nous	nous	nous
vous	vous	vous	vous
ils, elles	se	s'	

In the present tense (see Chapter 6), the reflexive pronoun goes in front of the verb, and the verb is conjugated according to its status as a regular, irregular, stem-changing, or spelling-change verb. (For info on different word-order situations, check out the following section.) For example, the pronominal verb **se doucher** means *to take a shower*. **Doucher** is a regular –**er** verb, so you conjugate the pronominal form as shown in the following table.

se doucher (to take a shower)

je me douche	nous nous douchons
tu te douches	vous vous douchez
il/elle/on se douche	ils/elles se douchent

Je me douche le soir. (*I shower at night.*)

TIP

Don't let the **nous** and **vous** forms of pronominal verbs weird you out. Yes, the subject and reflexive pronoun are identical, but they're both required.

When **me**, **te**, or **se** is followed by a word that begins with a vowel or mute **h**, you have to drop the –**e** and make a contraction. For instance, the pronominal verb **s'habiller** (*to get dressed*) is also a regular –**er** verb, so you use the conjugations in the following table.

s'habiller (to get dressed)	
je m'habille	nous nous habillons
tu t'habilles	vous vous habillez
il/elle/on s'habille	ils/elles s'habillent

Elle s'habille dans ta chambre. (*She's getting dressed in your room.*)

Te changes to **toi** when used in affirmative commands. For example:

» **Tu te couches** (*You're going to bed*) but **Couche-toi** (*Go to bed*).

» **Tu t'habilles** (*You're getting dressed*) but **Habille-toi** (*Get dressed*).

See Chapter 14 for more information about commands.

PRACTICE

Fill in the blanks with the correct reflexive pronoun.

Q. Il _____ lève.

A. Il se lève. (*He's getting up.*)

1. Je _____ baigne.

2. Marc _____ couche.

3. Ils _____ rasent.

4. Vous _____ reposez.

5. Tu _____ maquilles.

6. Nous _____ déshabillons.

7. Tu _____ approches du banc.

8. Elle _____ souvient de ce film.

9. Je _____ habille.

10. Annette _____ regarde.

REMEMBER

The reflexive pronoun always has to agree with the subject in all tenses and moods, including the present participle and the infinitive (Chapter 10 talks about both of these verb forms). Table 7-2 gives some examples with **je** as the subject.

Table 7-2   Reflexive Pronoun with Different Verb Forms

Verb Form	French	Translation
Present tense	**Je me coiffe.**	*I'm fixing my hair.*
Past tense	**Je me suis coiffé.**	*I fixed my hair.*
Present participle	**En me coiffant, je suis tombé.**	*While fixing my hair, I fell.*
Infinitive	**Je vais me coiffer.**	*I'm going to fix my hair.*

Understanding the Types of Pronominal Verbs

Just like ice cream, pronominal verbs come in many different flavors (though they may not taste as good). *Pronominal verbs* are all the different verbs that you have to use with a reflexive pronoun (see preceding section for more about these particular pronouns).

You can recognize a pronominal verb by the reflexive pronoun **se** that precedes the infinitive in the dictionary or your vocab lists: **se coucher** (*to go to bed*), **se laver** (*to wash oneself*), and so on. (Within sentences, you can tell a verb is pronominal when you see **se** or one of the other reflexive pronouns accompanying it.)

Although you can use most pronominal verbs without the reflexive pronoun, the meaning changes: Alone, **coucher** means *to put (someone else) to bed*, and **laver** means *to wash (someone/ something else)*. So to say what you mean to say in French, you need to know when to use the reflexive pronoun and when not to. The following sections cover the three types of pronominal verbs.

Reflexive verbs: Acting on oneself

Reflexive verbs tell you that someone is doing something to their own body or life. Table 7-3 shows some common reflexive verbs. Note that many of them have something to do with parts of the body or clothing, and the others have to do with personal circumstance or position.

Here are a couple of example sentences:

> **Je me marie avec Thérèse demain.** (*I'm marrying Thérèse tomorrow.*)

> **Il se rase une fois par semaine.** (*He shaves once a week.*)

DIFFERENCES

Reflexive verbs don't really exist in English — you just use regular verbs, and if you want to stress that you're doing something to yourself, you can tack on *myself*, as in *I got dressed by myself* or *I dressed myself*. In French, though, the idea of *by myself*, represented by the reflexive pronoun **me**, is not optional — you have to use it to distinguish from the non-reflexive meaning. See the section "Deciding Whether to Make a Verb Pronominal," later in this chapter, for more information on knowing when you need to use pronominal verbs.

Table 7-3   Common Reflexive Verbs

Verb	Translation	Verb	Translation
s'approcher de	to approach	se laver (les mains, les cheveux)	to wash (one's hands, hair)
s'asseoir	to sit down	se lever	to get up
se baigner	to bathe, swim	se maquiller	to put on makeup
se brosser (les dents,	to brush (one's teeth, hair)	se marier (avec)	to get married (to)
se casser (le bras, le doigt)	to break (one's arm, finger)	se moucher	to blow one's nose
se coiffer	to fix one's hair	se peigner	to comb one's hair
se coucher	to go to bed	se promener	to go for a walk
se couper	to cut oneself	se raser	to shave
se déshabiller	to get undressed	se regarder	to look at oneself
se doucher	to take a shower	se reposer	to rest
se fâcher	to get angry	se réveiller	to wake up
s'habiller	to get dressed	se souvenir de	to remember
s'inquiéter	to worry		

PRACTICE

Reflecting on reflexive verbs. Translate these sentences into French — and don't forget the reflexive pronouns!

Q. He is shaving.

A. Il se rase.

11 I'm getting angry. _____

12 They (m) are getting dressed. _____

13 You (pl) are worrying. _____

14 Sylvia is getting up. _____

15 We (**nous**) are going for a walk. _____

16 You (child) are going to bed. _____

Reciprocal verbs: What you do to each other

Reciprocal verbs are any verbs that you use reflexively to mean that two or more subjects are doing something to, at, or with each other. Table 7-4 lists some common reciprocal verbs.

The following sentences indicate reciprocal action:

Nous nous connaissons depuis 20 ans. (*We've known each other for 20 years.*)

Ils se parlent tous les jours. (*They talk to each other every day.*)

Table 7-4   Common Reciprocal Verbs

Verb	Translation	Verb	Translation
s'aimer	to love (each other)	se parler	to talk (to each other)
se comprendre	to understand (each other)	se promettre	to promise (each other)
se connaître	to know (each other)	se quitter	to leave (each other)
se détester	to hate (each other)	se regarder	to look (at each other)
se dire	to tell (each other)	se rencontrer	to meet (each other)
se disputer	to argue (with each other)	se sourire	to smile (at each other)
s'écrire	to write (each other)	se téléphoner	to call (each other)
s'embrasser	to kiss (each other)	se voir	to see (each other)

TIP

Many reciprocal verbs can also be used reflexively: **Je me parle** (*I'm talking to myself*), **elle se regarde** (*she's looking at herself*), and so on. Because these verbs have different meanings, when the subject is plural, you can find it difficult to know whether the verb is reflexive or reciprocal. In those cases, you really need to pay attention to the context. For example:

Nous nous parlons. (*We are talking to each other.* or *We are talking to ourselves.*)

Elles se regardent. (*They are looking at each other.* or *They are looking at themselves.*)

PRACTICE

It's time to get reciprocal! Translate these sentences into French — and don't forget the reflexive pronouns.

Q. You understand each other.

A. **Vous vous comprenez.**

17 They (f) love each other. _____

18 We are leaving (each other). _____ .

19 You hate each other. _____

20 They (m) see each other. _____

21 We are arguing. _____

22 You are kissing. _____

Idiomatic pronominal verbs: Figuratively speaking

Idiomatic pronominal verbs sound exciting, but *idiomatic* just means that the meaning of these verbs is distinctly different from their meaning when you use them non-reflexively. (An *idiom* is an expression whose meaning you can't determine just by literally translating the individual words because at least one of those words is used figuratively. See Chapter 2 for more info on idioms.)

Table 7-5 shows some common idiomatic pronominal verbs and their non-pronominal equivalents.

Table 7-5		Idiomatic Pronominal Verbs	
Non-Pronominal French Verb	Translation	Pronominal Verb	Translation
amuser	*to amuse*	**s'amuser**	*to have a good time*
appeler	*to call*	**s'appeler**	*to be named*
débrouiller	*to untangle*	**se débrouiller**	*to manage, get by*
décider	*to decide*	**se décider**	*to make up one's mind*
demander	*to ask*	**se demander**	*to wonder*
dépêcher	*to send, to dispatch*	**se dépêcher**	*to hurry*
endormir	*to put to sleep*	**s'endormir**	*to fall asleep*
ennuyer	*to bother, to annoy*	**s'ennuyer**	*to be bored*
entendre	*to hear*	**s'entendre**	*to get along*
installer	*to install*	**s'installer**	*to settle in (a home)*
mettre	*to place, put*	**se mettre à**	*to begin to*
rappeler	*to call back*	**se rappeler**	*to recall, remember*
rendre compte de	*to account for*	**se rendre compte de**	*to realize, to take into account*
réunir	*to gather, collect*	**se réunir**	*to meet, get together*
tromper	*to deceive*	**se tromper**	*to be mistaken*
trouver	*to find*	**se trouver**	*to be located*

Here's what these verbs look like pronominally:

> **Je m'appelle Laura.** (*My name is Laura.*)

> **Il s'amuse bien.** (*He's having a really good time.*)

See whether you can ID some idioms. Translate these verbs into English, making sure to distinguish the regular meaning from the pronominal one.

PRACTICE

Q. rappeler/se rappeler

A. *to call back/to recall, remember*

23 ennuyer _____/s'ennuyer _____

24 tromper _____/se tromper _____

25 entendre _____/s'entendre _____

26 débrouiller _____/se débrouiller _____

27 trouver _____/se trouver _____

28 amuser _____/s'amuser _____

Knowing Where the Words Go

When using pronominal verbs, you need to make sure you use the correct word order with the reflexive pronoun. If you don't, the person you're talking to may not understand who's doing what to whom.

Word order with the reflexive pronoun is very simple: You put the pronoun directly in front of the pronominal verb in nearly all tenses, moods, and constructions.

> **Je me lève à 9 h 00.** (*I get up at 9 a.m.*)

> **Il se baignait à 10 h 00.** (*He was bathing at 10 a.m.*)

When you have a conjugated verb followed by an infinitive, the reflexive pronoun goes in front of the infinitive because the infinitive is the pronominal verb. (See Chapter 10 for more about infinitives.)

> **Nous allons nous acheter de la glace.** (*We're going to buy ourselves some ice cream.*)

> **Tu peux t'asseoir ici.** (*You can sit here.*)

REMEMBER

In a few situations, you don't put the reflexive pronoun right in front of the pronominal verb:

» **Affirmative imperative:** In the *affirmative imperative* (commands), you place the reflexive pronoun after the verb and connect the two words with hyphens:

- **Lève-toi.** (*Get up.*)
- **Dépêchez-vous.** (*Hurry up.*)

Note that **te** changes to **toi**. As shown in Table 7-1 earlier in this chapter, **vous** does not change.

See Chapter 14 for more information about the imperative.

» **Compound tenses:** In the **passé composé**, the reflexive pronoun precedes the helping verb **être**:

- **Je me suis levé très tôt.** (*I got up really early.*)
- **Vous vous êtes trompé.** (*You made a mistake.*)

Go to Chapter 15 to read up on the **passé composé**.

» **Questions with inversion:** When you ask questions by using inversion with pronominal verbs, the reflexive pronoun precedes the inverted verb-subject, which means it usually goes at the beginning of the sentence.

- **Te douches-tu le matin ou le soir ?** (*Do you shower in the morning or at night?*)
- **Vous êtes-vous levés avant 7 h 00 ?** (*Did you get up before 7 a.m.?*)

See Chapter 8 for information about asking questions that use inversion.

PRACTICE

Determine which reflexive pronoun each sentence needs and where that pronoun goes; then rewrite the sentence.

Q. Jacques peigne les cheveux.

A. **Jacques se peigne les cheveux.** (*Jacques is combing his hair.*)

29 Nous demandons pourquoi.

_____

30 Elle va habiller après le petit-déjeuner.

_____

31 Tu regardes trop.

_____

32 Je vais laver les cheveux.

_____

33 Ils approchent lentement.

_____

34 Vous allez installer au Canada.

_____

Deciding Whether to Make a Verb Pronominal

Pronominal verbs tell you that the verb has a special meaning: The action is being done to the subject, two or more subjects are doing something to each other, or the verb has an idiomatic meaning. You can use pronominal verbs in all tenses and moods, and you conjugate them just like any other verb — the only difference between pronominal verbs and non-pronominal verbs is that pronominal verbs need a reflexive pronoun.

The important thing to understand about these verbs is that you can use the great majority of them without the reflexive pronoun, but then the verb has a different meaning. The extent of the difference in meaning depends on the type of pronominal verb. The following sections discuss the correct ways to use pronominal verbs.

Reflexive verbs: Oneself or something else?

Reflexive verbs indicate that the subjects are doing something to themselves — usually something to do with parts of the body (washing, brushing), clothing (dressing, undressing), personal circumstance (marriage, divorce), or position (sitting, getting up). Using those verbs without the reflexive pronoun means that the subject is doing that action to someone or something else. Compare the following sentences.

> **Yvette se marie avec François demain.** (*Yvette is marrying François tomorrow.*)

> **Le prêtre marie trois couples par semaine.** (*The priest marries three couples a week.*)

In the first sentence, Yvette herself is getting married, but in the second, the priest is performing the ceremony that joins two people — not including himself — to one another. Therefore, the latter does not have a reflexive pronoun.

Here is another set of examples comparing a pronominal verb with its non-pronominal counterpart:

> **Ils se lavent les mains.** (*They're washing their hands.*)

> **Ils lavent la voiture.** (*They're washing the car.*)

In the reflexive sentence, the subjects are washing a part of themselves; in the non-reflexive sentence, the subjects are washing something else. So the difference in meaning has nothing to do with the verb, which describes the same action in both sentences — the difference is just in who or what is affected by the verb.

DIFFERENCES

When you use reflexive verbs such as **se laver** (*to wash*), **se brosser** (*to brush*), and **se casser** (*to break*) with nouns that describe body parts, you use the definite article — not the possessive adjective — in front of the body part because the reflexive pronoun tells you whom it belongs to.

> **Je me suis cassé la jambe.** (*I broke my leg.*)

> **Il se brosse les dents.** (*He's brushing his teeth.*)

If you break someone else's leg or break something inanimate, you don't use the verb reflexively.

> **J'ai cassé la jambe de mon frère.** (*I broke my brother's leg.*)

> **J'ai cassé une assiette.** (*I broke a plate.*)

See Chapter 15 for information on using the **passé composé** as in the previous two examples.

WARNING

Not all pronominal verbs have a non-pronominal equivalent. **Se souvenir** (*to remember*), for example, is always reflexive. You never see **souvenir** used as a verb without a reflexive pronoun.

PRACTICE

Translate these sentences into French, paying careful attention to whether the verbs need to be reflexive. Write your answers in the spaces provided.

Q. He's cutting his hair.

A. **Il se coupe les cheveux.**

35 I'm getting dressed.

_____

36 You (tu) are combing your hair.

_____

37 We're walking the dog.

_____

38 Thierry is shaving.

_____

39 Sandrine is bathing her little brother.

_____

40 You (vous) are getting up.

_____

Reciprocal verbs: Returning the favor?

Reciprocal verbs tell you that two or more people are doing something to each other, sort of a grammatical mutual admiration society. Reciprocal verbs usually have to do with communication (reading/writing to each other), feeling (loving/hating each other), and being together or apart. You use them when you want to be clear that the subjects are both doing the same thing to each other. You can use all reciprocal verbs without the reflexive pronoun for normal, non-mutual actions. Compare these sentences:

» **Nous nous promettons.** (_We promise each other._)

Nous promettons à nos enfants. (_We promise our kids._)

» **Ils se sourient.** (_They're smiling at each other._)

Ils sourient en voyant le chiot. (_They smile upon seeing the puppy._)

The difference in meaning between reciprocal and non-reciprocal verbs isn't huge. The reciprocal verb indicates that multiple subjects are all treating each other the same way: They're making promises to each other, smiling at each other, and so on. The non-reciprocal verb indicates the same activity, but it's not returned.

PRACTICE

Your friend Charles hates inequality. He thinks these sentences are unfair because only one person is doing something. Rewrite them so that the two subjects are reciprocating. Note that you need to replace the singular subjects with plural subjects and then conjugate the verbs for the new subject.

Q. Je t'écris. (I'm writing to you.)

A. **Nous nous écrivons.** (*We're writing to each other.*)

NOTE DE SERVICE

À: _____

De: _____

41. Il m'aime. _____

42. Tu lui téléphones. _____

43. Elle l'embrasse. _____

44. Géraldine voit Michèle. _____

45. Elle me regarde. _____

46. Ils vous comprennent. _____

47. Je lui dis la vérité. _____

48. Tu me parles. _____

49. Elles me connaissent. _____

50. Il la déteste. _____

Idiomatic pronominal verbs: What's the meaning of all this?

Idiomatic pronominal verbs have the biggest difference in meaning between the pronominal and non-pronominal forms. If you use reflexive and reciprocal verbs (discussed in the preceding sections) without the reflexive pronoun, they just change who receives the action of the verb and whether the action is reciprocated. But idiomatic pronominal verbs have a meaning that's completely different from that of their non-pronominal counterparts. Therefore, you need to memorize the list in the section "Idiomatic pronominal verbs: Figuratively speaking," earlier in this chapter, to be sure you're saying the right thing. Compare these sentence pairs:

>> **Je m'entends bien avec mes parents.** (*I get along well with my parents.*)

J'entends du bruit. (*I hear some noise.*)

>> **Te rappelles-tu de son prénom ?** (*Do you remember his name?*)

Tu peux rappeler demain. (*You can call back tomorrow.*)

Even though the verb itself is the same, the meanings of these sentence pairs have nothing in common because the reflexive pronoun changes the literal meaning of the verb into an idiomatic meaning.

PRACTICE

Translate these sentences into French, paying special attention to the meanings of the words in italics and to whether you have to use normal verbs or idiomatic pronominal verbs. Write your answers in the spaces provided.

Q. *His name* is Jean.

A. Il s'appelle Jean.

51 You (tu) have *to hurry*!

_____

52 I'm *bored*.

_____

53 He can't *find* his keys.

_____

54 She's *deceiving* everyone.

_____

55 We're *settling* in our new apartment.

_____

56 Are you (vous) *making up your mind*?

_____

57 I'm *putting* this book on the table.

_____

58 You (tu) *are mistaken*.

_____

59 The bank *is located* next to the park.

_____

60 They *meet* on Mondays.

_____

Answer Key to "Sorting Out Pronominal Verbs" Practice Questions

1. **Je me baigne.** (*I'm bathing.*)
2. **Marc se couche.** (*Marc is going to bed.*)
3. **Ils se rasent.** (*They're shaving.*)
4. **Vous vous reposez.** (*You're resting.*)
5. **Tu te maquilles.** (*You're putting on makeup.*)
6. **Nous nous déshabillons.** (*We're getting undressed.*)
7. **Tu t'approches du banc.** (*You're approaching the bench.*)
8. **Elle se souvient de ce film.** (*She remembers this movie.*)
9. **Je m'habille.** (*I'm getting dressed.*)
10. **Annette se regarde.** (*Annette is looking at herself.*)
11. **Je me fâche.**
12. **Ils s'habillent.**
13. **Vous vous inquiétez.**
14. **Sylvia se lève.**
15. **Nous nous promenons.**
16. **Tu te couches.**
17. **Elle s'aiment.**
18. **Nous nous quittons./On se quitte.**
19. **Vous vous détestez.**
20. **Ils se voient.**
21. **Nous nous disputons./On se dispute.**
22. **Vous vous embrassez.**
23. to bother, to annoy/to be bored
24. to deceive/to be mistaken
25. to hear/to get along
26. to untangle/to manage, get by
27. to find/to be located
28. to amuse/to have a good time

29. **Nous nous demandons pourquoi.** (*We wonder why.*)

30. **Elle va s'habiller après le petit-déjeuner.** (*She's going to get dressed after breakfast.*)

31. **Tu te regardes trop.** (*You look at yourself too much.*)

32. **Je vais me laver les cheveux.** (*I'm going to wash my hair.*)

33. **Ils s'approchent lentement.** (*They are approaching slowly.*)

34. **Vous allez vous installer au Canada.** (*You are going to settle in Canada.*)

35. **Je m'habille.**

36. **Tu te peignes.**

37. **Nous promenons le chien./On promène le chien.**

38. **Thierry se rase.**

39. **Sandrine baigne son petit frère.**

40. **Vous vous levez.**

41. **Nous nous aimons.** (*We love each other.*)

42. **Vous vous téléphonez.** (*You call each other.*)

43. **Ils/Elles s'embrassent.** (*They're kissing each other.*)

44. **Elles se voient.** (*They see each other.*)

45. **Nous nous regardons.** (*We're looking at each other.*)

46. **Vous vous comprenez.** (*You understand each other.*)

47. **Nous nous disons la vérité.** (*We tell each other the truth.*)

48. **Nous nous parlons.** (*We're talking to each other.*)

49. **Nous nous connaissons.** (*We know each other.*)

50. **Ils se détestent.** (*They hate each other.*)

51. **Tu dois te dépêcher !**

52. **Je m'ennuie.**

53. **Il ne peut pas trouver ses clés.**

54. **Elle trompe tout le monde.**

55. **Nous nous installons dans notre nouvel appartement.**

56. **Est-ce que vous vous décidez ?/Vous décidez-vous ?**

57. **Je mets ce livre sur la table.**

58. **Tu te trompes.**

59. **La banque se trouve à côté du parc.**

60. **Ils se réunissent/se retrouvent le lundi.**

Chapter **8**

Asking and Answering Questions

Everyone knows that to connect with other people, you need to be a good listener; but if you want to have a real discussion, you can't just stand there and let others jabber on — you have to contribute, too. Questions are one of the foundations of a good conversation or letter, and knowing how to ask and answer questions can greatly improve both your spoken and written French. When you chat on the phone with your friend in Brussels and teleconference with your colleague in Montreal, don't let them do all the talking — ask some questions of your own.

DIFFERENCES

In French texts, you must precede with a space the question mark and all other two-part punctuation marks — exclamation points, **guillemets** (French quotation marks), colons, and semicolons.

This chapter explains how to ask and answer different types of questions, and it provides all the interrogative vocabulary that goes along with them.

Oui ou Non: Asking Yes-or-No Questions

If all you need is a simple *yes* or *no*, then asking questions in French couldn't be easier. You can ask yes-or-no questions in various ways, and which method you use depends on what kind of a conversation you're having or the type of correspondence you're writing. In most cases, you want to choose between the less formal **est-ce que** and the more formal inversion. The following sections help you make the right decision and show you how to use each form.

Posing informal questions

Using **est-ce que** (literally: *is it that*) is the easiest way to ask questions. All you have to do is stick **est-ce que** at the beginning of any statement and tack a question mark at the end.

> **Est-ce que tu es prêt ?** (*Are you ready?*)
>
> **Est-ce que David a mangé ?** (*Has David eaten?*)

When followed by a word that begins with a vowel, such as **il**, **elle**, and **on**, **est-ce que** contracts to **est-ce qu'**.

> **Est-ce qu'elle parle français ?** (*Does she speak French?*)
>
> **Est-ce qu'ils ont de l'argent ?** (*Do they have any money?*)

Est-ce que is somewhat informal, and it's rarely written — it's used mainly when speaking.

WARNING

Another very common way to ask questions informally when writing or speaking is just to tack a question mark at the end of a statement (and raise your tone, if speaking), such as **Tu veux venir avec nous ?** (*You want to come with us?*) However, this structure is very informal, so never use it in anything official or business-related. Inversion (see the following section) is the best way to ask questions in any kind of formal situation.

TIP

If you're pretty sure the answer to your question is *yes*, in a formal situation, you can stick **n'est-ce pas ?** (Literally: *isn't it that?*) on the end of a statement: **Vous comprenez, n'est-ce pas ?** (*You understand, right/don't you?*) Informally, you can just say **non ?** (*no?*).

PRACTICE

Turn each of the following statements into a question by using **est-ce que**.

Q. Elle est intéressante.

A. **Est-ce qu'elle est intéressante ?** (*Is she interesting?*)

1. Vous voulez étudier. _____

2. Tu es heureux. _____

3. Nous allons marcher. _____

4. Elle habite au Sénégal. _____

5. J'ai raison. _____

6. Ils sont prêts. _____

Asking formal questions with inversion

Inversion is a little bit more complicated than the informal methods of asking yes-or-no questions (covered in the preceding section). Whereas you can ask any question by using the informal **est-ce que**, the formal method, inversion, works only with a subject pronoun, not a noun or a name. Inversion is more formal than using **est-ce que**, so in a business setting, such as a job interview or conversation with your boss, use this option.

Asking questions with inversion requires you, at minimum, to change the word order of the subject and verb. You might need to make additional small changes including the following:

>> To ask a question by using inversion, you switch the order of the subject pronoun and verb, and then join them with a hyphen.

- **Vous êtes prêts** (*You are ready*) becomes **Êtes-vous prêts ?** (*Are you ready?*)
- **Il connaît Maryline** (*He knows Maryline*) becomes **Connaît-il Maryline ?** (*Does he know Maryline?*)

>> When the verb ends in a vowel and is followed by a third-person singular pronoun, you have to add **t–** between the verb and pronoun.

- **Elle parle français** (*She speaks French*) becomes **Parle-t-elle français ?** (*Does she speak French?*)
- **On a de l'argent** (*We have some money*) becomes **A-t-on de l'argent ?** (*Do we have any money?*)

>> When you have a conjugated verb plus an infinitive (like when talking about the near future, discussed in Chapter 10), inversion occurs with the conjugated verb, and then the infinitive follows.

- **Tu vas partir** (*You are going to leave*) becomes **Vas-tu partir ?** (*Are you going to leave?*)
- **Il sait nager** (*He knows how to swim*) becomes **Sait-il nager ?** (*Does he know how to swim?*)

>> Likewise, with compound tenses such as the **passé composé** (see Chapter 15), the auxiliary verb inverts with the subject pronoun, and then the past participle follows.

- **Il est parti** (*He left*) becomes **Est-il parti ?** (*Did he leave?*)
- **Vous avez travaillé aujourd'hui** (*You worked today*) becomes **Avez-vous travaillé aujourd'hui ?** (*Did you work today?*)

>> You can invert only subject pronouns (and interrogative pronouns, explained in the section "Interrogative pronouns," later in this chapter), not actual subjects that are nouns. So when you ask a question that includes a noun as the subject, such as **Hélène** or **le chat** (*the cat*), you have to either replace the noun with a pronoun or start the question with the noun, followed by the inverted verb and subject pronoun.

- **Hélène est prête** (*Hélène is ready*) becomes **Hélène est-elle prête ?** (*Is Hélène ready?*)
- **Le chat sait nager** (*The cat knows how to swim*) becomes **Le chat sait-il nager ?** (*Does the cat know how to swim?*)

Turn each of the following statements into a question by using inversion.

Q. Il est beau.

A. Est-il beau ? (*Is he handsome?*)

7 Tu as un chien. _____

8 Vous êtes prêts. _____

(9) Elle travaille ici. _____

(10) Ils aiment danser. _____

(11) Tu es triste. _____

(12) Vous devez partir. _____

(13) Nous sommes en retard. _____

(14) Elles habitent en France. _____

(15) Je suis en avance. _____

(16) Tu peux conduire. _____

Asking Who, What, Which, When, Where, Why, and How Questions

Questions that ask for information, such as *who*, *when*, *why*, and *how*, are often called *wh questions* in English because all these question words begin with *w* or *h*.

In French, these question words fall into three categories, and you need to understand the difference between them in order to ask the French version of *wh questions*.

Interrogative adverbs

Interrogative adverbs ask for more information about something that happens. French has five important interrogative adverbs:

» **comment** (*how*)

» **combien (de)** (*how much/many*)

» **quand** (*when*)

» **où** (*where*)

» **pourquoi** (*why*)

Comment

Comment usually means *how* at the beginning of a question.

> **Comment allez-vous ?** (*How are you?*)

> **Comment est-ce que tu as fait ça ?** (*How did you do that?*)

However, when used on its own, **Comment ?** can also mean *What?* — for example, when you need someone to repeat what they just said.

As I explain in Chapter 1, **comment** is also equivalent to *what* in the question **Comment vous-appelez vous ?** (*What is your name?* literally: *How do you call yourself?*)

Combien

Combien on its own or followed directly by **est-ce que** or inversion means *How many?* or *How much?*

> **Je veux des pommes. Combien ?** (*I want some apples. How many?*)
>
> **Combien gagne-t-il ?** (*How much does he earn?*)
>
> **Combien est-ce que tu dois ?** (*How much do you owe?*)

If a noun follows, the preposition **de** is required.

> **Combien de pommes voulez-vous ?** (*How many apples do you want?*)
>
> **Combien d'argent gagne-t-il ?** (*How much money does he earn?*)

Quand

Quand means *when*, and the answer can be a time or date.

> **Quand est-ce que vous êtes arrivés ? À midi.** (*When did you arrive? At noon.*)
>
> **Quand vas-tu en France ? Dans deux semaines.** (*When are you going to France? In two weeks.*)

However, if you want to know the exact time that something happened or will happen, use **À quelle heure ?** (*At what time?*). (**Quelle** is an interrogative adjective, which I explain in the section "Interrogative adjectives," later in this chapter.)

Où

Où means *where*.

> **Où habitez-vous ?** (*Where do you live?*)
>
> **Où va-t-on se retrouver ?** (*Where are we meeting?*)

Pourquoi

Pourquoi means *why*.

> **Pourquoi êtes-vous en retard ?** (*Why are you late?*)
>
> **Pourquoi est-ce que tu veux savoir ?** (*Why do you want to know?*)

Interrogation time! The police have caught you playing with fire, and they're full of questions. Fill in the missing interrogative adverb.

PRACTICE

Q. _____ vous appelez-vous ? (*What is your name?*)

A. Comment

17. _____ habitez-vous ? (Where do you live?)

18. _____ avez-vous emménagé ? (When did you move in?)

19. _____ payez-vous pour le loyer? (How much do you pay for rent?)

20. _____ est-il si cher? (Why is it so expensive?)

21. _____ feux avez-vous allumés ? (How many fires have you set?)

22. _____ aimez-vous le feu ? (Why do you like fire?)

23. Vous avez des complices ? _____ ? (Do you have accomplices? How many?)

24. _____ vous êtes-vous rencontrés ? (How did you meet?)

25. _____ sont-ils ? (Where are they?)

26. _____ allez-vous répondre ? (When are you going to answer?)

Interrogative pronouns

Interrogative pronouns ask *who* or *what*, and because they're pronouns, you can't use them in front of a noun: They stand in for the noun they're asking about.

Who in French is pretty easy — it's usually translated as **qui**.

> **Qui est à la plage ?** (*Who is at the beach?*)

> **Qui va inviter les voisins ?** (*Who is going to invite the neighbors?*)

> **À qui appartient ce livre ?** (*Whose book is this?* literally: *To whom does this book belong?*)

What is a lot more complicated.

>> If it's at the beginning of a question, the French translation is **que**:

  ● **Que veut dire « pamplemousse » ?** (*What does "**pamplemousse**" mean?*)

  ● **Que devez-vous faire aujourd'hui ?** (*What do you need to do today?*)

>> **Que** contracts to **qu'** in front of a vowel or mute **h**.

  ● **Qu'avez-vous fait ?** (*What have you done?*)

  ● **Qu'allons-nous regarder ?** (*What are we going to watch?*)

>> After a preposition, **que** changes to **quoi** (see Chapter 12 for details on prepositions).

  ● **À quoi pensez-vous ?** (*What are you thinking about?*)

  ● **De quoi parlent-ils ?** (*What are they talking about?*)

>> In addition, if you're asking *what* but you really mean *which*, you want an interrogative adjective, which I discuss in the following section.

WARNING

Don't get too attached to the idea that **qui** means *who* and **que** means *what*. They usually do, but not always. When asking questions, **qui** and **que** also indicate whether you're using *who* or *what* as the subject or object of the question — see the section "Asking wh questions with est-ce que," later in this chapter, for details.

PRACTICE

First date: The best way to get to know a potential soul mate is by asking questions. Fill in the missing interrogative pronouns.

Q. _____ es-tu ? (Who are you?)

A. Qui

27. _____ fais-tu dans la vie ? (What do you do in life [work/hobbies]?)

28. Sur _____ écris-tu ? (What do you write about?)

29. _____ lit tes livres ? (Who reads your books?)

30. _____ aimes-tu faire le week-end ? (What do you like to do on the weekend?)

31. De _____ rêves-tu ? (What do you dream about?)

32. À _____ fais-tu confiance ? (Whom do you trust?)

33. _____ allons-nous boire ? (What are we going to drink?)

34. _____ choisit le vin ? (Who is choosing the wine?)

35. _____ veux-tu manger ? (What do you want to eat?)

36. _____ va payer ? (Who is going to pay?)

Interrogative adjectives

DIFFERENCES

French interrogative adjectives are perhaps the most difficult question words for native English speakers to understand. In English, when you ask a question about two or more similar objects, you can just use *"what"* + noun, even though *"which"* may be the grammatically correct option, as in *What (Which) shirt do you like better?* But in French, you can't use the interrogative pronoun **que** in front of a noun — you have to use **quel** whenever you're asking someone to make a distinction between two or more nouns: **Quelle chemise préfères-tu ?** (*Which shirt do you like better?*)

Quel is an adjective, which means that it has to agree in gender and number with the noun it modifies (see Chapter 11 for more details about adjectives):

>> Masculine singular: **quel homme** (*what/which man*)

>> Feminine singular: **quelle femme** (*what/which woman*)

>> Masculine plural: **quels hommes** (*what/which men*)

>> Feminine plural: **quelles femmes** (*what/which women*)

PRACTICE

Which which is which: Fill in the blanks with the correct form of the interrogative adjective.

Q. _____ livre ? (m) (Which book?)

A. Quel

37. _____ voiture ? (f) (Which car?)

38. _____ papiers ? (m) (Which papers?)

39. _____ appartement ? (m) (Which apartment?)

40. _____ nations ? (f) (Which nations?)

41. _____ salutation ? (f) (Which greeting?)

42. _____ ordinateurs ? (m) (Which computers?)

43. _____ robe ? (f) (Which dress?)

44. _____ café ? (m) (Which coffee?)

Asking wh questions with est-ce que

You can ask *wh* questions by using interrogative adverbs + **est-ce que**. Just put the question word(s) at the beginning of the question, followed by **est-ce que**, then the subject and verb.

> **Où est-ce que tu vas ?** *(Where are you going?)*

> **Combien d'argent est-ce que vous avez ?** *(How much money do you have?)*

> **Pourquoi est-ce qu'il aime le jazz ?** *(Why does he like jazz?)*

> **Quand est-ce que Laura va arriver ?** *(When is Laura going to arrive?)*

When you're asking a question by using the interrogative pronouns *who* or *what*, **est-ce que** gets more complicated:

>> **Que** + **est-ce que** has to contract to **qu'est-ce que**.

>> If the question has *who* or *what* as the object of the question (meaning the action is done to them), the same basic rules of **est-ce que** as explained in the section "Posing informal questions," earlier in this chapter, still apply — just start with **qui** or **que**, then follow with **est-ce que** and the rest of the question.

> **Qui est-ce que nous cherchons ?** *(Whom are we looking for?)*

> **Qu'est-ce que tu veux faire ?** *(What do you want to do?)*

However, if *who* or *what* is the *subject* of the question (meaning they do the action), you have to change **est-ce que** to **est-ce qui**.

Qui est-ce qui veut m'aider ? (*Who wants to help me?*)

Qu'est-ce qui se passe ? (*What's happening?*)

Note that **qui** doesn't contract with **est-ce que** or any other word.

REMEMBER

In the preceding examples, the first word — the word that comes *before* **est-ce que** or **est-ce-qui** — determines the meaning:

>> If the first word is **qui**, you're asking *who?*

>> If the first word is **que**, you're asking *what?*

So far, so good. But this is where it gets tricky. You need to look at the word that comes after **est-ce** because it indicates the function of the word before **est-ce**:

>> If the word at the end is **qui**, the first word (whether **qui** or **que**) is the *subject.*

>> If the word at the end is **que**, the first word (whether **qui** or **que**) is the *direct object.*

Clear as mud, right? Here's a summary of the four possibilities:

>> **qu'est-ce qui** means *"what"* and is the subject

>> **qu'est-ce que** means *"what"* and is the direct object

>> **qui est-ce qui** means *"who"* and is the subject

This phrase usually contracts to just **qui**.

>> **qui est-ce que** means *"whom"* and is the direct object

So now it's time to do a little analysis:

>> **Qu'est-ce qui voit le chat ?** (*What [subject] sees the cat?*)

>> **Qu'est-ce que le chat voit ?** (*What [direct object] does the cat see?*)

>> **Qui est-ce qui voit le chat ?/Qui voit le chat ?** (*Who [subject] sees the cat?*)

>> **Qui est-ce que le chat voit ?** (*Whom [direct object] does the cat see?*)

TIP

If you're not sure how to tell whether something is a subject or object, try rewording the question. When you rearrange *What do you want to see?*, you get *You want to see what?*, which makes it clear that *you* is the subject and *what* is the direct object. Table 8-1 lays out this information for you.

Table 8-1   Interrogative Pronouns with Est-ce que

English Pronoun	Subject of Question	Object of Question
Who(m)	**Qui est-ce qui** (or **Qui**)	**Qui est-ce que**
What	**Qu'est-ce qui**	**Qu'est-ce que**

You can also ask questions by using a preposition + *whom* or *what*. **Remember:** After a preposition, **que** changes to **quoi**.

> **À qui est-ce que tu écris ?** (*Whom are you writing to?* or *To whom are you writing?*)
>
> **De quoi est-ce que vous parlez ?** (*What are you talking about?*)
>
> **À quelle heure est-ce que tu pars ?** (*[At] What time are you leaving?*)

PRACTICE

Your boss sent out an important memo, but you spilled coffee on it and some of the words are illegible. For each of the partial sentences provided here, ask a question by using **est-ce** to request the missing information.

Q. _____ va commencer un nouveau projet.

A. **Qui est-ce qui / Qui va commencer un nouveau projet ?** (Who is going to start a new project?)

NOTE DE SERVICE

À tous les employés :			
De la part du chef :			

Il s'agit de ▨▨▨▨
(45)

Il y aura ▨▨▨▨ employés dans l'équipe.
(46)

L'équipe sera basée à ▨▨▨▨
(47)

Elle travaillera avec ▨▨▨▨
(48)

Elle va faire ▨▨▨▨
(49)

Il faut commencer demain parce que ▨▨▨▨
(50)

L'équipe doit se réunir à ▨▨▨▨
heures . . .
(51)

. . . dans le bureau ▨▨▨▨
(52)

Le ▨▨▨▨ est très important.
(53)

Le projet durera ▨▨▨▨ mois.
(54)

Asking wh questions with inversion

To ask a *wh* question by using inversion, just put the interrogative term right at the beginning.

> **Où vas-tu ?** (*Where are you going?*)
>
> **Combien d'argent avez-vous ?** (*How much money do you have?*)
>
> **Pourquoi aime-t-il le jazz ?** (*Why does he like jazz?*)
>
> **Quand Laura va-t-elle arriver ?** (*When is Laura going to arrive?*)

Take a look at this comparison of *wh* questions with inversion and **est-ce que**:

Question with Inversion	Question with **est-ce que**	English Translation
Où habitez-vous ?	**Où est-ce que vous habitez ?**	*Where do you live?*
Pourquoi a-t-il 10 chiens ?	**Pourquoi est-ce qu'il a 10 chiens ?**	*Why does he have 10 dogs?*

TIP

Though most *yes-or-no* and *wh* questions can be asked with either **est-ce que** or inversion, certain common questions are virtually always asked with inversion. Table 8-2 lists these fixed questions. The ones that include "you" have two versions, one with **tu** and the other with **vous** (I explain the difference in Chapter 1).

Table 8-2　Common Questions that Use Inversion

English	French
Do you speak French/English?	**Parles-tu français/anglais ?** or
	Parlez-vous français/anglais ?
How are you?	**Comment vas-tu ?** or
	Comment allez-vous ?
How old are you?	**Quel âge as-tu ?** or
	Quel âge avez-vous ?
How's the weather?	**Quel temps fait-il ?**
What day is it?	**Quel jour sommes-nous ?**
What is your name?	**Comment t'appelles-tu ?** or
	Comment vous appelez-vous ?
What time is it?	**Quelle heure est-il ?**
Where are you going?	**Où vas-tu ?** or
	Où allez-vous ?
Who is it?	**Qui est-ce ?**

It's the old switcheroo! Rewrite these **est-ce que** questions with inversion instead.

Q. Qu'est-ce que vous mangez ?

A. **Que mangez-vous ?** (What are you eating?)

55 Où est-ce que tu vas ? (Where are you going?)

56 Combien d'argent est-ce qu'ils ont ? (How much money do they have?)

57 Pourquoi est-ce qu'elle aime voyager ? (Why does she like traveling?)

58 À qui est-ce que tu parles ? (Whom are you talking to?)

59 Quand est-ce que tu vas arriver ? (When are you going to arrive?)

60 À quelle heure est-ce que nous partons ? ([At] What time are we leaving?)

61 Quelle heure est-ce qu'il est ? (What time is it?)

62 Pourquoi est-ce que tu chantes ? (Why are you singing?)

63 Quand est-ce qu'ils mangent ? (When do they eat?)

64 Comment est-ce qu'il apprend l'espagnol ? (How is he learning Spanish?)

Answering Questions

Knowing how to ask questions is only half the battle. What kind of world would it be if questions got asked but never answered? (Would that make them rhetorical? What good would that do? Am I annoying you yet?) As you can see, you also have to know how to answer questions — and understand other people's answers, too. The following sections give you an overview of responding to different types of questions.

Answering yes-or-no questions

Yes-or-no questions aren't just easy to ask — they're also easy to answer. You can take the easy road and just answer **oui** (*yes*) or **non** (*no*).

> **Est-ce que tu es prêt ?** (*Are you ready?*) **Oui.** (*Yes.*)
>
> **Avez-vous mangé ?** (*Have you eaten?*) **Non.** (*No.*)

You can also reword the question as a statement after your answer.

> **Oui, je suis prêt.** (*Yes, I'm ready.*)
>
> **Non, je n'ai pas mangé.** (*No, I haven't eaten.*)

DIFFERENCES

French has another word for *yes*, **si**, which you use when someone asks a question in the negative but you want to respond in the affirmative. For example, if someone says, "Don't you like to swim?" and you do in fact like to swim, in English, you have to say, "Yes, I do like to swim." But in French, someone can ask **N'aimes-tu pas nager ?**, and you can just answer **Si**. (Check out Chapter 9 for more information about negatives.)

Of course, not all questions merit a simple yes or no. The following are some useful ways to answer questions:

» **oui** (*yes*)

» **si** (*yes* — in response to a negative)

» **bien sûr** (*of course*)

» **non** (*no*)

» **pas du tout** (*not at all*)

» **pas encore** (*not yet*)

» **peut-être** (*maybe*)

» **je ne sais pas** (*I don't know*)

» **ça m'est égal** (*I don't care*)

So very agreeable! Answer *yes* to all of these questions, and also write out the full response.

PRACTICE

Q. Est-ce que tu aimes lire ? (Do you like to read?)

A. **Oui, j'aime lire.** (Yes, I like to read.)

65 Est-ce que nous sommes en retard ?

66 Veulent-elles acheter une voiture ?

67 Allez-vous à la fête ?

68 As-tu faim ?

69 Est-ce que je peux partir tôt ?

70 Vont-ils nager ?

71 Veut-elle aller en France ?

72 Est-ce qu'il travaille aujourd'hui ?

Answering wh questions

The answers to *wh* questions are a lot more complicated than responses to *yes-or-no* questions. (I introduce the *wh* questions in the section "Asking Who, What, Which, When, Where, Why, and How Questions," earlier in this chapter.) Because these types of questions are asking for information, you have to respond with that information in place of the question words.

– **Quelle heure est-il ?** (*What time is it?*)
– **Il est midi.** (*It's noon.*)

– **Comment t'appelles-tu ?** (*What's your name?*)
– **Je m'appelle Jean.** (*My name is Jean.*)

You can use the following words to help you answer *wh* questions (see Chapter 5 for details on dates and times):

>> **à** (*at, in, to*)

>> **il est** (*it is* — with time)

>> **on est**, **nous sommes** (*it is* — with dates, as I explain in Chapter 5)

>> **parce que** (*because*)

>> **pendant** (*for* — with time)

PRACTICE

Try answering the following questions in French. Because they're personal, there are no right or wrong answers, but you can read some possible answers in the Answer Key (see the following section) to make sure your answers are in the correct format. (For info on negative sentences, see Chapter 9.)

Q. Comment vous appelez-vous ?

A. Je m'appelle Laura. (*My name is Laura.*)

73 Est-ce que vous habitez en France ? _____

74 Où est-ce que vous travaillez ? _____

75 Qu'est-ce que vous aimez faire le samedi ? _____

76 Savez-vous nager ? _____

77 Quelle musique aimez-vous ? _____

78 Qui est votre meilleur ami ? _____

79 Quelle est la date de votre anniversaire ? _____

80 Combien de frères et de sœurs avez-vous ? _____

Answer Key to "Asking and Answering Questions" Practice Questions

1. **Est-ce que vous voulez étudier ?** (*Do you want to study?*)

2. **Est-ce que tu es heureux ?** (*Are you happy?*)

3. **Est-ce que nous allons marcher ?** (*Are we going to walk?*)

4. **Est-ce qu'elle habite au Sénégal ?** (*Does she live in Senegal?*)

5. **Est-ce que j'ai raison ?** (*Am I right?*)

6. **Est-ce qu'ils sont prêts ?** (*Are they ready?*)

7. **As-tu un chien ?** (*Do you have a dog?*)

8. **Êtes-vous prêts ?** (*Are you ready?*)

9. **Travaille-t-elle ici ?** (*Does she work here?*)

10. **Aiment-ils danser ?** (*Do they like to dance?*)

11. **Es-tu triste ?** (*Are you sad?*)

12. **Devez-vous partir ?** (*Do you have to leave?*)

13. **Sommes-nous en retard ?** (*Are we late?*)

14. **Habitent-elles en France ?** (*Do they live in France?*)

15. **Suis-je en avance ?** (*Am I early?*)

16. **Peux-tu conduire ?** (*Can you drive?*)

17. **Où**

18. **Quand**

19. **Combien**

20. **Pourquoi**

21. **Combien de**

(22) Pourquoi

(23) Combien

(24) Comment

(25) Où

(26) Quand

(27) Que

(28) quoi

(29) Qui

(30) Qu'

(31) quoi

(32) qui

(33) Qu'

(34) Qui

(35) Que

(36) Qui

(37) Quelle

(38) Quels

(39) Quel

(40) Quelles

(41) Quelle

(42) Quels

(43) Quelle

(44) Quel

NOTE DE SERVICE

Á tous les employés :			
De la part du chef :			

(45) De quoi est-ce qu'il s'agit? (*What is it about?*) **(46) Combien d'**employés **est-ce qu'**il y aura dans l'équipe? (*How many employees will be on the team?*) **(47) Où est-ce que** l'équipe sera basée? (*Where will the team be based?*) **(48) Avec quoi** OR **qui est-ce qu'**elle travaillera? (*What* OR *Who will it work with?*) **(49) Qu'est-ce qu'**elle va faire? (*What will it do?*) **(50) Pourquoi est-ce qu'**il faut commencer demain? (*Why do we need to start tomorrow?*) **(51) À quelle heure** OR **Quand est-ce que** l'équipe doit se réunir (*At what time* OR *When does the team have to meet?*) **(52) Dans quel** bureau est-ce qu'elle doit se rassembler? (*In which office does it have to meet?*) **(53) Qu'est-ce qui** est très important? (*What is very important?*) **(54) Combien de** mois **est-ce que** le projet durera? (*How many months will the project last?*)

(55) Où vas-tu ?

(56) Combien d'argent ont-ils ?

(57) Pourquoi aime-t-elle voyager ?

(58) À qui parles-tu ?

(59) Quand vas-tu arriver ?

(60) À quelle heure partons-nous ?

(61) Quelle heure est-il ?

(62) Pourquoi chantes-tu ?

(63) Quand mangent-ils ?

(64) Comment apprend-il l'espagnol ?

(65) Oui, nous sommes en retard. (*Yes, we're late.*)

(66) Oui, elles veulent acheter une voiture. (*Yes, they want to buy a car.*)

(67) Oui, nous allons à la fête. (*Yes, we're going to the party.*)

(68) **Oui, j'ai faim.** (*Yes, I'm hungry.*)

(69) **Oui, tu peux / vous pouvez partir tôt.** (*Yes, you can leave early.*)

(70) **Oui, ils vont nager.** (*Yes, they are going to swim.*)

(71) **Oui, elle veut aller en France.** (*Yes, she wants to go to France.*)

(72) **Oui, il travaille aujourd'hui.** (*Yes, he's working today.*)

(73) **Oui, j'habite en France.** (*Yes, I live in France.*) or **Non, je n'habite pas en France.** (*No, I don't live in France.*)

(74) **Je travaille chez Google/dans une banque.** (*I work at Google/in a bank.*)

(75) **Le samedi j'aime aller à la plage/j'aime lire.** (*I like to go to the beach / read on Saturdays.*)

(76) **Oui, je sais nager.** (*Yes, I know how to swim.*) or **Non, je ne sais pas nager.** (*No, I don't know how to swim.*)

(77) **J'aime la musique classique/le rap.** (*I like classical music/rap.*)

(78) **Henri/Mon frère est mon meilleur ami.** (*Henri/My brother is my best friend.*)

(79) **Mon anniversaire est le 10 septembre.** (*My birthday is September 10.*)

(80) **J'ai deux frères et une sœur.** (*I have two brothers and one sister.*) or **Je n'ai pas de frères et sœurs.** (*I don't have any brothers or sisters.*)

Chapter **9**

Just Say No: The Negative

ven if you'd rather be a yes-man (or yes-woman), sometimes you just have to say *no*. Otherwise, you may discover that you've agreed to visit your pen pal in the sweltering Malian desert or accepted a weekend work assignment with no extra pay.

In French, being negative is twice as hard as it is in English because French requires at least two words, whereas English only needs one. This chapter explains all the different ways to be negative in French, as well as how to respond — whether you agree or disagree — when someone says something negative to you.

Using Negative Adverbs

Other than the short and sweet **non** (*no*), negative adverbs are the most common construction used to negate statements and questions. In English, the negative adverb is usually a single word, such as *not* or *never*. In French, it's at least two words, and one of them is always **ne**. The following sections take a closer look at the most common negative adverb, as well as some other options that you have.

The most common negative adverb: Ne ... pas

The French equivalent of *not*, as in *I do not sing*, is **ne ... pas**. These two words have to surround the verb — you put **ne** in front of it and **pas** after.

> **Je ne chante pas.** (*I don't sing.*)

> **Tu ne danses pas.** (*You don't dance.*)

Ne + a vowel or mute **h** contracts to **n'**.

> **Elle n'est pas là.** (*She's not there.*)

> **Il n'habite pas à Paris.** (*He doesn't live in Paris.*)

DIFFERENCES

In English, when you make most verbs negative, you have to add *do* as a helping verb: so the negation of *I smoke* is *I do not smoke*. You have one more verb in the English negative than in the affirmative. This is not the case in French: You always have the same number of verbs in the affirmative and negative: The negation of **Je fume** is **Je ne fume pas**.

REMEMBER

Partitive articles (**du, de la, des**) and indefinite articles (**un, une, des**) all change to **de** after a negation. (See Chapter 3 for more info on articles.)

> **Je veux du pain.** (*I want some bread.*) becomes **Je ne veux pas de pain.** (*I don't want any bread.*)

> **J'ai un frère.** (*I have a brother.*) changes to **Je n'ai pas de frère.** (*I don't have any brothers.*)

PRACTICE

Rewrite each of these statements in the negative.

Q. J'ai faim.

A. Je n'ai pas faim. (*I'm not hungry.*)

1. Elle parle français. _____

2. Il est en France. _____

3. Je travaille beaucoup. _____

4. Tu manges trop. _____

5. Vous avez raison. _____

6. Elles aiment danser. _____

7. Je vais en Italie. _____

8. Elle fume souvent. _____

⑨ Ils veulent des fraises. _____

⑩ Nous avons un enfant. _____

Using ne . . . pas in two-verb constructions

You use **ne . . . pas** when you have two verbs in much the same way that you do when you have one verb (see the preceding section).

When you have a verb + infinitive in a sentence, like with the near future construction (see Chapter 10), **ne . . . pas** surrounds just the conjugated verb.

> **Il ne va pas travailler.** (*He isn't going to work.*)
>
> **Tu ne dois pas venir.** (*You must not come.*)

Likewise, in compound tenses such as the **passé composé** (see Chapter 15), **ne . . . pas** surrounds the auxiliary verb.

> **Elles ne sont pas arrivées.** (*They haven't arrived.*)
>
> **Je n'ai pas fini.** (*I didn't finish.*)

In informal, spoken French, **ne** is often dropped, so **pas** carries the full weight of negation.

TIP

> **Je ne sais pas.** becomes **Je sais pas.** (*I don't know.*)
>
> **Il n'a pas étudié.** turns into **Il a pas étudié.** (*He didn't study.*)

PRACTICE

Rewrite each of these statements in the negative.

Q. J'ai mangé.

A. **Je n'ai pas mangé.** (*I haven't eaten.*)

⑪ Elle sait coudre. _____

⑫ Ils ont fait la lessive. _____

⑬ Tu peux aller à la banque. _____

⑭ Nous avons fini le projet. _____

⑮ Je vais acheter un chien. _____

⑯ Ils peuvent étudier à midi. _____

⑰ Elle va arriver ce matin. _____

⑱ Tu es parti tôt. _____

19 Nous aimons manger ensemble. _____

20 Je sais conduire. _____

Following word order with ne . . . pas

In more complex constructions, figuring out word order when using **ne . . . pas** is a bit trickier.

When negating questions by using inversion (check out Chapter 8), the **ne . . . pas** surrounds the inverted verb–plus–subject.

> **Ne viennent-ils pas ?** (*Aren't they coming?*)
>
> **N'as-tu pas faim ?** (*Aren't you hungry?*)

TIP

Ne . . . pas can't be used in **est-ce que** questions. In a formal situation, if you're pretty sure that the answer to your question is *yes*, you can say something and then end the sentence with **n'est-ce pas ?**, which means *right?* or *isn't that so?* For instance, **Vous avez faim, n'est-ce pas ?** means *You're hungry, right?* Informally, you can use **non ?** (*no?*) the same way.

REMEMBER

When your negative statement or question has reflexive, object, or adverbial pronouns (see Chapter 13 to find out all about pronouns), those pronouns have to stay directly in front of the verb. So that means **ne** precedes the whole group of them, and **pas** follows the conjugated verb as usual in the present tense.

> **Je ne te crois pas.** (*I don't believe you.*)
>
> **Il ne le veut pas.** (*He doesn't want it.*)

The same idea applies to compound verb tenses, such as the **passé composé** (see Chapter 15).

> **Ils ne nous ont pas parlé.** (*They didn't talk to us.*)
>
> **Tu ne me l'as pas donné.** (*You didn't give it to me.*)

WARNING

For two–part verbal constructions, such as the near future, where you have a conjugated verb + infinitive, the negation surrounds the first (conjugated) verb, but the pronoun(s) stays in front of the *infinitive*. (See Chapter 10 for more details on infinitives.) For example:

> **Tu ne vas pas le faire.** (*You're not going to do it.*)
>
> **Ils ne veulent pas nous les donner.** (*They don't want to give them to us.*)

PRACTICE

Quiz yourself on complex negative structures by turning these French statements and questions negative. Rewrite each sentence in the space provided.

Q. Je te vois.

A. Je ne te vois pas. (*I don't see you.*)

21 Elle le veut. _____

22 Veux-tu partir ? _____

23 Nous te parlons. _____

24 Ils vont travailler demain. _____

25 Mangez-vous ? _____

26 Je l'ai. _____

27 Allons-nous conduire ensemble ? _____

28 Vous m'aimez. _____

29 T'habilles-tu ? _____

30 Je peux l'entendre. _____

Other negative adverbs

Although **ne . . . pas** is the most common negative adverb, several others are also very useful. Take a look at the following:

> » **ne . . . jamais** (*never*)
> » **ne . . . nulle part** (*nowhere*)
> » **ne . . . pas du tout** (*not at all*)
> » **ne . . . pas encore** (*not yet*)
> » **ne . . . pas que** (*not only*)
> » **ne . . . pas toujours** (*not always*)
> » **ne . . . plus** (*not anymore, no more, no longer*)
> » **ne . . . que** (*only*)

All negative adverbs follow the same placement rules as **ne . . . pas**, with **ne** preceding the conjugated verb and **jamais**, **plus**, or whatever else following it.

> **Elle ne ment jamais.** (*She never lies.*)
>
> **Je ne suis pas encore prêt.** (*I'm not ready yet.*)
>
> **Nous n'avons que cinq euros.** (*We have only five euros.*)

Like with **ne . . . pas**, in informal spoken French, you can drop the **ne** with other negative adverbs:

> **Je ne fume plus.** becomes **Je fume plus.** (*I don't smoke any more.*)
>
> **Je n'y suis jamais allé.** becomes **J'y suis jamais allé.** (*I've never gone there.*)

Be careful when dropping **ne** because the second part of the adverb can have a different meaning when used affirmatively. **Plus**, for example, can mean **more** when it's not used with **ne**, so make sure that you add any other info necessary to get your point across.

WARNING

Rewrite each of these sentences in the negative by using the negative adverb provided.

PRACTICE

Q. J'ai soif. (ne . . . plus)

A. **Je n'ai plus soif.** (*I'm no longer thirsty.*)

31 Elle parle grec. (ne . . . que) _____

32 Il vient chez nous. (ne . . . jamais) _____

33 Je peux travailler. (ne . . . plus) _____

34 Tu dois partir. (ne . . . pas encore) _____

35 Ils jouent au foot. (ne . . . jamais) _____

36 Elle le veut. (ne . . . pas du tout) _____

37 J'ai un frère. (ne . . . que) _____

38 Il est en avance. (ne . . . pas toujours) _____

39 Nous pouvons conduire. (ne . . . plus) _____

40 Elles aiment voyager. (ne . . . pas du tout) _____

Using Negative Pronouns

If you want to negate nouns, you need negative pronouns — words that replace nouns. The following sections point out what you need to know when you use these negative structures in French.

Ne . . . personne

One important French negative pronoun is **ne . . . personne** (*no one, not anyone*). It can serve three different functions in the sentence:

>> As the direct object, the word order for **ne . . . personne** is the same as for **ne . . . pas**. **Ne** precedes the verb and **personne** follows it:

- **Je ne connais personne.** (*I don't know anyone.*)

- **Nous n'aimons personne.** (*We don't like anyone.*)

» When **ne . . . personne** is the object of a preposition (see Chapter 12 for the lowdown on prepositions), the word order is almost the same — you just need to stick the preposition in front of **personne**:

- **Je ne parle à personne.** (*I'm not talking to anyone.*)

- **Il ne rit de personne.** (*He doesn't laugh at anyone.*)

» Using **ne . . . personne** as the subject is the trickiest of the bunch. In this usage, **personne** goes to the head of the sentence, and **ne** goes right after it, followed by the verb:

- **Personne ne veut de pain.** (*No one wants any bread.*)

- **Personne n'est prêt.** (*No one is ready.*)

You use the same word order in two-verb constructions, whether verb + infinitive (as in the near future) or auxiliary verb + past participle (as in the **passé composé**):

Personne ne va danser. (*No one is going to dance.*)

Personne n'est arrivé à l'heure. (*No one arrived on time.*)

Ne . . . rien

The other essential negative pronoun is **ne . . . rien** (*nothing, not anything*). It can serve three different functions in the sentence, just like **ne . . . personne** (see the preceding section):

» When **ne . . . rien** is the direct object, the word order is the same as with **ne . . . personne**: **Ne** precedes the verb and **rien** follows it:

- **Je ne veux rien.** (*I don't want anything.*)

- **Ils ne mangent rien.** (*They're not eating anything.*)

» You have the same deal when **ne . . . rien** is the object of a preposition as when it's the direct object — you just need to put the preposition in front of **rien**:

- **Nous ne rêvons à rien.** (*We're not dreaming about anything.*)

- **Tu ne te souviens de rien.** (*You don't remember anything.*)

Just like with **ne . . . personne** (see the preceding section), in both simple and two-verb constructions, **rien** goes to the head of the sentence when it's the subject, followed by **ne**:

Rien ne marche bien. (*Nothing works right.*)

Rien n'est parfait. (*Nothing is perfect.*)

Rien ne va me convaincre. (*Nothing is going to convince me.*)

Rien n'est arrivé. (*Nothing happened.*)

Negatives and their indefinite opposites

Negative pronouns mean *no one* and *nothing*. Their *antonyms* (or opposites) are called *indefinite pronouns* and are particularly useful for answering and asking questions. For example:

– **Est-ce que quelqu'un a acheté du pain ?** (*Did someone buy bread?*)

– **Non, personne n'a acheté de pain.** (*No, no one bought bread.*)

Table 9-1 shows negative pronouns and their antonyms, indefinite pronouns.

Table 9-1   Negative and Indefinite Pronouns

Negative Pronouns	Translations	Indefinite Pronouns	Translations
ne . . . personne	*no one*	quelqu'un	*someone*
		tout le monde	*everyone*
ne . . . rien	*nothing*	quelque chose	*something*
		tout	*everything*

Practice using negative pronouns

PRACTICE

Your colleagues are just too nosy! Respond to all of their questions using negative pronouns.

Q. Qu'est-ce que tu fais ?

A. **Je ne fais rien.** (*I'm not doing anything.*)

41 Qui est au téléphone ? _____

42 Qu'est-ce que tu vas faire ce soir ? _____

43 Avec qui est-ce que tu habites ? _____

44 Que veux-tu faire demain ? _____

45 Qui habite à côté de chez toi ? _____

46 À quoi penses-tu ? _____

47 Qu'est-ce que tu fais le samedi ? _____

48 Avec qui sors-tu ? _____

49 Qu'est-ce qui va arriver demain ? _____

50 Est-ce que tu as quelqu'un dans ta vie ? _____

Responding to Negative Questions and Statements

Negative questions and statements aren't necessarily correct — sometimes you agree, and sometimes you don't. Because these sentences are in the negative, responding to them accurately can be a little bit confusing. The following sections explain the correct ways to answer these types of questions and statements. (To figure out how to say no to regular questions, see Chapter 8.)

Replying with no

When someone asks you a negative question or makes a negative statement that you agree with, you can respond with just **non**.

> – **Tu n'as pas soif ?** (*Aren't you thirsty?*)
> – **Non.** (*No.*)

> – **Pierre n'est pas prêt.** (*Pierre isn't ready.*)
> – **Non.** (*No.*)

Using just the one word can feel a bit abrupt, so you might like to reword the question as a negative statement.

> – **Tu n'as pas faim ?** (*Aren't you hungry?*)
> – **Non, je n'ai pas faim.** (*No, [that's correct] I'm not hungry.*)

> – **Danièle n'est pas timide.** (*Danièle isn't shy.*)
> – **Non, elle n'est pas timide.** (*No, [you're right] she's not shy.*)

You can add emphasis by using a negative adverb or pronoun.

> – **Le nouveau chef n'est pas très sympa.** (*The new boss isn't very nice.*)
> – **Non, pas du tout.** (*No, not at all.*)

> – **Personne dans cette classe ne fait les devoirs.** (*No one in this class does the homework.*)
> – **Non, personne.** (*No, no one.*)

You can also add emphasis by using an expression such as **c'est vrai** (*that's true*) or **exact** (*right, exactly*).

> – **Ce film n'est pas très bon.** (*This movie isn't very good.*)
> – **C'est vrai.** (*That's true.*)

> – **Le service client n'est plus ce qu'il était.** (*Customer service isn't what it used to be.*)
> – **Exact.** (*Exactly.*)

Of course, you can also use the various negative constructions to answer affirmative questions (see Chapter 8) in the negative.

- **Est-ce que vous voyagez souvent ?** (*Do you travel often?*)
- **Non, jamais.** (*No, never.*)

- **Vois-tu quelqu'un sur la scène ?** (*Do you see anyone on the stage?*)
- **Non, personne.** (*No, no one.*)

Answering with yes

DIFFERENCES

In English, if someone says, *Are you not hungry?* but in fact you are hungry, you can't just say *yes* because they won't know whether you mean *yes, that's right* or *yes, I am.* You have to spell it out: *Yes, that's right, I'm not hungry* or *Yes, [actually] I am hungry.* Not so in French.

When someone asks or says something negative that you don't agree with, French has a unique word, **si**, which all by its lonesome means *yes, I am* or *yes, I do,* or *yes, the opposite of whatever you just said.* Of course, you can still repeat the statement as part of your answer if you want, but in French you don't have to. However, when you do agree with the negative, you can just say **non** (*no*).

- **N'est-il pas prêt ?** (*Isn't he ready?*)
- **Si (il est prêt).** (*Yes [he is ready].*)
- **Non (il n'est pas prêt).** (*No [he's not ready].*)

- **Tu ne veux pas savoir.** (*You don't want to know.*)
- **Si (je veux savoir).** (*Yes [I do want to know].*)
- **Non (je ne veux pas savoir).** (*No [I don't want to know].*)

DIFFERENCES

English has only one word for *yes*, but French has two: **oui** and **si**. You use **oui** to say *yes* to a regular question and **si** to say *yes* to a negative question. Note that **si** (*yes*) never contracts, unlike **si** (*if*), which contracts with **il**.

si, il est prêt (*yes, he is ready*)

s'il est prêt (*if he is ready*)

PRACTICE

Respond to these questions and statements in complete sentences, using the answer in parentheses. If the question has **tu**, you need to respond with **je**.

Q. Sais-tu la réponse ? (no)

A. **Non, je ne sais pas la réponse.** (*No, I don't know the answer.*)

51 Veux-tu nager ? (no) _____

52 Vont-ils voyager ensemble ? (no) _____

53 N'a-t-elle pas une suggestion ? (yes) _____

54 Ne lis-tu pas ? (never) _____

55 Ne peut-il pas travailler ? (yes) _____

56 N'aimes-tu pas danser ? (not at all) _____

57 Il ne va jamais arriver ! (yes) _____

58 Ne vas-tu pas aller à la plage ? (yes) _____

59 N'aime-t-elle pas le chocolat ? (no) _____

60 Tu ne manges pas ? (yes) _____

Answer Key to "Just Say No: The Negative" Practice Questions

(1) **Elle ne parle pas français.** (*She doesn't speak French.*)

(2) **Il n'est pas en France.** (*He's not in France.*)

(3) **Je ne travaille pas beaucoup.** (*I don't work a lot.*)

(4) **Tu ne manges pas trop.** (*You don't eat too much.*)

(5) **Vous n'avez pas raison.** (*You're not correct.*)

(6) **Elles n'aiment pas danser.** (*They don't like to dance.*)

(7) **Je ne vais pas en Italie.** (*I'm not going to Italy.*)

(8) **Elle ne fume pas souvent.** (*She doesn't smoke often.*)

(9) **Ils ne veulent pas de fraises.** (*They don't want any strawberries.*)

(10) **Nous n'avons pas d'enfant.** (*We don't have any kids.*)

(11) **Elle ne sait pas coudre.** (*She doesn't know how to sew.*)

(12) **Ils n'ont pas fait la lessive.** (*They didn't do the laundry.*)

(13) **Tu ne peux pas aller à la banque.** (*You can't go to the bank.*)

(14) **Nous n'avons pas fini le projet.** (*We didn't finish the project.*)

(15) **Je ne vais pas acheter de chien.** (*I'm not going to buy a dog.*)

(16) **Ils ne peuvent pas étudier à midi.** (*They can't study at noon.*)

(17) **Elle ne va pas arriver ce matin.** (*She's not going to arrive this morning.*)

(18) **Tu n'es pas parti tôt.** (*You didn't leave early.*)

(19) **Nous n'aimons pas manger ensemble.** (*We don't like to eat together.*)

(20) **Je ne sais pas conduire.** (*I don't know how to drive.*)

(21) **Elle ne le veut pas.** (*She doesn't want it.*)

(22) **Ne veux-tu pas partir ?** (*Don't you want to leave?*)

(23) **Nous ne te parlons pas.** (*We're not talking to you.*)

(24) **Ils ne vont pas travailler demain.** (*They're not going to work tomorrow.*)

(25) **Ne mangez-vous pas ?** (*Aren't you eating?*)

(26) **Je ne l'ai pas.** (*I don't have it.*)

27) **N'allons-nous pas conduire ensemble ?** (*Aren't we going to drive together?*)

28) **Vous ne m'aimez pas.** (*You don't love me.*)

29) **Ne t'habilles-tu pas ?** (*Aren't you getting dressed?*)

30) **Je ne peux pas l'entendre.** (*I can't hear it.*)

31) **Elle ne parle que grec.** (*She speaks only Greek.*)

32) **Il ne vient jamais chez nous.** (*He never comes to our house.*)

33) **Je ne peux plus travailler.** (*I can no longer work/I can't work anymore.*)

34) **Tu ne dois pas encore partir.** (*You must not leave yet.*)

35) **Ils ne jouent jamais au foot.** (*They never play soccer.*)

36) **Elle ne le veut pas du tout.** (*She doesn't want it at all.*)

37) **Je n'ai qu'un frère.** (*I have only one brother.*)

38) **Il n'est pas toujours en avance.** (*He's not always early.*)

39) **Nous ne pouvons plus conduire.** (*We can't drive anymore.*)

40) **Elles n'aiment pas du tout voyager/Elles n'aiment pas voyager du tout.** (*They don't like traveling at all.*)

41) **Personne n'est au téléphone.** (*No one is on the phone.*)

42) **Je ne vais rien faire ce soir.** (*I'm not going to do anything tonight.*)

43) **Je n'habite avec personne.** (*I don't live with anyone.*)

44) **Je ne veux rien faire demain.** (*I don't want to do anything tomorrow.*)

45) **Personne n'habite à côté de chez moi.** (*No one lives next to me.*)

46) **Je ne pense à rien.** (*I'm not thinking about anything.*)

47) **Je ne fais rien le samedi.** (*I don't do anything on Saturdays.*)

48) **Je ne sors avec personne.** (*I'm not going out with anyone.*)

49) **Rien ne va arriver demain.** (*Nothing is going to happen tomorrow.*)

50) **Non, je n'ai personne dans ma vie.** (*No, I don't have anyone in my life.*)

51) **Non, je ne veux pas nager.** (*No, I don't want to swim.*)

52) **Non, ils ne vont pas voyager ensemble.** (*No, they're not going to travel together.*)

53) **Si, elle a une suggestion.** (*Yes, she has/does have a suggestion.*)

54) **Non, je ne lis jamais.** (*No, I never read.*)

55 Si, il peut travailler. (*Yes, he can work.*)

56 Non, je n'aime pas du tout danser/je n'aime pas danser du tout. (*No, I don't like to dance at all.*)

57 Si, il va arriver. (*Yes, he's going to arrive.*)

58 Si, je vais aller à la plage. (*Yes, I'm going to go to the beach.*)

59 Non, elle n'aime pas le chocolat. (*No, she doesn't like chocolate.*)

60 Si, je mange. (*Yes, I'm eating.*)

IN THIS CHAPTER

» **Going back to the basics with infinitives**

» **Working with present participles**

Chapter **10**

"To Be" or "Being" Is the Question: Infinitives and Present Participles

Infinitives and present participles are *impersonal* verb forms, but that doesn't mean they don't have any friends. It just means that they each have only one form — you don't conjugate them for the different grammatical persons like you do with other verb tenses and moods. In English, the infinitive is the word *to* + a verb, and the present participle ends in *–ing*. In French, the infinitive is a single word that ends in *–er*, *–ir*, or *–re*, while the present participle ends in *–ant*.

Although infinitives and present participles exist in both French and English, you use them very differently in the two languages. Both verb forms can act as other parts of speech: nouns and adjectives. French uses the present participle as a verb much less commonly than English does; in fact, the English present participle is often equivalent to the French infinitive.

This chapter explains how to recognize French infinitives, how to form present participles, and how to use them both.

Working with French Infinitives

The *infinitive* is the default form of a verb — its basic, unconjugated state. When you don't know what a verb means, you look up the infinitive in the dictionary (see Chapter 2 for some tips on using a French dictionary), and when you need to conjugate a verb, you often start with the infinitive.

In English, the infinitive has two parts — *to* + a verb — such as *to go*, *to choose*, and *to hear*. In French, the infinitive is a single word that ends in **–er**, **–ir**, or **–re**: such as **aller**, **choisir**, and **entendre**. You use these infinitive endings to classify French verbs because many verbs in each group follow the same conjugation rules. (To get in on the conjugation fun, flip to Chapter 6.)

DIFFERENCES

According to some dusty old grammar books, the English infinitive isn't supposed to be split; meaning no word is supposed to come between the *to* and its verb. For example, *to boldly go* has an adverb (*boldly*) which, ahem, boldly splits the infinitive *to go*. Because the French infinitive is a single word, it truly can't be split: In French, *to boldly go* is **aller courageusement**.

In addition to using the infinitive as the starting point for conjugating many verb tenses, you can also use the infinitive itself as a verb or noun. The following sections show you how.

As a verb: Expressing action

You use the French infinitive most often as a verb. To do this, you conjugate a verb for the subject of the sentence (such as **je veux** or **vous devez**) and follow that subject–verb combo with an infinitive (such as **aller** or **réserver**).

> **Je veux aller en France.** (*I want to go to France.*)
>
> **Vous devez réserver à l'avance.** (*You have to book in advance.*)

Even though the French infinitive already includes the idea of *to*, many French verbs require a preposition between the conjugated verb and the infinitive. When you translate these French phrases into English, the extra preposition has no English equivalent.

> **J'ai décidé de partir.** (*I decided to leave.*)
>
> **J'hésite à parler.** (*I hesitate to speak.*)

REMEMBER

The preposition you have to use in French — if any — depends on the conjugated verb, not on the infinitive. In other words, in the above examples, you don't have to precede **partir** with **de**, but rather, you have to follow **j'ai décidé** with **de**. Likewise, **j'hésite** has to be followed by **à**. On the other hand, **je veux** (*I want*) doesn't need a preposition. See Chapter 12 for an explanation of prepositions and Appendix B for a list of verbs that require them — and those that don't.

The English verbs *can* and *must* are *modal verbs*, meaning that they are followed directly by the verb, without *to*. The French equivalents of these verbs, **pouvoir** and **devoir**, have full sets of conjugations and are followed directly by the infinitive.

> **Peux-tu partir ?** (*Can you leave?*)
>
> **Je dois travailler.** (*I must work.*)

Another useful French verb is the impersonal **falloir** (*to be necessary*), which has only one conjugation: **il faut** (*it is necessary*) and is often followed by an infinitive.

> **Il faut manger.** (*It's necessary to eat.*)
>
> **Il faut dormir.** (*It's necessary to sleep.*)

The verb **il faut** is often used with an indirect object pronoun (Chapter 13 talks all about pronouns) to indicate who has to do something.

> **Il te faut manger.** (*It's necessary for you to eat./You have to eat.*)
>
> **Il nous faut dormir.** (*It's necessary for us to sleep./We have to sleep.*)

When the infinitive is a *pronominal verb* (a verb that needs a reflexive pronoun — see Chapter 7 for more on these types of verbs), the reflexive pronoun has to agree with the subject, as with **Je dois me lever** (*I have to get up*) or **Vas-tu t'habiller ?** (*Are you going to get dressed?*).

TIP

You can often translate the French infinitive as either the English present participle or the English infinitive:

> **J'aime chanter.** (*I like singing/to sing.*)
>
> **Il préfère marcher.** (*He prefers walking/to walk.*)

In French, you can also use the infinitive to give impersonal commands, such as on signs and in instructions (Chapter 14 explains how to give orders in French):

> **Marcher lentement.** (*Walk slowly.*)
>
> **Agiter avant emploi.** (*Shake before use.*)

To infinity and beyond! Complete these sentences by translating the verbs into French infinitives.

PRACTICE

Q. J'aime _____. (dance)

A. J'aime **danser** (*I like to dance.*)

1. Est-ce que tu veux _____ ce soir ? (go out)

2. Il sait _____. (drive)

3. Pouvez-vous _____ la porte ? (open)

4. Nous voulons _____ ensemble. (work)

5. Elle doit _____ demain. (leave)

6. Savez-vous _____ ? (swim)

7. J'aime _____ au football. (play)

8) Nous devons _____ avant 19 h 00. (eat)

9) Elles veulent _____ en France. (study)

10) Est-ce qu'il peut _____ ? (understand)

Using aller to say what's going to happen

Where there's a will, there's a **vais**! You can talk about the near future with the present tense of **aller** (see the following table) + the infinitive. This **futur proche** (*near future*) construction is equivalent to saying *to be going to do* something in English. The **futur proche** is just slightly informal and is most commonly used when what's going to happen is going to happen soon.

aller (to go)	
je vais	nous allons
tu vas	vous allez
il/elle/on va	ils/elles vont

Il va travailler toute la journée. (*He's going to work all day.*)

Consider another example:

> **Alexandre et Laurent vont être déçus.** (*Alexandre and Laurent are going to be disappointed.*)

With pronominal verbs (which I talk about in Chapter 7), the reflexive pronoun goes in front of the infinitive:

> **Nous allons nous promener sur la plage.** (*We're going to take a walk on the beach.*)

> **Vas-tu t'habiller ?** (*Are you going to get dressed?*)

Object and adverbial pronouns (see Chapter 13) also precede the infinitive.

> **Je vais le faire demain.** (*I'm going to do it tomorrow.*)

> **Ils vont en manger.** (*They're going to eat some.*)

You can read more about word order with reflexive, object, and adverbial pronouns in Chapter 13.

PRACTICE

Whatever is going to be, is going to be. Translate these sentences into French using the near future.

Q. I'm going to eat at noon. _____

A. Je vais manger à midi.

11) She is going to be happy. _____

12) Are you (tu) going to be late? _____

13   We are going to travel to Spain. _____

14   They (f) are going to watch TV. _____

15   I am going to get dressed. _____

16   Is he going to speak? _____

17   Are we going to have enough time? _____

18   I am going to call Paul. _____

19   She is going to wash her hair. _____

20   They (m) are going to write to each other. _____

As a noun: Infinitives as subjects

In English, you often use the *gerund* — the *–ing* form of a verb, identical to the English present participle — as if it's a noun. The French equivalent to this is the infinitive, and when you use it as a noun in this way, the infinitive always takes the third-person singular conjugation of the verb. So you use the infinitive in your sentence where you'd put any other noun, and then you follow it with a verb conjugated in the third-person singular.

> **Avoir des amis est important.** (*Having friends is important.*)
>
> **Pleurer ne sert à rien.** (*Crying doesn't do any good.*)
>
> **Voir, c'est croire.** (*Seeing is believing.*)

The infinitive is the only French verb form that can be used as a subject. All other verb forms need a separate subject; for example, **J'ai des amis** (*I have some friends*) has **je** as the subject and **avoir** conjugated as the verb.

WARNING

Even though you're using French infinitives as nouns in these sentences, they still have to act like verbs: The infinitives refer to the action of a verb, so you can't use them with articles or adjectives or make them plural. However, some French infinitives are also legitimate nouns with non-verby (that's the technical term) meanings. These *infinitive nouns* act just like regular nouns, meaning that you can modify them with articles, adjectives, and plurals — and they are always masculine. See Table 10-1 for some common examples.

DIFFERENCES

You also use the French infinitive after prepositions, where you'd use the present participle in English, such as with **sans attendre** (*without waiting*) and **avant de manger** (*before eating*). The French preposition **à** + an infinitive often means *for*, as with **à vendre** (*for sale*) and **à louer** (*for rent*).

Table 10-1 Common French Infinitive Nouns

French Verb	English Verb	French Noun	English Noun
déjeuner	to have lunch	le déjeuner	lunch
devoir	must, to have to	le devoir	duty
dîner	to have dinner	le dîner	dinner
être	to be	l'être	(living) being
goûter	to taste	le goûter	snack
pouvoir	can, to be able to	le pouvoir	power
rire	to laugh	le rire	laughter
savoir	to know	le savoir	knowledge
sourire	to smile	le sourire	smile

PRACTICE

Your boss has written up a strict new set of guidelines for the office, but the file got corrupted. Fill in the blanks to complete each sentence.

Q. _____ ces directives est obligatoire. (*Following these guidelines is obligatory.*)

A. **Suivre**

21 _____ à l'heure est essentiel. (*Being on time is essential.*)

22 _____ votre voiture derrière le bâtiment est important. (*Parking your car behind the building is important.*)

23 _____ du café est déconseillé. (*Drinking coffee is discouraged.*)

24 _____ des vêtements professionnels est nécessaire. (*Wearing professional clothing is necessary.*)

25 _____ vos propres photocopies est requis. (*Making your own copies is required.*)

26 _____ pendant votre heure de déjeuner est encouragé. (*Working during your lunch break is encouraged.*)

27 _____ des photos sur votre bureau n'est pas permis. (*Having photos on your desk is not permitted.*)

28 _____ réparer votre propre ordinateur est idéal. (*Knowing how to fix your own computer is ideal.*)

29 _____ à vos amis au téléphone est un motif de renvoi. (*Talking to your friends on the phone is a fireable offense.*)

30 _____ tôt est interdit. (*Leaving early is forbidden.*)

Understanding word order with infinitives

When your sentence has a conjugated verb followed by an infinitive, you have to pay attention to where you put some of the smaller sentence elements. For instance, object and adverbial pronouns (which I explain in Chapter 13), such as **le** (*it*) and **y** (*there*), always come right before the infinitive, not the conjugated verb.

> **Je peux le faire.** (*I can do it.*)

> **Il va nous téléphoner.** (*He's going to call us.*)

In a negative sentence that includes an infinitive (see Chapter 9 for more on negatives), you have to consider the meaning of your sentence: Are you negating the conjugated verb or the infinitive?

Most of the time, you're negating the main (conjugated) verb, so the negative structure surrounds that. Think about where you'd put the negative word in English. If *not* or another negative word goes with the conjugated verb, including a form of *be* or *do*, you're negating the conjugated verb in French.

> **Il n'aime pas lire.** (*He doesn't like to read.*)

> **Je ne peux pas trouver mon portefeuille.** (*I can't find my wallet.*)

If you're saying anything with *not to* in English, you're negating the French infinitive. In that case, both parts of the negative structure stay together in front of the infinitive.

> **Je t'ai dit de ne pas commencer sans moi.** (*I told you not to start without me.*)

> **Il préfère ne pas parler.** (*He prefers not to talk.*)

> **Être ou ne pas être . . .** (*To be or not to be . . .*)

PRACTICE

Your landlord has published new bylaws for your apartment building. Translate the missing bits into French.

Q. Nouvelles directives : Vous _____. (New guide-lines: You must follow them.)

A. devez les suivre

31. Voitures : Vous _____ uniquement dans la rue. (Parking: You can park them only on the street.)

32. Porte extérieure : Il est important de _____ ouverte. (Exterior door: It's important not to leave it open.)

33. Ascenseur : _____ après 19 h 00. (Elevator: No one can use it after 7 p.m.)

34. Chaussures : Il est obligatoire de _____ dans les couloirs. (Shoes: It's obligatory to wear them in the hallways.)

(35) Fenêtres : Quelqu'un _____ le samedi. (Windows: Someone is going to wash them on Saturdays.)

(36) Appareils électroménagers : Il faut _____ neufs. (Appliances: You must buy them new.)

(37) Votre porte : Prenez soin de _____. (Your door: Take care not to slam it.)

(38) Jouets : Les enfants _____ dehors. (Toys: Children cannot leave them outside.)

(39) Peinture : Vous _____ toutes les dix ans. (Paint: You can change it every 10 years.)

(40) Des questions ? Vous _____ cette semaine. (Any questions? You must ask them this week.)

Presenting Present Participles

In English, the present participle ends in *–ing*, and in French, it ends in **–ant**. The present participle is all over the place, grammatically speaking. It can be a verb, gerund, adjective, or noun. It's also something of a misnomer because the present participle doesn't actually have a tense; you can use it in the present, past, and future.

In French, the present participle is *variable* (it has different forms for masculine, feminine, singular, and plural) when it's an adjective or noun, but the present participle is invariable when it's a verb or gerund. In the following sections, I discuss how to create the present participle and how to correctly use it.

Forming present participles

For nearly all verbs — regular, stem-changing, spelling-change, and irregular (see Chapter 6 where I talk about these verb forms) — you form the French present participle by taking the present-tense **nous** form of the verb, dropping **–ons**, and adding **–ant**. See Table 10-2.

Table 10-2   Creating Present Participles

Infinitive	Nous Form	Present Participle
parler (*to talk, speak*)	**parlons**	**parlant** (*talking, speaking*)
choisir (*to choose*)	**choisissons**	**choisissant** (*choosing*)
entendre (*to hear*)	**entendons**	**entendant** (*hearing*)
aller (*to go*)	**allons**	**allant** (*going*)
manger (*to eat*)	**mangeons**	**mangeant** (*eating*)
commencer (*to begin*)	**commençons**	**commençant** (*beginning*)
voir (*to see*)	**voyons**	**voyant** (*seeing*)

This rule has only three exceptions. These present participles all still end in –ant, but the first two aren't conjugated from the **nous** form of the verb. The third has two participles, depending on how it's used:

>> **avoir** (*to have*): **ayant** (*having*)

>> **être** (*to be*): **étant** (*being*)

>> **savoir** (*to know*): **savant** (*knowing; as a noun or adjective*)/**sachant** (*knowing; as a verb or gerund*)

The present participle of pronominal verbs (see Chapter 7) is preceded by the reflexive pronoun when you use it as a gerund or verb:

>> **se lever** (*to get up*): **se levant** (*getting up*)

>> **se coucher** (*to go to bed*): **se couchant** (*going to bed*)

>> **s'habiller** (*to get dressed*): **s'habillant** (*getting dressed*)

PRACTICE

Find the present participle for these verbs.

Q. travailler

A. **travaillant** (*working*)

41 vendre _____

42 finir _____

43 aller _____

44 ouvrir _____

45 être _____

46 bouger _____

47 savoir _____

48 lancer _____

49 agir _____

50 avoir _____

Using present participles

In both French and English, you can use the present participle as an adjective or a noun. The following sections show you how to use present participles in different situations.

Present participles as adjectives

When you use the French present participle as an adjective, it acts just like most other adjectives, meaning that it follows the noun it modifies and has to agree in gender and number. (Remember that you add **–e** for feminine adjectives, **–s** for masculine plural adjectives, and **–es** for feminine plural adjectives — see Chapter 11 for more information about adjectives.)

> **un livre intéressant** (*an interesting book*)
>
> **une soucoupe volante** (*a flying saucer*)
>
> **des appartements charmants** (*some charming apartments*)
>
> **des tables pliantes** (*some folding tables*)

WARNING

You can't turn just any French verb into a present-participle adjective. This form is far less common in French than in English — always check your adjectives by looking them up in a French dictionary. See Chapter 2 for tips on using bilingual dictionaries.

Nouns that are present participles

You can use some French present participles as nouns that refer to people. Therefore, like the present participle as an adjective (see the preceding section), the present participle as a noun has different forms for masculine, feminine, singular, and plural. You follow the same rules for making these present participles feminine and plural as for other nouns: **assistant** is masculine, **assistante** is feminine, **assistants** is masculine plural, and **assistantes** is feminine plural. (See Chapter 3 for more information about nouns.)

> » **dirigeant**, **dirigeante** (*leader*); **dirigeants**, **dirigeantes** (*leaders*)
>
> » **étudiant**, **étudiante** (*student*); **étudiants**, **étudiantes** (*students*)

DIFFERENCES

In English, you can use an *–ing* word as a noun that refers to the action of a verb; for example, *Running is good exercise* or *Smoking is bad for you*. An *–ing* word that you use as a noun is called a *gerund* in English, and it's identical to the present participle. However, you can't use the French present participle to translate the English gerund. You can translate this use of the English gerund only with the French infinitive (as explained in the section "As a noun: Infinitives as subjects," earlier in this chapter) or an equivalent French noun. See Table 10-3 for some examples of French translations for English gerunds.

Here you can see a couple of these pairs in action:

> **J'aime la pêche.** or **J'aime pêcher.** (*I like fishing.*)
>
> **L'écriture est difficile.** or **Écrire est difficile.** (*Writing is difficult.*)

The French present participle is much rarer than the English one, and its use as a noun is extremely limited. If you have any doubts at all about whether to use the French present participle as a noun in a particular sentence, don't — that use is probably wrong.

Table 10-3   English –ing Nouns and Their French Counterparts

English Gerund	French Noun	Infinitive
dancing	la danse	danser
fishing	la pêche	pêcher
hunting	la chasse	chasser
reading	la lecture	lire
running	la course	courir
smoking	le tabagisme	fumer
swimming	la natation	nager
writing	l'écriture	écrire

PRACTICE

Determine how to create the present participle and make it agree, then write the correct form in the blank.

Q. C'est une idée _____. (choquer)

A. **C'est une idée choquante.** (*It's a shocking idea.*)

51 Paulette et Francine sont mes _____. (assister)

52 Il a raconté une histoire _____. (intéresser)

53 Les _____ de cette ville n'aiment pas les étrangers. (habiter)

54 Il a une voix _____. (chanter)

55 C'est une décision _____ ! (effrayer)

56 Nous avons un _____ pour la classe aujourd'hui. (remplacer)

57 Elle connaît beaucoup de blagues _____. (amuser)

58 Anne est une enfant _____. (obéir)

59 J'espère que les _____ sont contentes. (gagner)

60 Ah, les couleurs _____ sont si belles ! (changer)

Using other verb forms in lieu of the French present participle

DIFFERENCES

In English, you often use a conjugated verb followed by the present participle, such as to create the *present progressive.* For example, *I am reading.* You can't use the French present participle this way — that grammatical structure simply doesn't exist. Here are some tips for translating the English present participle into French:

>> The English verb *am/are/is* + *–ing*: The French equivalent is the simple present (see Chapter 6).

   I am reading a book. (**Je lis un livre.**)

>> The English verb *was/were* + *-ing*: The French equivalent is the imperfect (see Chapter 16).

I was reading a book. (**Je lisais un livre.**)

>> A conjugated English verb other than a form of *be* + *-ing* (or an English *-ing* word at the beginning of the sentence): The French equivalent is the infinitive (see the section "As a noun: Infinitives as subjects," earlier in this chapter).

I like reading. (**J'aime lire.**)

Reading is important. (**Lire est important.**)

Translate each of these sentences into French. See Chapter 16 to read about the imperfect conjugations you need to translate some of these.

PRACTICE

Q. I like dancing.

A. J'aime danser.

61 He hates fishing. _____

62 We (nous) are leaving at noon. _____

63 Do you (tu) like running? _____

64 Writing is difficult. _____

65 Are you (vous) waiting? _____

66 They (m) were working yesterday. _____

67 Smoking is dangerous. _____

68 I am eating. _____

69 Were you (vous) driving? _____

70 They (m) are traveling together. _____

Answer Key to "Infinitives and Present Participles" Practice Questions

1. **Est-ce que tu veux sortir ce soir ?** (*Do you want to go out tonight?*)

2. **Il sait conduire.** (*He knows how to drive.*)

3. **Pouvez-vous ouvrir la porte ?** (*Can you open the door?*)

4. **Nous voulons travailler ensemble.** (*We want to work together.*)

5. **Elle doit partir demain.** (*They have to leave tomorrow.*)

6. **Savez-vous nager ?** (*Do you know how to swim?*)

7. **J'aime jouer au football.** (*I like playing soccer.*)

8. **Nous devons manger avant 19 h 00.** (*We have to eat before 7 p.m.*)

9. **Elles veulent étudier en France.** (*They want to study in France.*)

10. **Est-ce qu'il peut comprendre ?** (*Can he understand?*)

11. **Elle va être contente/heureuse.**

12. **Est-ce que tu vas être en retard ? Vas-tu être en retard ? Tu vas être en retard ?**

13. **Nous allons voyager en Espagne.**

14. **Elles vont regarder la télé.**

15. **Je vais m'habiller.**

16. **Est-ce qu'il va parler ? Va-t-il parler ? Il va parler ?**

17. **Est-ce que nous allons avoir assez de temps ?/Allons-nous avoir assez de temps ? Nous allons avoir assez de temps ?**

18. **Je vais téléphoner à Paul./Je vais appeler Paul.**

19. **Elle va se laver les cheveux.**

20. **Ils vont s'écrire.**

21. **Être**

22. **Garer**

23. **Boire**

24. **Porter**

25. **Faire**

Answer Key to "Infinitives and Present Participles" Practice Questions

(26) **Travailler**

(27) **Avoir**

(28) **Savoir**

(29) **Parler**

(30) **Partir**

(31) **pouvez les garer**

(32) **ne pas la laisser**

(33) **Personne ne peut l'utiliser**

(34) **les porter**

(35) **va les laver**

(36) **les acheter**

(37) **ne pas la claquer**

(38) **ne peuvent pas les laisser**

(39) **pouvez la changer**

(40) **devez les poser**

(41) **vendant** (*selling*)

(42) **finissant** (*finishing*)

(43) **allant** (*going*)

(44) **ouvrant** (*opening*)

(45) **étant** (*being*)

(46) **bougeant** (*moving*)

(47) **savant/sachant** (*knowing*)

(48) **lançant** (*throwing*)

(49) **agissant** (*acting*)

(50) **ayant** (*having*)

(51) **assistantes** (*Paulette and Francine are my assistants.*)

(52) **intéressante** (*He told an interesting story.*)

(53) **habitants** (*The inhabitants of this town don't like strangers.*)

(54) **chantante** (*He has a lilting voice.*)

(55) **effrayante** (*It's a frightening decision!*)

(56) **remplaçant** (*We have a substitute for class today.*)

(57) **amusantes** (*She knows a lot of amusing jokes.*)

(58) **obéissante** (*Anne is an obedient child.*)

(59) **gagnantes** (*I hope the winners are happy.*)

(60) **changeantes** (*Oh, the changing colors are so beautiful!*)

(61) **Il déteste pêcher/la pêche.** (English gerunds referring to actions are equivalent to the French infinitive or a noun.)

(62) **Nous partons à midi.** (*Be* + *−ing* is equivalent to the French present tense.)

(63) **Aimes-tu courir/la course ? Est-ce que tu aimes courir/la course ? Tu aimes courir/la course ?** (English gerunds referring to actions are equivalent to the French infinitive or a noun.)

(64) **Écrire/L'écriture est difficile.** (English gerunds referring to actions are equivalent to the French infinitive or a noun.)

(65) **Attendez-vous ? Est-ce que vous attendez ? Vous attendez ?** (*Be* + *−ing* is equivalent to the French present tense.)

(66) **Ils travaillaient hier.** (*Be* in the past +*−−ing* is equivalent to the French imperfect.)

(67) **Fumer/La tabagisme est dangereux.** (English gerunds referring to actions are equivalent to the French infinitive or a noun.)

(68) **Je mange.** (*Be* + *-ing* is equivalent to the French present tense.)

(69) **Conduisiez-vous ? Est-ce que vous conduisiez ? Vous conduisez ?** (*Be* in the past + *−ing* is equivalent to the French imperfect.)

(70) **Ils voyagent ensemble.** (*Be* + *−ing* is equivalent to the French present tense.)

3

Writing with Panache: Dressing Up Your Sentences

Chapter **11**

Describing and Comparing with Flair: Adjectives and Adverbs

*A*djectives are descriptive words, and *adverbs* sometimes help them out. Although nouns (flip back to Chapter 3) and verbs (covered in Chapters 6 and 7) are the building blocks and actions of language, adjectives (which modify nouns and pronouns) and adverbs (which affect verbs, adjectives, and other adverbs) are the colors, shapes, sizes, speeds, frequencies, and styles that bring those blocks and actions to life. For example, in the first sentence, *descriptive* is an adjective, and *sometimes* is an adverb. You can see that without them, the sentence would've been missing some important information (and boring): *Adjectives are words, and adverbs help them out.* So adjectives and adverbs provide detail and clarification to the nouns, verbs, and other words they modify.

This chapter explains all about French adjectives and adverbs, including how to use them, where to put them in the sentence, the different types, and how to use them to make comparisons.

Describing All the Things with Adjectives

Adjectives describe nouns and pronouns. They can tell you what something looks, tastes, feels, sounds, and smells like, as well as how smart it is, where it's from, what it's for, and possibly even why you should or shouldn't care about it. The following sections focus on what you need to know about adjectives to use them correctly in your French writing and speaking.

DIFFERENCES

Adjectives that refer to nationalities, languages, and religions aren't capitalized in French: **américain** (*American*), **français** (*French*), **chrétien** (*Christian*), and so on.

Making your adjectives agree

DIFFERENCES

In French, most adjectives come after the noun they modify — rather than before the noun, like they do in English — and they have to agree with the noun in gender and number.

In order to make adjectives agree, you add and/or change certain letters. Most of the rules for making adjectives feminine and plural are the same as for making nouns feminine and plural. (Chapter 3 explains noun gender and number in detail.)

When ensuring that adjectives agree, you need to know that most French adjectives have four forms:

>> Masculine singular

>> Feminine singular

>> Masculine plural

>> Feminine plural

REMEMBER

The *masculine singular* is the default form of the adjective — that's what you'd look up in the dictionary. For example, **vert** (*green*) and **beau** (*beautiful*) are masculine; your dictionary likely doesn't have entries for the feminine equivalents, **verte** and **belle**, or the plurals, **verts/vertes** and **beaux/belles**; instead, those variants appear somewhere in the listing for the default (masculine singular) form.

Converting masculine adjectives to the feminine form

In order to make a masculine adjective feminine, all you have to do for many adjectives is add an –**e** to the end:

>> **petit** (*small*) becomes **petite**

>> **joli** (*pretty*) becomes **jolie**

>> **préféré** (*favorite*) becomes **préférée**

>> **bleu** (*blue*) becomes **bleue**

If the masculine adjective already ends in **–e**, you don't make any changes to get the feminine form:

> » **grave** (*serious*) remains **grave**
>
> » **rouge** (*red*) remains **rouge**

Like nouns, certain adjective endings have irregular feminine forms. Many of these words involve a doubling of the final consonant before adding the **–e**:

> » For adjectives that end in **–el**, **–il**, or **–ul**, add **–le** for the feminine:
>   - **formel** (*formal*) becomes **formelle**
>   - **pareil** (*similar*) becomes **pareille**
>   - **nul** (*none*) becomes **nulle**
>
> » For masculine adjectives that end in **–en** or **–on**, add **–ne** for the feminine form:
>   - **tunisien** (*Tunisian*) becomes **tunisienne**
>   - **bon** (*good*) becomes **bonne**
>
> » For most adjectives that end in **–s**, add **–se** for the feminine:
>   - **bas** (*low*) becomes **basse**
>   - **gros** (*big*) becomes **grosse**
>
>   However, for adjectives that refer to nationalities, just add **–e** without doubling the **s**:
>   - **français** (*French*) becomes **française**
>   - **chinois** (*Chinese*) becomes **chinoise**

French also has several other irregular feminine forms, which follow these patterns:

> » **–ais** to **–aîche**: **frais** (*fresh*) becomes **fraîche**
>
> » **–c** to **–che**: **blanc** (*white*) becomes **blanche**
>
> » **–eau** to **–elle**: **nouveau** (*new*) becomes **nouvelle**
>
> » **–er** to **–ère**: **cher** (*expensive*) becomes **chère**
>
> » **–et** to **–ète**: **secret** (*secret*) becomes **secrète**
>
> » **–eux** to **–euse**: **heureux** (*happy*) becomes **heureuse**
>
> » **–f** to **–ve**: **vif** (*lively*) becomes **vive**
>
> » **–x** to **–ce**: **doux** (*sweet*) becomes **douce**

PRACTICE

It's Ladies' Night! Turn these masculine adjectives feminine.

Q. grand

A. grande (*big*)

1. lent _____

2. amer _____

(3) sportif _____

(4) actuel _____

(5) malheureux _____

(6) moyen _____

(7) allemand _____

(8) facile _____

(9) beau _____

(10) frais _____

Making adjectives plural

In order to make most French adjectives plural, all you do is add an **–s** to the masculine or feminine singular form; see the preceding section to read more about these. For instance, **joli** and **jolie** (*pretty*) become **jolis/jolies**; **blanc/blanche** (*white*) change to **blancs/blanches**; and **triste** (*sad*) becomes **tristes**.

REMEMBER

Here are a few more guidelines to keep in mind when making masculine adjectives plural:

>> Masculine adjectives that end in **–s** or **–x** have the same singular and plural masculine forms. For example, **français** (*French*) and **vieux** (*old*) can modify both singular and plural masculine nouns.

>> Masculine adjectives that end in **–eau** add an **–x** for the plural: **nouveau** (*new*) becomes **nouveaux**, and **beau** (*beautiful*) switches to **beaux**.

>> Masculine adjectives that end in **–al** become plural by transforming to **–aux**: **social** (*social*) becomes **sociaux**, and **idéal** (*ideal*) changes to **idéaux**.

TIP

These patterns for making adjectives feminine and plural are exactly the same as for making nouns feminine and plural; see Chapter 3 for more about nouns.

To make adjectives feminine and plural, just follow these steps:

REMEMBER

1. **Make the adjective feminine.**

   Follow the rules in the preceding section.

2. **Make the feminine adjective plural.**

   For this change, follow the rules in this section.

For example, take the masculine singular **grand** (*big, tall*)

>> Make it feminine by adding **–e: grande** (f singular)

>> Make it plural by adding **–s: grandes** (f plural)

PRACTICE

For each of these singular masculine adjectives, provide the feminine singular, masculine plural, and feminine plural forms.

Q. noir

A. **noire, noirs, noires** (*black*)

11 difficile _____

12 gras _____

13 gentil _____

14 premier _____

15 heureux _____

16 neuf _____

17 anglaise _____

18 intéressant _____

19 nouveau _____

20 bon _____

Identifying French adjectives that have fewer than four forms

French adjectives usually have four forms; however, some have fewer. Consider Table 11-1, which sums up these rules with examples of French adjectives in all their forms.

Table 11-1   French Adjectives, Ready to Agree

English	Masc. Sing.	Fem. Sing.	Masc. Pl.	Fem. Pl.
green	vert	verte	verts	vertes
gray	gris	grise	gris	grises
red	rouge	rouge	rouges	rouges
white	blanc	blanche	blancs	blanches
ideal	idéal	idéale	idéaux	idéales

Note the French adjectives in Table 11-1 that have fewer than four forms:

» Adjectives that end in **-s**, such as **gris**, have only three forms because the masculine singular and plural are the same.

» Adjectives that end in **-e**, such as **rouge**, have only two forms because the masculine and feminine forms are the same.

You always need to consider the spelling of the masculine singular adjective, as I explain in the previous sections "Converting masculine adjectives to the feminine form" and "Making adjectives plural," in order to know what changes it needs — if any — to become feminine and/or plural.

Correctly positioning adjectives around nouns

Using adjectives with nouns is a great way to add description to a sentence. But in order to put adjectives in their correct places, you need to think about the type of adjective and what it means.

DIFFERENCES

Most descriptive French adjectives — that is, adjectives that describe the nature or appearance of a noun, such as color, shape, or origin — follow the nouns they modify:

>> **une voiture verte** (*a green car*)

>> **un garçon mince** (*a slender boy*)

>> **des accords européens** (*European agreements*)

>> **une fille heureuse** (*a happy girl*)

In addition, present and past participles used as adjectives always follow nouns (see Chapter 10 to discover the joys of present participles and Chapter 15 to dive into past participles):

>> **des yeux étincelants** (*sparkling eyes*)

>> **une histoire compliquée** (*a complicated story*)

TIP

However, a few descriptive adjectives, as well as all other types of French adjectives, come before nouns. Descriptive adjectives that refer to the following qualities have to come in front of the nouns they modify (you can remember them with the acronym BAGS):

>> Beauty: **une jolie femme** (*a pretty woman*), **un beau paysage** (*a beautiful landscape*)

>> Age: **un jeune homme** (*a young man*), **une nouvelle voiture** (*a new car*)

>> Goodness and badness: **une bonne idée** (*a good idea*), **un mauvais rhume** (*a bad cold*)

>> Size: **un petit appartement** (*a small apartment*), **une grande voiture** (*a big car*)

REMEMBER

Grand is an exception to this rule. When it precedes the noun, it means *big* (for an object) or *great* (for a person): **une grande maison** (*a big house*), **un grand homme** (*a great man*). But to say that a person is tall, **grand** has to follow the noun it modifies: **un homme grand** (*a tall man*). See the section "Identifying adjectives that have changing meanings," later in this chapter, for details.

All non-descriptive adjectives (possessive, demonstrative, interrogative, and numerical adjectives) come before the noun. (You can read more about possessive and demonstratives in Chapter 4, interrogatives in Chapter 8, and numbers in Chapter 3.) Here are some examples of non-descriptive adjective uses:

>> **ma fille** (*my daughter*)

>> **cette voiture** (*this car*)

>> **Quelle maison ?** (*Which house?*)

>> **quatre livres** (*four books*)

PRACTICE

Where do they go? Write out each phrase, taking care to put the adjective in the correct position either before or after the noun. And don't forget to make the adjective agree with the noun.

Q. rouge; un livre

A. **un livre rouge** (*red book*)

21 difficile; une décision _____

22 bon; une idée _____

23 cher; un ordinateur _____

24 important; les papiers _____

25 ce; maison _____

26 jaune; une chaise _____

27 beau; les cheveux _____

28 notre; enfants _____

29 fascinant; un film _____

30 nouveau; une école _____

Using special forms for six adjectives that precede nouns

Most French adjectives have four different forms: masculine singular, feminine singular, masculine plural, and feminine plural. But six French adjectives have a fifth: a special form that you use only in very specific constructions. This masculine singular form exists for six of the adjectives that go in front of nouns, and you use it only in front of a vowel or mute **h**. Its purpose is to make pronunciation easier so that you don't have to say back-to-back vowel sounds. See Table 11-2.

Table 11-2   Adjectives with Special Masculine Singular Forms

English	Masc. Sing.	Masc. Sing. before a Vowel or Mute h	Fem. Sing.	Masc. Pl.	Fem. Pl.
beautiful	beau	bel	belle	beaux	belles
this	ce	cet	cette	ces	ces
new	nouveau	nouvel	nouvelle	nouveaux	nouvelles
crazy	fou	fol	folle	fous	folles
soft	mou	mol	molle	mous	molles
old	vieux	vieil	vieille	vieux	vieilles

You use this special form *only* with masculine nouns and *only* when the adjective directly precedes a vowel or mute **h**. All three of these conditions must be met:

- » The noun is masculine.
- » The noun is singular.
- » The word that directly follows the adjective — whether it's the noun itself or another adjective — begins with a vowel or mute **h**.

For example:

- » **un bel homme** (*a handsome man*)
- » **mon nouvel avocat** (*my new lawyer*)
- » **cet ingénieur** (*this engineer*)

If a second adjective that doesn't begin with a vowel or mute **h** is used between the two words, you can't use the special form, such as with **ce grand ingénieur** (*this great engineer*).

On the other hand, if you precede a masculine noun that *doesn't* begin with a vowel or mute **h** with another adjective that does, you *do* use the special form, such as with **cet ancien maire** (*this former mayor*).

REMEMBER

The letter that the noun itself starts with doesn't necessarily tell you whether you have to use the special form. Here are some examples:

- » **Special form adjective + noun with vowel/mute h:** If the adjective directly precedes **homme** (*man*) or **éclair** (*flash of lightning*), for example, you use the special form: **cet homme** (*this man*)

- » **Special form adjective + adjective with vowel/mute h:** If the potentially special form adjective precedes a second adjective, such as **intéressant** (*interesting*) or **ancien** (*old*), you use the special form as long as the noun is masculine (even if the noun itself begins with a consonant): **cet ancien bâtiment** (*this old building*)

- » **No special form adjective + adjective with consonant/aspirated h:** If a second adjective such as **jeune** (*young*) or **grand** (*big*) comes between the potentially special form adjective and noun, you can't use the special form of the adjective — even if the noun begins with a vowel or mute **h**: **ce jeune homme** (*this young man*).

How very special! Decide which form of the adjective to use in these phrases.

PRACTICE

Q. un _____ anorak (nouveau)

A. un **nouvel** anorak (*a new windbreaker*)

31 un _____ homme (beau)

32 _____ ananas (ce)

33 un _____ espoir (fou)

34 le _____ anglais (vieux)

35 une _____ histoire (nouveau)

36 un _____ âge (beau)

37 _____ joli appartement (ce)

38 une _____ idée (fou)

39 un _____ arbre (vieux)

40 un _____ hôpital (nouveau)

Identifying adjectives that have changing meanings

Some French adjectives have different meanings depending on whether they precede or follow the noun. Generally speaking, when these adjectives have a *figurative* or *subjective* meaning, you place them before the noun. When they have a *literal* or *objective* meaning, you place them after the noun:

>> **un ancien médecin** (*former doctor*) versus **un médecin ancien** (*old doctor*)

>> **la pauvre femme** (*poor, wretched woman*) versus **la femme pauvre** (*poor, penniless woman*)

See Table 11-3 for some common French adjectives that can have meaning changes.

Table 11-3   Adjectives with Meaning Changes

Adjective	Meaning before Noun (figurative or subjective)	Meaning after Noun (literal or objective)
brave	good, decent	brave
cher	dear	expensive
curieux	odd, strange	inquisitive
dernier	final	previous
franc	real, genuine	frank
grand	great	tall
premier	first	basic, primary
prochain	following	next
propre	(my, his, our) own	clean
triste	sorry, pathetic	sad

PRACTICE

Translate the following phrases into French, paying careful attention to the placement of the French adjectives.

Q. an orange book

A. un livre orange

41 a yellow house _____

42 a beautiful country _____

43 a funny movie _____

44 a young girl _____

45 an interesting story _____

46 a new apartment _____

47 a great doctor _____

48 a small car _____

49 a tall woman _____

50 an old friend _____

Using Adverbs Accurately

Like adjectives (see the section "Describing All the Things with Adjectives," earlier in this chapter), adverbs are descriptive words. But instead of describing nouns, adverbs describe verbs, adjectives, or other adverbs. Adverbs tell you when, where, why, how, how often, and how much. Unlike adjectives, which have to agree with the nouns they modify, adverbs are *invariable*: They have only one form. The following sections cover what you need to know — including recognizing types of adverbs, forming adverbs, and positioning them — so that you can correctly use French adverbs in your writing and speech.

Identifying types of adverbs

Different types of adverbs have different purposes, and the type that you want to use depends on what you want to say. Are you talking about how often something happens, where it happens, when . . . ? The following sections cover adverbs of frequency, place, time, quantity, and manner. French has two other types of adverbs that you need to know about. They are interrogative adverbs (see Chapter 8) and negative adverbs (see Chapter 9).

Adverbs of frequency

Adverbs of frequency express *how often* or *how consistently* something happens:

>> **encore** (*again*)

>> **généralement** (*usually*)

>> **parfois/quelquefois** (*sometimes*)

>> **rarement** (*rarely*)

>> **souvent** (*often*)

>> **toujours** (*always, still*)

Check out some examples:

> **Je vais souvent au musée.** (*I often go to the museum.*)

> **Prends-tu toujours l'avion pour aller au Québec ?** (*Do you always fly to Quebec?*)

PRACTICE

Frequent fliers? Choose the correct adverb for each of these people.

Q. Je voyage _____. (I travel often.)

A. souvent

51 Jean prend _____ le train. (Jean always takes the train.)

52 Aline va _____ au parc à pied. (Aline sometimes goes to the park on foot.)

53 Nicolas voyage _____ seul. (Nicolas rarely travels alone.)

54 Jacques préfère _____ prendre le bateau. (Jacques sometimes prefers to go by boat.)

55 Céline se rend _____ dans les Caraïbes en hélicoptère. (Céline often goes to the Caribbean by helicopter.)

56 Ils voyagent _____ ensemble. (They usually travel together.)

Adverbs of place

Adverbs of place tell you where something happens:

French Adverb	Translation	French Adverb	Translation
à côté	next door	en bas	down below, downstairs
autour	around	en haut	up above, upstairs
dedans	inside	ici	here
dehors	outside	là	here, there
derrière	behind, in the back	loin	far away
dessous	below	partout	everywhere
dessus	on top (of)	près	nearby, close
devant	in front	quelque part	somewhere

Take a look at some example sentences:

> **Je préfère m'asseoir derrière.** (*I prefer sitting in the back.*)
>
> **Qui habite en haut ?** (*Who lives upstairs?*)

REMEMBER

Many adverbs of place are also prepositions. The difference is that an adverb acts by itself to modify a verb — **J'habite en bas** (*I live below*) — and a preposition joins its object (the noun that follows it) with another word — **J'habite en bas de chez Michel** (*I live below Michel*). See Chapter 12 for more information about French prepositions.

PRACTICE

Here and there: Choose the correct adverb for each sentence.

Q. J'habite _____. (*I live here.*)

A. **ici**

57 Natalie est allée trop _____. (*Nathalie went too far.*)

58 Le musée est _____. (*The museum is next door.*)

59 Les enfants jouent _____. (*The kids are playing outside.*)

60 Yves habite _____. (*Yves lives downstairs.*)

61 Tu connais le lycée ? Le café est juste _____. (*Do you know the high school? The café is right in front [of it].*)

62 Nous voyons des boulangeries _____. (*We see bakeries everywhere.*)

Adverbs of time

Adverbs of time explain *when* something happens:

French Adverb	Translation	French Adverb	Translation
actuellement	*currently*	**depuis**	*since*
après	*after*	**enfin**	*at last, finally*
aujourd'hui	*today*	**ensuite/puis**	*next, then*
aussitôt	*immediately*	**hier**	*yesterday*
autrefois	*formerly, in the past*	**immédiatement**	*immediately*
avant	*before*	**longtemps**	*for a long time*
bientôt	*soon*	**maintenant**	*now*
d'abord	*first, at first*	**récemment**	*recently*
déjà	*already*	**tard**	*late*
demain	*tomorrow*	**tôt**	*early*

WARNING

Actuellement means *currently*, not *actually*. **En fait** means *actually*.

Here are some sentences with adverbs of time:

Nous allons partir demain. (*We're going to leave tomorrow.*)

J'ai enfin visité Paris. (*I finally visited Paris.*)

PRACTICE Now and then: Choose the correct adverb for each sentence.

Q. Je travaille _____ à Genève. (*I currently work in Geneva.*)

A. actuellement

63 Philippe est arrivé _____. (*Philippe arrived yesterday.*)

64 L'épicerie ouvre _____. (*The grocery store is opening soon.*)

65 Mon fils habite au Maroc depuis _____. (*My son has lived in Morocco for a long time.*)

66 Le chat a _____ mangé. (*The cat has already eaten.*)

67 Je vais finir ce livre _____. (*I'm going to finish this book today.*)

68 _____, vous devez lire les instructions. (*First, you need to read the instructions.*)

Adverbs of quantity

Adverbs of quantity tell you *how many* or *how much*:

French Adverb	Translation	French Adverb	Translation
assez (de)	*rather, fairly, enough (of)*	pas mal de	*quite a few*
autant (de)	*as much, as many*	(un) peu (de)	*few, little, not very*
beaucoup (de)	*a lot, many*	la plupart de	*most*
bien des	*quite a few*	plus (de)	*more*
combien (de)	*how many, how much*	tant (de)	*so much, so many*
très	*very*	moins (de)	*less, fewer*
trop (de)	*too much, too many*		

Here are some sentences with adverbs of quantity:

Ils ont pas mal de chiens. (*They have quite a few dogs.*)

Je parle très vite. (*I speak very quickly.*)

Note: The parentheses around **de** in many of these phrases indicate that the **de** is required only if followed by a noun. **J'ai assez mangé** (*I ate enough*) doesn't need **de** because **assez** is followed by a verb, but **j'ai assez de temps** (*I have enough time*) does need **de** because **temps** is a noun.

Il y a trop de circulation. (*There's too much traffic.*)

Elle a beaucoup d'amis. (*She has a lot of friends.*)

REMEMBER When most adverbs of quantity are followed by a noun, as in the preceding two examples, you need to include the preposition **de** between them, and you usually don't use an article in front of the noun. However, there are a couple of exceptions:

>> When the noun after **de** refers to specific people or things, you need an article. In general, if the English translation includes *of the* rather than just *of*, you need the article. Compare these two sentences:

- **Cette ville a beaucoup de circulation.** (*This town has a lot of traffic.*)

- **Beaucoup de la circulation à Marseille est à destination de l'aéroport.** (*A lot of the traffic in Marseilles is going toward the airport.*)

>> **Bien des, encore de**, and **la plupart de** always precede a plural noun, such as in **La plupart des plages sont rocheuses** (*Most of the beaches are rocky*).

A little or a lot: Choose the correct adverb for each sentence.

PRACTICE

Q. J'ai _____ questions pour vous. (I have a lot of questions for you.)

A. **beaucoup de**

69 Nous sommes _____ contents. (We are very happy.)

70 Les oiseaux font _____ bruit ! (The birds are making too much noise!)

71 Elle travaille _____. (She works a lot.)

72 Ils ont _____ amis en Grèce. (They have quite a few friends in Greece.)

73 Est-ce que nous avons _____ vin ? (Do we have enough wine?)

74 Je n'ai jamais vu _____ arbres fruitiers ! (I've never seen so many fruit trees!)

Turning adjectives into adverbs of manner

Many adverbs are formed from adjectives, in both French and English. These are usually adverbs of manner and express *how* something happens. They usually end in *–ly* in English (*clearly, quickly, frankly*), whereas their French equivalents end in **–ment** (**clairement, rapidement, franchement**).

The rules for turning adjectives into adverbs are fairly straightforward. For masculine adjectives that end in a single vowel, just add **–ment**:

>> **poli** (*polite*) becomes **poliment** (*politely*)

>> **carré** (*square*) becomes **carrément** (*squarely*)

>> **triste** (*sad*) becomes **tristement** (*sadly*)

Other words need a little more tweaking. Keep the following rules in mind when forming adverbs:

>> When the masculine adjective ends in a consonant (except for **–ant** or **–ent**) or multiple vowels, take the feminine form of the adjective and add **–ment**. Most French adjectives of manner are formed like this:

- **certain** (*certain*, m)/**certaine** (f) becomes **certainement** (*certainly*)
- **heureux** (*happy*, m)/**heureuse** (f) becomes **heureusement** (*happily, fortunately*)
- **dernier** (*last*, m)/**dernière** (f) becomes **dernièrement** (*lastly*)
- **nouveau** (*new*, m)/**nouvelle** (f) becomes **nouvellement** (*newly*)

>> For adjectives that end in **–ant** or **–ent**, replace that ending with **–amment** or **–emment**:

- **constant** (*constant*) becomes **constamment** (*constantly*)
- **intelligent** (*intelligent*) becomes **intelligemment** (*intelligently*)

However, remember a few specific exceptions to the preceding rules:

>> **continu** (*continuous*) becomes **continûment** (*continuously*)

>> **énorme** (*enormous*) becomes **énormément** (*enormously*)

>> **gentil** (*nice, kind*) becomes **gentiment** (*nicely, kindly*)

>> **lent** (*slow*) becomes **lentement** (*slowly*)

>> **vrai** (*true*) becomes **vraiment** (*truly*)

Some French adverbs of manner don't end in **–ment**:

>> **bien** (*well*)

>> **debout** (*standing up*)

>> **exprès** (*on purpose*)

>> **mal** (*poorly, badly*)

>> **mieux** (*better*)

>> **pire** (*worse*)

>> **vite** (*quickly*)

>> **volontiers** (*gladly*)

Here are some example sentences with adverbs of manner.

Elle parle très poliment. (*She speaks very politely.*)

Tu l'as fait exprès ! (*You did it on purpose!*)

PRACTICE Turn these adjectives into adverbs.

Q. joli

A. joliment (*prettily*)

(75) naturel _____

(76) clair _____

(77) lent _____

(78) malheureux _____

(79) vrai _____

(80) premier _____

(81) abondant _____

(82) gentil _____

(83) affreux _____

(84) prudent _____

Positioning adverbs

The position of French adverbs depends on what they're modifying, as well as the type of adverb.

Adverbs after the verb

When French adverbs modify a verb, they usually follow it.

> **Je le fais volontiers !** (*I'm happy to do it!*)

> **Nous voyageons souvent en été.** (*We often travel in the summer.*)

If there are two verbs, the adverb goes after the conjugated verb, rather than after the infinitive or past participle (see Chapter 10 for more about the infinitive and Chapter 15 for the **passé composé**).

> **J'aime beaucoup nager.** (*I like swimming a lot.*)

> **Il a déjà mangé.** (*He has already eaten.*)

When you negate a sentence that contains an adverb following a verb, the second part of the negative structure (explained in Chapter 9) comes before the adverb.

> **Je ne me sens pas bien.** (*I don't feel well.*)

> **Il ne travaille jamais vite.** (*He never works quickly.*)

Adverbs in other spots

You can usually put adverbs that refer to a point in time — such as **aujourd'hui** (*today*) and **hier** (*yesterday*) — at the beginning or end of the sentence, as in **Aujourd'hui, je dois travailler/Je dois travailler aujourd'hui** (*Today, I have to work/I have to work today*). The same is true for long adverbs, as in **Normalement, je me lève à 7 h 00/Je me lève à 7 h 00 normalement** (*Usually, I get up at 7 a.m./I get up at 7 a.m., usually*).

However, when you want to stress the meaning of the adverb, you put it after the conjugated verb, as in **Il a violemment critiqué la nouvelle loi.** (*He strongly criticized the new law.*) The adjective **violemment** (*strongly*) follows the conjugated helping verb **a**. (See Chapter 15 for more about helping verbs.)

Adverbs that modify adjectives or other adverbs go in front of those words.

> **Elle est très belle.** (*She is very beautiful.*)
>
> **J'habite ici depuis assez longtemps.** (*I've lived here for a fairly long time.*)

PRACTICE

Your colleague Marianne asked you to look over a memo she wrote, and you think it's a bit dull and imprecise because she didn't use any adverbs. Help her out by adding the adverb in parentheses to each of these sentences.

Q. Nous allons parler de la fête annuelle. (aujourd'hui)

A. **Aujourd'hui, nous allons parler de la fête annuelle.** (*Today, we're going to talk about the annual party.*)

NOTE DE SERVICE

À:	Tous les employés		
De:	Marianne		
Sujet:	Fête annuelle		

85. Elle se tient dans le bureau. (normalement)

_____

86. Mais cette fois, nous pouvons trouver un endroit intéressant. (plus)

_____

87. À mon avis, un restaurant est un bon choix. (très)

_____

88. Comme ça, nous mangeons ce que nous voulons. (exactement)

_____

89. J'ai téléphoné à plusieurs restaurants ... (hier)

_____

90. ... et j'en ai trouvé trois qui semblent idéaux. (presque)

_____

91. Le premier a du charme. (beaucoup)

_____

92. Le deuxième est ici. (près de)

_____

93. Et le troisième est fréquenté par des célébrités. (souvent)

_____

94. Répondez pour me dire lequel vous préférez. (immédiatement)

_____

Comparing with Comparatives and Superlatives

The two kinds of comparisons you can make in French are *comparatives* and *superlatives*:

>> **Comparatives:** Say that something is *more [something] than, [something]–er than, less [something] than,* or *as [something] as* something else.

>> **Superlatives:** Proclaim that something is *the most [something], the [something]–est,* or *the least [something] of all.*

Read on for more info about both kinds!

More or less, equal: Relating two things with comparatives

Comparatives can indicate one of three things:

>> Superiority

>> Inferiority

>> Equality

You use the comparative **plus . . . que** in French to indicate superiority — that something is *more [something] than* or *[something]–er than* something else. The construction works for both adjectives and adverbs.

> **Elle est plus belle que ma sœur.** (*She is more beautiful than my sister.*)

> **Jacques parle plus rapidement que Martin.** (*Jacques speaks more quickly than Martin.*)

TIP

In French comparatives and superlatives, you use stressed pronouns, rather than subject pronouns, after **que**. *Stressed pronouns* are special forms that you use after prepositions (see Chapter 12) and in comparatives or superlatives. See Table 11-4.

Table 11-4   Stressed Pronouns that Follow Que in Comparatives and Superlatives

Person	Singular	Plural
First	moi	nous
Second	toi	vous
Third	lui/elle	eux

In the following examples, stressed pronouns are used instead of nouns after the comparative and superlative structures:

> **Elle est plus belle que moi.** (*She is more beautiful than I am.*)

> **Jacques parle plus rapidement que toi.** (*Jacques speaks more quickly than you.*)

If the object to which you're comparing your subject is implied or has already been mentioned, you can leave out the phrase starting with **que**.

> **J'ai lu ton livre, mais le mien est plus intéressant [que le tien].** (*I read your book, but mine is more interesting [than yours].*)

REMEMBER

The adjective in a comparative has to agree with the noun or pronoun it is comparing. In order to do so, follow the agreement rules in the section "Making your adjectives agree," earlier in this chapter. However, remember that like other adverbs (see "Using Adverbs Accurately" earlier in this chapter), the comparative adverb itself (**plus**, **moins**, **aussi**) is *invariable* (does not change to agree with the noun). For example:

> **Paul est plus grand que Paulette.** (*Paul is taller than Paulette.*)
>
> **Paulette est plus grande que Paul.** (*Paulette is taller than Paul.*)

To say that something is inferior — *less [something] than* — use the comparative **moins . . . que**.

> **Yvette est moins ennuyeuse que son frère.** (*Yvette is less boring than her brother.*)
>
> **Ce livre est moins intéressant [que l'autre].** (*This book is less interesting [than the other one].*)
>
> **Il chante moins distinctement que son ami.** (*He sings less distinctly than his friend.*)

You express equality with **aussi . . . que** in French, which is equivalent to *as [something] as* in English.

> **L'activité physique est aussi importante que la nutrition.** (*Physical activity is as important as nutrition.*)
>
> **Ma mère est aussi grande que mon père.** (*My mother is as tall as my father.*)
>
> **Vous vivez aussi bien qu'un roi.** (*You live as well as a king.*)

All these comparatives are between two people or things, but you can also make comparisons with two adjectives.

> **Je suis plus agacé que fâché.** (*I'm more annoyed than [I am] angry./I'm annoyed, rather than angry.*)
>
> **Il est aussi audacieux que courageux.** (*He's as audacious as [he is] courageous.*)

PRACTICE

Your friend Élise is so competitive! Whenever you describe anything at all, she claims that she and everything of hers is bigger, better, or just more of whatever. For each phrase, write what Élise's response would be. For the positive attributes, use **plus**, and for the negative ones, use **moins**.

Q. Ma voiture est rouge et vieille.

A. **Ma voiture est plus rouge et moins vieille !** (*My car is redder and less old!*)

95 Ce livre est intéressant. _____

96 Mes amis sont paresseux. _____

97 Nicolas nage mal. _____

(98) J'ai une question importante. _____

(99) Martin s'habille professionnellement. _____

(100) Je regarde un film stupide. _____

(101) Ma sœur est belle. _____

(102) Anne travaille consciencieusement. _____

(103) J'ai mangé une huître dégoûtante. _____

(104) Il parle le français couramment. _____

Supersizing with superlatives

Superlatives talk about the two extremes: *the most, the least, the [something]–est.* In order to form the superlative, you need to know the three parts involved:

>> The definite article (see Chapter 3)

>> **Plus** (*most*) or **moins** (*least*)

>> The adjective or adverb

Superlatives with adjectives

The definite article and the adjective both have to be masculine or feminine, and singular or plural, to agree with the noun that they're modifying. Then, to form the superlative, use this formula:

definite article + **plus** or **moins** + adjective

REMEMBER

Before you can use superlatives, you also have to know whether the adjective you're using goes before or after the noun (see the section "Correctly positioning adjectives around nouns," earlier in this chapter) because adjectives that follow the noun have to be in that same position in superlatives. Once you know that, here's what you need to do:

>> When the superlative follows the noun, you have to use the definite article twice — it precedes both the noun and the superlative:

   • **C'est la solution la plus équitable.** (*That's the fairest solution.*)

   • **Mon frère est l'homme le moins sportif du monde.** (*My brother is the least athletic man in the world.*)

>> Adjectives that precede the noun can either precede or follow the noun in superlatives. When they precede it, you use only one definite article:

   • **Il est l'homme le plus beau./Il est le plus bel homme.** (*He is the most handsome man.*)

   • **Nous avons trouvé les options les moins mauvaises/Nous avons trouvé les moins mauvaises options.** (*We've found the least bad options.*)

Superlatives with adverbs

Superlatives with adverbs are a little different from superlatives with adjectives (see the preceding section). Because adverbs don't agree with the words they modify, the definite article in superlatives doesn't either, so it's always **le**, the masculine singular. Also, because most adverbs follow verbs, comparative and superlatives adverbs always follow verbs, and superlatives with adverbs never have two definite articles in the way that superlatives with adjectives sometimes do. Instead, superlatives with adverbs simply take the form **le** + **plus** or **moins** + adverb.

> **Elle danse le plus parfaitement.** (*She dances the most perfectly.*)

> **Ils conduisent le moins lentement.** (*They drive the least slowly.*)

Élise is insisting that she's the best and has the best of everything! For each phrase, write what Élise's response would be.

PRACTICE

Q. Mon vélo est vert mais rouillé.

A. **Mon vélo est le plus vert et le moins rouillé !** (*My bike is the greenest and the least rusty!*)

105 Karine parle clairement. _____

106 Mes enfants sont bruyants. _____

107 Étienne travaille dur. _____

108 Il a acheté un chiot mignon. _____

109 J'ai des étudiants agaçants. _____

110 Je vois une jolie fleur. _____

111 Cet article est fascinant. _____

112 Nous marchons prudemment. _____

113 Ma maison est moche. _____

114 Sophie réagit méchamment. _____

For better or worse: Special comparative and superlative forms

Two French adjectives have special forms in the *superior* comparative and superlative: **bon** (*good*) and **mauvais** (*bad*). The superior comparative of **bon** is **meilleur** (*better*) and the superior superlative is **le meilleur** (*the best*). Like all adjectives, they have to agree with the nouns they modify.

> **Ton vélo est meilleur que le mien.** (*Your bike is better than mine.*)

> **Ma question est la meilleure.** (*My question is the best.*)

Note: The inferior comparative/superlative and the equal comparative keep the regular form and follow the normal rules:

> **Leurs idées sont moins bonnes.** (*Their ideas are less good/aren't as good.*)
>
> **C'est la solution la moins bonne.** (*This is the least good solution.*)
>
> **Ta cuisine est aussi bonne que la mienne.** (*Your cooking is as good as mine.*)

Mauvais has two superior comparative and superlative forms. You can say **plus mauvais** (*literally,* "more bad") or **pire** (*worse*).

> **Cette décision est plus mauvaise que l'autre.** or **Cette décision est pire que l'autre.** (*This decision is worse than the other one.*)
>
> **Ces problèmes sont les plus mauvais.** or **Ces problèmes sont les pires.** (*These problems are the worst.*)

The inferior comparative/superlative and the equal comparative have only one form, following the normal rules.

> **Cette possibilité est moins mauvaise que l'autre.** (*This possibility is less bad than/not as bad as the other.*)
>
> **C'est vin le moins mauvais de la sélection.** (*This is the least bad wine in the selection.*)
>
> **Ils sont aussi mauvais que tes élèves.** (*They're as bad as your pupils.*)

French also has special forms for the superior comparative and superlative of the French adverb **bien** (*well*). The comparative is **mieux** (*better*), and the superlative is **le mieux** (*the best*).

> **Philippe comprend mieux que moi.** (*Philippe understands better than I do.*)
>
> **C'est en France que je me sens le mieux.** (*It's in France that I feel best.*)

But the inferior comparative and superlative follow the regular rules:

> **Tu écris moins bien.** (*You write less well./You don't write as well.*)
>
> **Il écrit le moins bien de la classe.** (*He writes the least well in the class.*)

PRACTICE

Supercharge these sentences: Use the comparative for numbers 116 through 120 and the superlative for numbers 121 through 125.

Q. J'ai une bonne idée.

A. J'ai une meilleure idée. (*I have a better idea.*)

115 Il a trouvé une mauvaise chaise. _____

116 Voici un bon ordinateur. _____

117 Je vous entend bien. _____

118 Ces problèmes sont mauvais. _____

119 Elle ne joue pas bien. _____

120 Je cherche un bon livre. _____

121 Nous avons une mauvaise voiture. _____

122 Qui connaît bien Jean-Marc ? _____

123 Elle va à une bonne boulangerie. _____

124 Ces pommes sont mauvaises. _____

Answer Key to "Adjectives and Adverbs" Practice Questions

1. **lente** (*slow*)
2. **amère** (*bitter*)
3. **sportive** (*athletic*)
4. **actuelle** (*current*)
5. **malheureuse** (*unhappy, unfortunate*)
6. **moyenne** (*medium, average*)
7. **allemande** (*German*)
8. **facile** (*easy*)
9. **belle** (*beautiful*)
10. **fraîche** (*cool, fresh*)
11. **difficile, difficiles, difficiles** (*difficult*)
12. **grasse, gras, grasses** (*fatty*)
13. **gentille, gentils, gentilles** (*kind*)
14. **première, premiers, premières** (*first*)
15. **heureuse, heureux, heureuses** (*happy*)
16. **neuve, neufs, neuves** (*new*)
17. **anglaise, anglais, anglaises** (*English*)
18. **intéressante, intéressants, intéressantes** (*interesting*)
19. **nouvelle, nouveaux, nouvelles** (*new*)
20. **bonne, bons, bonnes** (*good*)
21. **une décision difficile** (*a difficult decision*)
22. **une bonne idée** (*a good idea*)
23. **un ordinateur cher** (*an expensive computer*)
24. **les papiers importants** (*the important papers*)
25. **cette maison** (*this/that house*)
26. **une chaise jaune** (*a yellow chair*)

27. **les beaux cheveux** (*the beautiful hair*)

28. **nos enfants** (*our kids*)

29. **un film fascinant** (*a fascinating movie*)

30. **une nouvelle école** (*a new school*)

31. **un bel homme** (*a handsome man*)

32. **cet ananas** (*this pineapple*)

33. **un fol espoir** (*a mad hope*)

34. **le vieil anglais** (*Old English*)

35. **une nouvelle histoire** (*a new story*)

36. **un bel âge** (*a lovely age*)

37. **ce joli appartement** (*this nice apartment*)

38. **une folle idée** (*a crazy idea*)

39. **un vieil arbre** (*an old tree*)

40. **un nouvel hôpital** (*a new hospital*)

41. **une maison jaune**

42. **un beau pays**

43. **un film amusant/drôle**

44. **une jeune fille**

45. **une histoire intéressante**

46. **un nouvel appartement**

47. **un grand médecin/docteur**

48. **une petite voiture**

49. **une femme grande**

50. **un vieil ami/un vieux copain**

51. **toujours**

52. **parfois/quelquefois**

53. **rarement**

54. **parfois/quelquefois**

55. **souvent**

56. **généralement**

57. **loin**

58. **à côté**

59. **dehors**

60. **en bas**

61. **devant**

62. **partout**

63. **hier**

64. **bientôt**

65. **longtemps**

66. **déjà**

67. **aujourd'hui**

68. **D'abord**

69. **très**

70. **trop de**

71. **beaucoup**

72. **bien des/pas mal d'**

73. **assez de**

74. **autant d'**

75. **naturellement** (*naturally*)

76. **clairement** (*clearly*)

77. **lentement** (*slowly*)

78. **malheureusement** (*unfortunately*)

79. **vraiment** (*really/truly*)

80. **premièrement** (*firstly/in the first place*)

81. **abondamment** (*abundantly*)

82. **gentiment** (*kindly*)

83. **affreusement** (*terribly/horribly*)

84. **prudemment** (*prudently*)

(85) **Elle se tient normalement dans le bureau.** (*It is normally held in the office.*)

(86) **Mais cette fois, nous pouvons trouver un endroit plus intéressant.** (*But this time, we can find a more interesting spot.*)

(87) **À mon avis, un restaurant est un très bon choix.** (*In my opinion, a restaurant is a very good choice.*)

(88) **Comme ça, nous mangeons exactement ce que nous voulons.** (*That way, we eat exactly what we want.*)

(89) **Hier, j'ai téléphoné à plusieurs restaurants . . .** (*Yesterday, I called several restaurants . . .*)

(90) **. . . et j'en ai trouvé trois qui semblent presque idéaux.** (*. . . and I found three that seem almost perfect.*)

(91) **Le premier a beaucoup de charme.** (*The first has a lot of charm.*)

(92) **Le deuxième est près d'ici.** (*The second is near here.*)

(93) **Et le troisième est souvent fréquenté par des célébrités.** (*And the third is often frequented by celebrities.*)

(94) **Répondez immédiatement pour me dire lequel vous préférez.** (*Respond immediately to tell me which one you prefer.*)

(95) **Mon livre est plus intéressant !** (*My book is more interesting!*)

(96) **Mes amis sont moins paresseux !** (*My friends are less lazy!*)

(97) **Je nage moins mal !** (*I swim less badly!*)

(98) **J'ai une question plus importante !** (*I have a more important question!*)

(99) **Je m'habille plus professionnellement !** (*I dress more professionally!*)

(100) **Je regarde un film moins stupide !** (*I'm watching a less stupid movie!*)

(101) **Ma sœur est plus belle !** (*My sister is more beautiful!*)

(102) **Je travaille plus consciencieusement !** (*I work more conscientiously!*)

(103) **J'ai mangé une huître plus dégoûtante !** (*I ate a more disgusting oyster!*)

(104) **Je parle le français plus couramment !** (*I speak French more fluently!*)

(105) **Je parle le plus clairement !** (*I speak the most clearly!*)

(106) **Mes enfants sont les moins bruyants !** (*My kids are the least noisy!*)

(107) **Je travaille le plus dur !** (*I work the hardest!*)

(108) **J'ai acheté le chiot le plus mignon !** (*I bought the cutest puppy!*)

(109) **J'ai les étudiants les moins agaçants !** (*I have the least annoying students!*)

(110) **Je vois la plus jolie fleur !/Je vois la fleur la plus jolie !** (*I see the prettiest flower!*)

(111) **Mon article est le plus fascinant !** (*My article is the most fascinating!*)

(112) **Je marche le plus prudemment !** (*I walk the most carefully!*)

(113) **Ma maison est la moins moche !** (*My house is the least ugly!*)

(114) **Je réagis le moins méchamment !** (*I react the least meanly!*)

(115) **Il a trouvé une plus mauvaise chaise./Il a trouvé une pire chaise.** (*He found a worse chair.*)

(116) **Voici un meilleur ordinateur.** (*Here's a better computer.*)

(117) **Je vous entend mieux.** (*I hear you better.*)

(118) **Ces problèmes sont plus mauvais./Ces problèmes sont pires.** (*These problems are worse.*)

(119) **Elle ne joue pas mieux.** (*She doesn't play better.*)

(120) **Je cherche le meilleur livre.** (*I'm looking for the best book.*)

(121) **Nous avons la plus mauvaise voiture./Nous avons la pire voiture.** (*We have the worst car.*)

(122) **Qui connaît le mieux Jean-Marc ?** (*Who knows Jean-Marc the best?*)

(123) **Elle va à la meilleure boulangerie.** (*She goes to the best bakery.*)

(124) **Ces pommes sont les plus mauvaises./Ces pommes sont les pires.** (*These apples are the worst.*)

Chapter **12**

An Ode to Prepositions

Prepositions are joining words — they connect nouns to other nouns or to verbs in order to show the relationship between those words, such as what something is about, whom someone is working for, or how your keys always manage to hide from you. Prepositions can be tricky in foreign languages because you can't memorize them like you do vocabulary lists.

Many French prepositions have more than one English translation — and vice versa — because it's not a simple matter of knowing what they mean, but rather how you use them in each language. The job of prepositions is to explain how one word affects another, such as by talking *to*, *about*, or *over* it, and those uses can vary widely between French and English. This chapter explains the most common French prepositions and how to use them with places, time, and verbs, as well as how and when to form contractions.

Identifying Common Prepositions

The most common French prepositions are **à** and **de**, but knowing how to use them isn't a simple matter of translation. **À** often means *to*, *at*, or *in*, and **de** usually means *of*, *from*, or *about*, but you also use these prepositions to indicate other concepts, such as possession or purpose. Therefore, you have to understand not only what they mean, but also how you use them in French. No need to worry, though — the following sections explain how to use the most common prepositions.

The preposition à

À is the French equivalent of *to*, *at*, or *in* — at least, most of the time. It often indicates current location or future destination.

Je suis à l'hôpital. (*I'm at/in the hospital.*)

Je vais à la banque. (*I'm going to the bank.*)

DIFFERENCES

English makes a distinction between whether you're going *to* a place or are currently *at* or *in* it, but French doesn't. **À** covers both of those concepts.

You can also use **à** to mean at a point in time (see Chapter 5 for more on time).

Notre vol est à 14 h 00. (*Our flight is at 2 p.m.*)

Je suis parti à 5 h 30. (*I left at 5:30 a.m.*)

À is also found in expressions related to saying goodbye temporarily, such as **à bientôt** (*see you soon*) and **à la prochaine** (*until next time*).

The preposition **à** has some other uses, as well — you can read about them in the sections "When to use à or de" and "Giving Verbs the Prepositions They Need," later in this chapter.

The preposition de

De is the French equivalent of *of*, *from*, and *about* — usually.

J'ai acheté une bouteille de vin. (*I bought a bottle of wine.*)

Nous parlons de l'école. (*We're talking about school.*)

You use **de** for all these meanings:

>> Cause: **Je meurs de soif !** (*I'm dying of thirst!*)

>> Description: **un guide de voyage** (*a travel guide*)

>> Origin: **Il est de Dakar.** (*He is from Dakar.*)

>> Possession: **le voyage de Simone** (*Simone's trip*)

>> Method or means: **un choc de front** (*head-on crash*)

DIFFERENCES

In English, you use *'s* or *s'* for possession: *Jean's book, my kids' bedroom*. To translate this into French, you have to reverse the words and join them with the preposition **de**: **le livre de Jean, la chambre de mes enfants**. See Chapter 4 for more information about expressing possession in French.

De contracts to **d'** in front of a vowel or mute **h**, such as **la voiture d'Anne** (*Anne's car*).

You need the preposition **de** in other constructions, as well — see the sections "Distinguishing between Prepositions" and "Giving Verbs the Prepositions They Need," later in this chapter.

PRACTICE

Translate these sentences into French, taking care to choose the correct preposition, either **à** or **de**.

Q. I'm talking to Guillaume.

A. Je parle à Guillaume.

1 Let's leave at noon. _____

2 They're from Rabat. _____

3 He's going to the bank. _____

4 Dominique's car is at the beach. _____

5 She wants to go to the grocery store. _____

6 I don't like my friends' cat. _____

7 We bought a history book. _____

8 I'm using my colleague's computer. _____

9 Are you (vous) at the house? _____

10 She arrived from Montreal. _____

Forming contractions with prepositions

When you follow the prepositions **à** and **de** with the definite articles **le** and **les**, you have to contract them. But you don't form contractions with the definite articles **la** and **l'** — see Table 12-1.

Table 12-1   Prepositions, With and Without Contractions

à + Article	Contraction/No Contraction	de + Article	Contraction/No Contraction
à + le	au	**de + le**	du
à + les	aux	**de + les**	des
à + la	à la	**de + la**	de la
à + l'	à l'	**de + l'**	de l'

Take a look at some of these contractions in action:

Je vais [à + le] au marché. (*I'm going to the store.*)

Il se plaint [de + les] des mouches. (*He's complaining about the flies.*)

 WARNING À and **de** contract only with the definite articles **le** and **les**. They don't contract with the direct objects **le** and **les**. (See Chapter 3 for information about definite articles and check out Chapter 13 for more on direct objects).

>> **Je parle du problème.** (*I'm talking about the problem*)

In this sentence, **du [de + le]** means *about the.*

>> **Il m'a dit de le faire.** (*He told me to do it.*)

In this sentence, **le** is what's being done, so **le** is the direct object of **faire** and therefore doesn't contract with **de**.

PRACTICE

Translate these sentences into French. Pay attention to which preposition you need, either **à** or **de**, and whether it has to contract.

Q. I'm going to the museum.

A. Je vais au musée.

11 We're eating at the restaurant. _____

12 They're talking about the dogs. _____

13 She's going to the supermarket. _____

14 My kids are at the park. _____

15 They like going to supermarkets. _____

16 Where are the students' books? _____

17 He's going to see Marie at the café. _____

18 I have the magazines from the office. _____

19 Are you (tu) going to the stores? _____

20 They arrived from the newsstand. _____

Identifying other useful prepositions

Although **à** and **de** are the most common French prepositions, you may hear, read, and use many others on a daily basis. The following list gives you a couple of other useful prepositions that you need to know:

>> **Chez** is one of the most interesting French prepositions. It has several meanings and no simple English equivalent — in different contexts, you can translate it as *at/to the home of, at/to the office of, in the mind of,* or *among.*

  • **Je suis rentré chez moi.** (*I went back [to my] home.*)

  • **Elle va chez le dentiste.** (*She's going to the dentist's office.*)

  • **Chez Sartre, l'enfer, c'est les autres.** (*According to Sartre, hell is other people.*)

  • **Manger en famille est très important chez les Français.** (*Eating as a family is very important to/among the French.*)

>> **En** is another preposition that has multiple meanings — you may translate it as *in* or *to* (for more detailed information about **en**, see the section "When to use dans or en," later in this chapter).

- **Je l'ai fait en 5 minutes.** (*I did it in 5 minutes.*)
- **Je suis en France.** (*I'm in France.*)
- **Nous allons en Algérie.** (*We're going to Algeria.*)

The other important French prepositions have simpler, more one-to-one meanings — see Table 12-2.

Table 12-2 French Prepositions

French Preposition	English Preposition	Example	Translation
après	after	Je suis parti après minuit.	I left after midnight.
avant	before	J'ai mangé avant la fête.	I ate before the party.
avec	with	Il voyage avec sa copine.	He's traveling with his girlfriend.
contre	against	J'ai voté contre lui.	I voted against him.
dans	in	Mets-le dans le tiroir.	Put it in the drawer.
pour	for	Je l'ai acheté pour vous.	I bought it for you.
sans	without	Elle mange sans parler.	She eats without speaking.
sous	under	Cet animal habite sous terre.	This animal lives under the ground.
sur	on	Il y a un carton sur mon lit.	There's a box on my bed.
vers	toward	Continuez vers la plage.	Continue toward the beach.

PRACTICE

Pay careful attention to which preposition you need as you translate these sentences into French.

Q. He's walking toward the park.

A. Il marche vers le parc.

21 Your sweater is in a box. _____

22 The dog is under the table. _____

23 They want to leave before midnight. _____

24 She is at Michel's place. _____

25 We are going toward the park. _____

26 You can eat after the party. _____

27 My books are on the desk. _____

28 I'm going to the dentist's office. _____

29 Are you (tu) for or against this solution? _____

30 I'm leaving with or without you. _____

Distinguishing between Prepositions

Part of the difficulty with French prepositions is that some of them have more than one meaning, and some of them share a meaning with other prepositions — at least, when you translate them into English. In fact, French prepositions are very precise. The ones that seem to share a meaning have specific rules governing their uses. The following sections help you determine how to use the right preposition in the correct manner.

When to use à or de

The French prepositions **à** and **de** have overlapping or complementary meanings, which can be confusing. The key is to understand what they mean in French before you try to translate them into English. The following list spells out when to use each one:

» **Location:** The preposition **à** tells you where something is or will be, and **de** tells you where it was, whether originally or just a little while ago.

- **Je suis à Paris.** (*I'm in Paris.*)
- **Il est de Paris.** (*He is from Paris.*)
- **Je vais à Nice.** (*I'm going to Nice.*)
- **Il arrive de Nice.** (*He is arriving from Nice.*)

» **Description:** When you use **à** between two nouns, the second noun explains the purpose of the first. In comparison, when **de** goes between two nouns, the second noun specifies the contents.

- **une cuillère à thé** (*teaspoon*)
- **une cuillère de thé** (*spoonful of tea*)
- **un verre à eau** (*water glass, glass for water*)
- **un verre d'eau** (*glass of water*)

In addition, many French verbs require either **à** or **de** — see the section "Giving Verbs the Prepositions They Need," later in this chapter.

Purpose or contents? Decide which preposition is needed for the meaning provided: either **à** or **de**.

PRACTICE

Q. une cuillère à / de thé (teaspoon)

A. à

31 une tasse à / de café (coffee cup)

32 une tasse à / de thé (cup of tea)

33 un verre à / de bière (glass of beer)

(34) un verre à / de vin (wine glass)

(35) une assiette à / de dessert (dessert plate)

(36) une assiette à / de fromages (plate of cheeses)

When to use dans or en

Dans and **en** both mean *in*, but they're not interchangeable:

>> **Dans:** Means *in* in reference to both location and time.

>> **En:** In terms of location, **en** can only mean *in a country* or *to a country*. In reference to time, **en** means *in a certain amount of time* or *in a given time period*.

The following list spells out when to use **dans** or **en**:

>> **Location: Dans** means *inside of* something, such as a box, bag, or house.

- **Il y a une souris dans ma chambre !** (*There's a mouse in my bedroom!*)

- **As-tu un stylo dans ton sac ?** (*Do you have a pen in your bag?*)

En can't mean *in* something concrete, such as a box or a bag. It can only mean *in* a country, which you can read about in the following section.

>> **Time:** When you use **dans** followed by a period of time, it means that you'll do something that far in the future.

- **Je vais le faire dans dix minutes.** (*I'm going to do it in ten minutes./I'm going to do it ten minutes from now.*)

- **Nous allons partir dans un mois.** (*We're going to leave in a month.*)

In reference to time, **en** explains how long something takes.

- **Je l'ai fait en dix minutes.** (*I did it in ten minutes./It took me ten minutes to do it.*)

- **Je peux écrire cet article en un mois.** (*I can write this article in a month./It will take me a month to write this article.*)

En can also tell you when something happens — in which month, season, or year.

- **Nous ne travaillons pas en été.** (*We don't work in the summer.*)

- **Il a écrit cet article en 2017.** (*He wrote this article in 2017.*)

PRACTICE Your boss wrote you an e-mail about an upcoming meeting with employees — some of whom have very particular requirements — from other branch offices. Unfortunately, your printer has been acting up, and it left out all the prepositions when you printed it off. Fill in the blanks with the correct preposition: **à**, **de**, **dans**, or **en**.

Q. La réunion va commencer _____ 14 h 00.

A. **La réunion va commencer à 14 h 00.** (*The meeting is going to begin at 2 p.m.*)

New Message

File   Edit   View   Insert   Format   Tools   Message   Help

Send   Cut   Copy   Paste   Undo   **abc✔** Check

From: Françoise Dupré

To: Juliette LaCroix

Cc:

Subject

M. Boumani va arriver **(37)** _____ (from) Tanger **(38)** _____
13h00. Il préfère boire son café dans une tasse **(39)** _____
thé. Sa collègue, Mme Labiya, a besoin d'un verre **(40)** _____
eau dans un verre **(41)** _____ vin. Mlle Leblanc vient
(42) _____ Genève. Elle peut manger tous les hors-d'œuvre
(43) _____ cinq minutes, donc elle ne devrait pas être
assise à côté de la buvette. Les trois employés **(44)** _____
Paris, qui sont déjà venus ici **(45)** _____ mai, n'ont pas
de besoins particuliers. Venez dans mon bureau **(46)** _____
une heure et je peux vous donner les autres détails.

Using Prepositions with Places

In French, you use all kinds of different prepositions with places, depending on whether you're talking about a city or a country — and in the case of a country, depending on the gender, number, and first letter of that country. The following sections clarify the rules so that you can figure out which preposition to use the next time you're traveling or talking about a specific place.

Prepositions with countries

REMEMBER

When choosing between the prepositions to use with countries, you can't just put your hand in the preposition grab bag and pull one out. You have to look at the following three things to determine which preposition to use:

» The gender of the country

» The first letter of the country

» Whether the country is singular or plural

TIP

Determining the gender of countries is simple. Countries that end in –e are feminine: **la France** (*France*), **l'Italie** (*Italy*), and so on. Countries that don't end in –e are masculine: **le Canada** (*Canada*), **le Koweït** (*Kuwait*), and so on. There are only five exceptions — these countries end in –e but are still masculine:

>> **le Bélize** (*Belize*)

>> **le Cambodge** (*Cambodia*)

>> **le Mexique** (*Mexico*)

>> **le Mozambique** (*Mozambique*)

>> **le Zimbabwe** (*Zimbabwe*)

After you determine all of the necessary information for the country in question, you can use the info in the following sections to help you determine which preposition to use in any situation.

Going to or being in a country

DIFFERENCES

English has different prepositions depending on whether you're on your way somewhere or you're already there, but French doesn't. The same preposition expresses both of these ideas.

To say *in* or *to* a singular feminine country, you use the preposition **en** with no article.

Je vais en France. (*I'm going to France.*)

Il habite en Algérie. (*He lives in Algeria*)

You also use **en** for singular masculine countries that begin with a vowel:

Quand vas-tu en Angola ? (*When are you going to Angola?*)

Je veux bien voyager en Ouganda. (*I'd really like to travel to Uganda.*)

To say *in* or *to* a singular masculine country that begins with a consonant or aspirate **h**, you use the preposition **à** plus the definite article **le**, which contracts to **au**.

Nous voyageons au Maroc. (*We're traveling to Morocco.*)

Il veut rester au Honduras. (*He wants to stay in Honduras.*)

For plural countries of either gender, you use **à** plus the plural definite article **les**, which contracts to **aux**.

Nous habitons aux États-Unis. (*We live in the United States.*)

Il va aux Seychelles. (*He's going to the Seychelles.*)

Coming from or being from a country

To say that you're arriving *from*, or are originally *from*, a singular feminine country, use the preposition **de** with no article:

Il arrive de Belgique. (*He's arriving from Belgium.*)

Nous venons de Suisse. (*We are from Switzerland.*)

If the feminine country begins with a vowel, **de** contracts to **d'**:

> **Il arrive d'Islande.** (*He's arriving from Iceland.*)

> **Venez-vous d'Égypte ?** (*Are you from Egypt?*)

When you're arriving or you're originally from a masculine country, use **du** or **d'**:

> **Elle vient du Canada.** (*She is from Canada.*)

> **J'arrive d'Oman.** (*I'm arriving from Oman.*)

To say that you're arriving from or are originally from a plural country, use **des** (**de** plus the plural definite article **les**).

> **Elle arrive des îles Fidji.** (*She's arriving from Fiji.*)

> **Nous venons des États-Unis.** (*We are from the United States.*)

Prepositions with cities

The prepositions you use with cities are much more straightforward. You use **à** to mean *in* or *to* a city and **de** to mean *from*:

> **Nous allons à Genève.** (*We're going to Geneva.*)

> **Ils sont à Casablanca.** (*They're in Casablanca.*)

> **Elle vient de Bruxelles.** (*She's from Brussels.*)

> **Je suis arrivé d'Alger.** (*I arrived from Algiers.*)

PRACTICE

Fill in the blanks with the correct preposition and article, if necessary, for the meaning in parentheses.

Q. Je viens _____ (from) France.

A. Je viens de France. (*I am from France.*)

47) Il va _____ (to) Australie.

48) Nous voyageons _____ (in) Canada.

49) Elle revient _____ (from) Italie.

50) Ils arrivent _____ (from) Mali.

51) Je vais _____ (to) Londres.

52) Elle est _____ (in) Paris.

53) Nous allons _____ (to) Espagne.

54 Elles viennent _____ (from) Irlande.

55 Ils vont _____ (to) Pointe-à-Pitre.

56 Vas-tu _____ (to) États-Unis ?

Giving Verbs the Prepositions They Need

Many French verbs need a preposition when they're followed by an object or an infinitive. English has some verbs that need prepositions, called *phrasal verbs*, but they're not at all the same thing as in French. English phrasal verbs require different prepositions depending on meaning, such as *to move on* and *to move in*.

French has a few verbs that have different meanings, depending on which preposition follows, but most verbs just require a certain preposition that, confusingly, often has no English translation or has a meaning that doesn't correspond to the "normal" meaning of the preposition. This section points out some of the more common verbs and the prepositions that go with them.

Verbs with à

Hundreds of French verbs require the preposition **à**; Appendix B shows some of the most common ones. The preposition doesn't make any difference in the verb conjugation, so to use these verbs, just conjugate each verb according to its status as a regular, stem-changing, irregular, or pronominal verb (check out Chapters 6 and 7 for more on all these verbs), and then follow with the preposition.

> **Fais attention aux instructions.** (*Pay attention to the instructions.*)
>
> **Vas-tu m'inviter à la fête ?** (*Are you going to invite me to the party?*)
>
> **Il a volé cette idée à son collègue.** (*He stole this idea from his colleague.*)

TIP

The French infinitive after **à** often translates more naturally as the present participle in English (you can read more about the difference between French and English infinitives and present participles in Chapter 10).

> **Je m'amuse à regarder les touristes.** (*I enjoy watching the tourists.*)

Verbs with de

Hundreds of French verbs require the preposition **de** (see Appendix B). To use these verbs, just conjugate them (which I explain how to do in Chapters 6 and 7) and follow them with the preposition **de**.

> **Nous refusons de partir.** (*We're refusing to leave.*)
>
> **Il a oublié de se raser.** (*He forgot to shave.*)
>
> **Je viens de manger.** (*I just ate.*)

Verbs with other prepositions

Although **à** and **de** are the most common prepositions after verbs (see the preceding sections), other French prepositions are also required with certain verbs. Just conjugate them, add the preposition, and go! See Appendix B.

> **Il boit toujours sa bière dans une tasse à thé.** (*He always drinks his beer out of a teacup.*)

> **J'ai cassé l'assiette en 10 morceaux.** (*I broke the plate into 10 pieces.*)

> **Notre avocat va parler pour nous.** (*Our lawyer is going to speak for us/on our behalf.*)

Verbs with different prepositions

Although most verbs always require one specific preposition, a few have different meanings according to which preposition you use. See Table 12-3 for some examples. Just conjugate these verbs and follow that conjugated verb with the appropriate preposition. No simple shortcut exists to know which verb uses which preposition, but you can more easily remember them if you include in your vocabulary lists the prepositions that each verb needs and the different translations.

Table 12-3 Verbs with Different Meanings per Preposition

Verb + à	Translation	Verb + Another Preposition	Translation
aller à	*to go to*	**aller vers**	*to go toward, in the direction of*
donner à	*to give to*	**donner contre**	*to trade for, exchange*
être à [quelqu'un]	*to belong to [someone]*	**être**	*to be*
jouer à	*to play a game/sport*	**jouer de**	*to play an instrument*
manquer à quelqu'un	*to miss someone*	**manquer de**	*to almost to do something, to lack*
parler à	*to talk to*	**parler de**	*to talk about*
penser à	*to think about, reflect upon*	**penser de**	*to have an opinion on*
profiter à	*to benefit, be profitable to*	**profiter de**	*to make the most of*
téléphoner à quelqu'un	*to call someone*	**téléphoner pour quelque chose**	*to phone about/regarding something*
tenir à	*to insist on/to care for*	**tenir de**	*to resemble*

Here are some examples showing how the meaning of the verbs in Table 12-3 change when with different prepositions.

> **Je parle à mon frère.** (*I'm talking to my brother.*)

> **Nous parlons de la France.** (*We're talking about France.*)

> **J'ai donné mon vélo à Daniel.** (*I gave Daniel my bike.*)

> **J'ai donné mon vélo contre des écouteurs.** (*I traded my bike for earphones.*)

You can translate both **penser à** and **penser de** as *to think about*, but there's a big difference. **Penser à** means *to have in mind, to consider*, and **penser de** means *to have an opinion on.*

> **Je pense à mes vacances.** (*I'm thinking about my vacation.*)

> **Que penses-tu de cette idée ?** (*What do you think about this idea?*)

Prepositional panic: Determine which preposition to use for the meaning provided.

PRACTICE

Q. Je vais _____ la pharmacie. (*I'm going to the pharmacy.*)

A. à

57 Je joue _____ la guitare. (I play the guitar.)

58 Il veut me donner son vélo _____ mon portable. (He wants to trade his bike for my cellphone.)

59 Cette voiture est _____ ma fille. (This car belongs to my daughter.)

60 Tu tiens vraiment _____ ton papa ! (You look just like your dad!)

61 Ils ont manqué _____ perdre leur emploi. (They almost lost their jobs.)

62 _____ quoi est-ce que tu penses ? (What are you thinking about?)

63 Elle joue _____ la pétanque. (She's playing boules.)

64 Il a téléphoné _____ confirmer le rendez-vous. (He called to confirm the appointment.)

65 Qu'est-ce que vous pensez _____ ma suggestion ? (What do you think of my suggestion?)

66 Nous tenons _____ te parler immédiatement. (We insist on speaking to you immediately.)

Verbs with no preposition

Some French verbs are followed directly by the infinitive or direct object, even though their English equivalents need a preposition. For example, **attendre** means *to wait for* + noun, not *to wait*. To remember these verbs (see Appendix B), in your vocabulary list, be sure to include the English preposition and note whether it's followed by a noun or verb.

> **Je cherche mon sac à dos.** (*I'm looking for my backpack.*)

> **Il ignore mon dilemme.** (*He is unaware of my dilemma.*)

> **Tu es censé travailler aujourd'hui.** (*You're supposed to work today.*)

Answer Key to "An Ode to Prepositions" Practice Questions

1. Partons à midi.

2. Ils/Elles sont de Rabat.

3. Il va à la banque.

4. La voiture de Dominique est à la plage.

5. Elle veut aller à l'épicerie.

6. Je n'aime pas le chat de mes amis/amies.

7. Nous avons/On a acheté un livre d'histoire.

8. J'utilise l'ordinateur de mon/ma collègue.

9. Êtes-vous à la maison ?/Est-ce que vous êtes à la maison ?/Vous êtes à la maison ?

10. Elle est arrivée de Montréal.

11. Nous mangeons/On mange au restaurant.

12. Ils/Elles parlent des chiens.

13. Elle va au supermarché.

14. Mes enfants sont au parc.

15. Ils/Elles aiment aller aux supermarchés.

16. Où sont les livres des étudiants ?/Où est-ce que sont les livres des étudiants ?

17. Il va voir Marie au café.

18. J'ai les magazines du bureau.

19. Est-ce que tu vas aux magasins ?/Vas-tu aux magasins ?/Tu vas aux magasins ?

20. Ils sont arrivés du kiosque.

21. Ton pull est dans un carton./Ton pull est dans une boîte.

22. Le chien est sous la table.

23. Ils/Elles veulent partir avant minuit.

24. Elle est chez Michel.

25. Nous allons vers le parc.

26. Tu peux/Vous pouvez manger après la fête.

(27) Mes livres sont sur le bureau.

(28) Je vais chez le dentiste.

(29) Es-tu pour ou contre cette solution ?/Est-ce que tu es pour ou contre cette solution ?/Tu es pour ou contre cette solution ?

(30) Je pars avec ou sans toi/vous.

(31) une tasse à café

(32) une tasse de thé

(33) un verre de bière

(34) un verre à vin

(35) une assiette à dessert

(36) une assiette de fromages

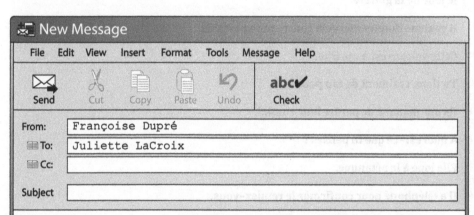

New Message

File   Edit   View   Insert   Format   Tools   Message   Help

Send   Cut   Copy   Paste   Undo   abc✔ Check

From: Françoise Dupré
To: Juliette LaCroix
Cc:
Subject:

M. Boumani va arriver **(37) de** Tanger **(38) à** 13h00. Il préfère boire son café dans une tasse **(39) à** thé. Sa collègue, Mme Labiya, a besoin d'un verre **(40) d'**eau dans un verre **(41) à** vin. Mlle Leblanc vient **(42) de** Genève. Elle peut manger tous les hors- d'œuvre **(43) en** cinq minutes, donc elle ne devrait pas être assise à côté de la buvette. Les trois employés **(44) de** Paris, qui sont déjà venus ici **(45) en** mai, n'ont pas de besoins particuliers. Venez dans mon bureau **(46) dans** une heure et je peux vous donner les autres détails.

(Mr. Boumani will arrive from Tangiers at 1 p.m. He prefers to drink his coffee from a teacup. His colleague, Mrs. Labiya, needs a glass of water in a wine glass. Miss Leblanc is from Genève. She can eat all the hors d'oeuvres in five minutes, so she should not be seated next to the buffet. The three employees from Paris, who already came here in May, don't have any special needs. Come to my office in an hour and I can give you the other details.)

(47) **Il va en Australie.** (*He's going to Australia.*)

(48) **Nous voyageons au Canada.** (*We're traveling in Canada.*)

(49) **Elle revient d'Italie.** (*She's coming back from Italy.*)

(50) **Ils arrivent du Mali.** (*They're arriving from Mali.*)

(51) **Je vais à Londres.** (*I'm going to London.*)

(52) **Elle est à Paris.** (*She is in Paris.*)

(53) **Nous allons en Espagne.** (*We are going to Spain.*)

(54) **Elles viennent d'Irlande.** (*They are from Ireland.*)

(55) **Ils vont à Pointe-à-Pitre.** (*They're going to Pointe-à-Pitre.*)

(56) **Vas-tu aux États-Unis ?** (*Are you going to the U.S.?*)

(57) **Je joue de la guitare.**

(58) **Il veut me donner son vélo contre mon portable.**

(59) **Cette voiture est à ma fille.**

(60) **Tu tiens vraiment de ton papa !**

(61) **Ils ont manqué de perdre leur emploi.**

(62) **À quoi est-ce que tu penses ?**

(63) **Elle joue à la pétanque.**

(64) **Il a téléphoné pour confirmer le rendez-vous.**

(65) **Qu'est-ce que vous pensez de ma suggestion ?**

(66) **Nous tenons à te parler immédiatement.**

Chapter **13**

Getting a Hold on Pronouns

Object and adverbial pronouns are little words that provide a lot of information. Direct and indirect objects tell you who or what is being looked at, spoken to, or otherwise acted upon, such as in *I gave the book to Tim* (*book* is the direct object and *Tim* is the indirect object); object pronouns replace them to keep you from repeating the same words over and over (and over and over), as in *I gave it to him* (*it* and *him* are object pronouns). Similarly, adverbial pronouns replace certain phrases to give you the same amount of information in less space. For instance, in *We went to France and lived there for two months*, the word *there* would be translated by the adverbial pronoun **y** in French.

To use object and adverbial pronouns effectively, you have to understand what they mean and where they go in the sentence, as well as what order they go in when you use two at the same time. This chapter explains direct object, indirect object, and adverbial pronouns, as well as the correct order for two pronouns working together.

Using Object Pronouns

As I explain in Chapter 1, pronouns replace nouns. An object pronoun is a specific type of pronoun that replaces an *object* in the grammatical sense of a noun that a verb acts upon.

Despite the objectified nature of the word, the grammatical term *objects* doesn't mean you're always talking about things like books and trees — they can, and often do, refer to people and animals. So watch out: If you don't know your French object pronouns, you may end up saying something like "I ate you" instead of "I ate it"!

In a rare case of linguistic logic, direct object pronouns replace direct objects, and indirect object pronouns replace indirect objects. The following sections spell out how to use direct and indirect object pronouns so everyone knows exactly what you're writing or talking about.

Presenting direct object pronouns

A *direct object* is a person or thing that a verb is acting on. When a direct object is a noun (as opposed to a pronoun), the direct object usually comes after the verb in both French and English, and you can tell it's a direct object because it doesn't have a preposition in front of it. For example, **Je vois un chien** (*I see a dog*).

TIP

To use a direct object pronoun, you first need to be able to identify the direct object, which you can do by asking the question, "Who or what is + [whatever the verb is]?" For example, in the sentence, **Lise connaît l'athlète** (*Lise knows the athlete*), **Lise** is the *subject* of the sentence — she's the person who knows. To find the direct object, you ask, "Who is known?" **Athlète** is the *object* — the person Lise knows.

Or in this sentence, **Mon frère déteste les glaces à l'eau** (*My brother hates popsicles*), ask "Who hates?" **Mon frère.** So **mon frère** is the *subject* — the person who hates. Ask, "What does he hate?" The answer — **les glaces à l'eau** — is the *object*, the things that he hates.

Asking "who or what is . . . ?" with these two examples, you discover the direct objects: Who is known? The athlete. What is hated? Popsicles. (And who is clearly bonkers? The guy who hates popsicles!)

REMEMBER

Transitive verbs are verbs that need direct objects — verbs such as *to like* and *to watch*. You can't say *I like* without a direct object — the sentence isn't complete. You have to say *I like you, I like chocolate, I like polka-dot slippers.* Verbs that don't need direct objects, such as *to walk* and *to travel*, are *intransitive verbs.*

Of course, some verbs, such as *to read*, can be both transitive and intransitive: *I read the newspaper* (transitive) versus *I read every day* (intransitive). Knowing the difference between transitive and intransitive helps you figure out whether you need a direct object as well as choose the right translation when you look up verbs in a dictionary (see Chapter 2).

In the same way that you can replace the subjects **Lise** and **mon frère** with subject pronouns (see Chapter 1), you can replace the direct objects **l'athlète** and **les glaces à l'eau** with direct object pronouns.

DIFFERENCES

In English, both direct objects and direct object pronouns follow the verb. In French, too, direct objects (the actual nouns) follow the verb. However, French direct object pronouns precede the verb.

Lise le connaît. (*Lise knows him.*)

Mon frère les déteste. (*My brother hates them.*)

When you choose a direct object pronoun, you have to consider the gender and number of the object you're replacing, as well as the grammatical person, because each of these genders, numbers, and persons have different forms. See Table 13-1 for the French direct object pronouns.

Table 13-1   Direct Object Pronouns

Subject Pronoun	Direct Object Pronoun	Translation
je	me (m', moi)	me
tu	te (t', toi)	you
il	le (l')	him, it
elle	la (l')	her, it
nous	nous	us
vous	vous	you
ils, elles	les	them

Word order with direct object pronouns

When asking a question (see Chapter 8) with **est-ce que**, the direct object pronoun stays in front of the verb.

> **Est-ce qu'elle le connaît ?** (*Does she know him?*)
>
> **Est-ce qu'il les déteste ?** (*Does he hate them?*)

Likewise with inversion (see Chapter 8), the direct object pronoun precedes the verb.

> **Le connaît-elle ?** (*Does she know him?*)
>
> **Les déteste-t-il ?** (*Does he hate them?*)

PRACTICE

Rewrite these sentences, replacing the underlined phrase with a direct object pronoun.

Q. Je vois <u>mon frère</u>.

A. **Je le vois.** (*I see him.*)

1. Il cherche <u>ses clés</u>. _____

2. Nous connaissons <u>cette ville</u>. _____

3. Avez-vous <u>la réponse</u> ? _____

4. Je finis <u>notre itinéraire</u>. _____

5. Qui connaît <u>Anne</u> ? _____

6. Elle veut <u>le livre</u>. _____

7. Nous voyons les chiens. _____

8. Cherches-tu la viande ? _____

9. Je sais la vérité. _____

10. Ils achètent les provisions. _____

When you have two verbs (a conjugated verb + an infinitive) in French (see Chapter 10), the pronoun precedes the infinitive, as in **Je dois le faire** (*I have to do it*).

In the **passé composé** (see Chapter 15), the direct object pronoun precedes the auxiliary verb, like with **Je l'ai fait** (*I did it*).

Whenever they precede a vowel, a mute **h**, or the adverbial pronoun **y**, the pronouns **me** and **te** contract to **m'** and **t'**, respectively, and both **le** and **la** contract to **l'**.

> **Je t'aime.** (*I love you.*)
>
> **Il l'adore.** (*He adores him/her/it.*)

In the affirmative imperative (see Chapter 14), the word order is different: Like reflexive pronouns, direct object pronouns follow the verb and are attached to it with hyphens.

> **Trouvez-le.** (*Find it.*)
>
> **Aide-nous.** (*Help us.*)

In addition, **me** changes to **moi** and **te** changes to **toi**:

> **Écoute-moi !** (*Listen to me!*)
>
> **Habille-toi.** (*Get dressed.*)

Translate these sentences into French. The parentheticals (m) and (f) indicate the gender of the preceding word, while (**tu**) and (**vous**) let you know which version of "you" to use. (See Chapter 1 for the different ways to say "you" in French.)

Q. He knows me.

A. Il me connaît.

11. I can see you. (vous) _____

12. My friends don't understand me. _____

13. Look (vous) at me. _____

14. Are they (f) listening to us? _____

15. I love them. _____

16 We have it. (f) _____

17 They (m) are going to drink it. (f) _____

18 I saw it. (m) _____

19 Do you (tu) want them? _____

20 We have to buy it. (m) _____

Giving you indirect object pronouns

Indirect objects are the people or animals that a verb is happening to or for. Indirect objects usually follow a preposition, such as **à** (*to*) or **pour** (*for*). (See Chapter 12 to read more about prepositions.)

Before you can correctly use an indirect object pronoun, you first need to have a firm grasp of what an indirect object pronoun is. To figure out the indirect object, you can ask, "To whom?" or "For whom?"

> **Elle parle à ses amis.** (*She's talking to her friends.*)

Elle is the subject of the preceding sentence — she's the person who's talking. And **ses amis** is the indirect object — the people she's talking to.

> **J'achète des livres pour ma nièce.** (*I'm buying some books for my niece./I'm buying my niece some books.*)

Je is the subject of the preceding sentence — the person who's buying. And **ma nièce** is the indirect object — the person I'm buying books for.

So now you can replace the indirect objects in the preceding examples with indirect object pronouns:

> **Elle leur parle.** (*She's talking to them.*)

> **Je lui achète des livres.** (*I'm buying her some books.*)

REMEMBER

When using indirect object pronouns, you need to figure out the grammatical person of the object you want to replace, and then choose the corresponding indirect object pronoun.

See Table 13-2 for the French indirect object pronouns.

TIP

The French indirect object pronouns for first and second person, singular and plural, are the same as the direct ones (**me, te, nous, vous**) — only the third-person singular and plural are different.

Lui is the indirect object pronoun for both men and women.

> **Il parle à David.** (*He's talking to David.*) becomes **Il lui parle.** (*He's talking to him.*)

> **Je parle à ma mère.** (*I'm talking to my mother.*) becomes **Je lui parle.** (*I'm talking to her.*)

Table 13-2   Indirect Object Pronouns

Subject Pronoun	Indirect Object Pronoun	Translation
je	me (m', moi)	me
tu	te (t', toi)	you
il, elle	lui	him, her
nous	nous	us
vous	vous	you
ils, elles	leur	them

Note that the third–person plural indirect object is **leur**, not to be confused with the possessive adjective **leur/leurs** (see Chapter 4).

> **Nous leur parlons.** (*We're talking to them.*)

The word order for indirect object pronouns is exactly the same as for direct object pronouns (see the preceding section). Here's a rundown of how indirect object pronouns are positioned:

>> **With a single verb:** In front of the verb, including in questions

>> **With two verbs:** In front of the second verb

>> **In the passé composé:** In front of the auxiliary verb

>> **In the affirmative imperative:** After the verb, joined by a hyphen

Take a look at some indirect object pronouns in action according to the preceding rules:

> **Lui parlez-vous souvent ?** (*Do you talk to him/her often?*)
>
> **Je vais leur donner des conseils.** (*I'm going to give them some advice.*)
>
> **Il nous a envoyé une lettre.** (*He sent a letter to us./He sent us a letter.*)
>
> **Parlons-lui.** (*Let's talk to him/her.*)

WARNING

Some verbs that have direct objects in French have an indirect object in English, and some English verbs that have direct objects have indirect objects in French. You don't use a preposition after **regarder** and **écouter**, for example, so the person or thing being looked at or listened to is a direct object in French. But in English, you say *look at* and *listen to*, which means the person or thing being looked at or listened to *isn't* a direct object. See Chapter 12 for more information about verbs with prepositions.

> **Tu le regardes.** (*You're looking at him.*) Not ~~Tu lui regardes.~~
>
> **Je les écoute.** (*I'm listening to them.*) Not ~~Je leur écoute.~~

PRACTICE

Rewrite sentences 21 through 25, replacing the underlined phrase with an indirect object pronoun. Then translate sentences 26 through 30 into French.

Q. Je parle à mes parents.

A. Je leur parle. (*I'm talking to them.*)

21. Il téléphone à Pierre. _____

22. Nous demandons de l'argent <u>à notre entraîneur</u>. _____

23. Vas-tu acheter cette bicyclette <u>pour moi</u> ? _____

24. Parlez <u>à vos collègues</u>. _____

25. J'ai emprunté un stylo <u>à Sylvie</u>. _____

26. He told me to leave. _____

27. He advises us. _____

28. They stole some money from us. _____

29. She didn't talk to me. _____

30. I'm asking you (guys) to help. _____

Understanding Adverbial Pronouns

Adverbial pronouns are similar to indirect object pronouns in that they replace a preposition + noun. However, the nouns that *adverbial pronouns* replace aren't indirect objects — they're prepositional phrases. (For example, in English, *to the beach* is a prepositional phrase.) *Prepositional phrases* provide additional information about the verb, but unlike indirect objects, they're not acted upon by the verb. The following sections give you the lowdown on the two adverbial pronouns and how to use them correctly.

Getting there with the adverbial pronoun y

You can use the adverbial pronoun **y** to replace the prepositions **à**, **chez**, **dans**, or **en** + [a place] to mean *there*. The adverbial pronoun **y** goes in exactly the same place as direct and indirect object pronouns.

> **Je vais à la plage.** (*I'm going to the beach.*) becomes **J'y vais.** (*I'm going there.*)

> **Elle a passé deux jours en France.** (*She spent two days in France.*) becomes **Elle y a passé deux jours.** (*She spent two days there.*)

DIFFERENCES In the same way that transitive verbs need a direct object to be complete, French verbs that need the preposition **à** (such as **aller** [*to go*]), need either **à** + noun or the adverbial pronoun **y** to be complete. In English, you can simply say, "I'm going," but in French, that's not a complete sentence — you have to do one of two things:

➤➤ Say where you're going, as in **Je vais chez moi.** (*I'm going home.*)

➤➤ Use **y**, such as **J'y vais.** (*I'm going [there].*)

You can also use **y** to replace **à** + [a thing] when the verb in the sentence requires the preposition **à**. In the section "Giving you indirect object pronouns," earlier in this chapter, I explain that you can replace **à** + noun with an indirect object pronoun. So what's the difference?

>> The indirect object tells you **whom** (person or animal) something is being done to or for.

>> The adverbial pronoun **y** tells you **what** (inanimate object) something is being done to or for.

In French, indirect object pronouns can replace only people and animals; you have to replace places and things with the adverbial pronoun **y**. (See Chapter 12 to read about verbs that need a preposition.) The following sentences talk about things.

> **Je réponds à la lettre.** (*I'm responding to the letter.*) becomes **J'y réponds.** (*I'm responding to it.*)

> **Nous obéissons aux lois.** (*We obey the laws.*) becomes **Nous y obéissons.** (*We obey them.*)

But these sentences talk about people:

> **Je réponds à mon ami.** (*I'm responding to my friend.*) becomes **Je lui réponds.** (*I'm responding to him.*)

> **Nous obéissons à nos parents.** (*We obey our parents.*) becomes **Nous leur obéissons.** (*We obey them.*)

PRACTICE

Rewrite sentences 31 through 35, replacing the underlined phrase with **y**. Then translate sentences 36 through 40 into French.

Q. Nous allons à Montréal.

A. Nous y allons. (*We're going [there].*)

31 Il travaille <u>dans la bibliothèque</u>. _____

32 Je réfléchis <u>à ma vie</u>. _____

33 Vas-tu conduire <u>en Europe</u> tout seul ? _____

34 Je suis <u>à la banque</u>. _____

35 Je ne suis jamais allé <u>aux îles Caraïbes</u>. _____

36 Did you (guys) attend it? _____

37 He entered it. _____

38 They are going to answer it. _____

39 We're thinking about them (the books). _____

40 I'm going now. _____

Adverbial grammar: Picking up more of it with the pronoun en

The adverbial pronoun **en** usually translates to *some* or *of it/them*. To use the adverbial pronoun **en**, you replace one or more words with **en**. The word order for **en** is the same as for object pronouns and the adverbial pronoun **y** (see the section "Presenting direct object pronouns," earlier in this chapter, for details).

WARNING

Be careful not to mix up the adverbial pronoun **en** with the preposition **en** — see Chapter 12 for discussion of **en** as a preposition.

You can use **en** to replace

>> **De** + noun

>> Partitive article + noun

>> Noun after a number

>> Noun after an adverb of quantity

See Chapter 3 for info about articles and nouns.

En replaces de + noun

When you have the preposition **de** or the partitive article (**du**, **de la**, **de l'**, or **des**), **en** replaces the preposition or article, as well as the noun following it:

> **Nous parlons d'amour.** (*We're talking about love.*) becomes **Nous en parlons.** (*We're talking about it.*)

> **Je veux des fraises.** (*I want some strawberries.*) becomes **J'en veux.** (*I want some [of them].*)

TIP

In English you say, *I want some*. You can't just say *I want* — at least, not if you're older than four. Likewise, in French, **je veux** is incomplete. Like in the preceding example sentence, if you don't include **des fraises**, you have to replace it with **en**.

En with numbers

When you use **en** in a sentence with a number + noun, it replaces only the noun — you still need to keep the number after the verb.

> **Il a trois voitures.** (*He has three cars.*) becomes **Il en a trois.** (*He has three [of them].*)

> **J'ai acheté une douzaine de livres.** (*I bought a dozen books.*) becomes **J'en ai acheté une douzaine.** (*I bought a dozen [of them].*)

DIFFERENCES

In English, *of it* or *of them* is usually optional. As long as everyone knows you're talking about cars or books, you can just say, *he has three* or *I bought a dozen*. But in French, **il a trois** and **j'ai acheté une douzaine** are incomplete — if you don't include the nouns, you have to replace them with **en**.

En with adverbs of quantity

With adverbs of quantity, **en** replaces **de** + noun, but you still need the adverb, so you tack it on the end (see Chapter 11 for more info on adverbs).

Avez-vous beaucoup de temps libre ? (*Do you have a lot of spare time?*) becomes **En avez-vous beaucoup ?** (*Do you have a lot [of it]?*)

Je mange très peu d'avocats. (*I eat very few avocados.*) becomes **J'en mange très peu.** (*I eat very few [of them].*)

PRACTICE

Rewrite these sentences, replacing all or part of the underlined phrase with **en**.

Q. Je veux <u>de la salade</u>.

A. **J'en veux.** (*I want some.*)

(41) Nous connaissons <u>beaucoup d'artistes</u>. _____

(42) Elle a <u>pas mal d'idées</u>. _____

(43) J'ai besoin de <u>six chaises</u>. _____

(44) Avez-vous <u>un stylo</u> ? _____

(45) Il a bu <u>du thé</u>. _____

(46) Que penses-tu <u>du résultat</u> ? _____

(47) Je n'ai pas <u>d'enfants</u>. _____

(48) Elle connaît <u>quatre mécaniciens</u>. _____

(49) Nous cherchons <u>des chaussures</u>. _____

(50) Est-ce que tu veux <u>une pomme</u> ? _____

Positioning Double Pronouns

In English, you can't say, "I bought for him it" — you have to say, "I bought it for him." This word order is non-negotiable. The same is true in French: Pronouns have to go in a certain order.

Object pronouns and adverbial pronouns, as well as reflexive pronouns (see Chapter 7), all go in the same place: in front of the verb — except in the affirmative imperative (flip to Chapter 14 for talk of imperatives). But you have more to consider when you have two of these pronouns in the same sentence. They both go in front of the verb, but which comes first? The following sections spell it out.

Lining up: Standard pronoun order

Using any combination of two object, adverbial, and/or reflexive pronouns together requires a very specific word order, but before I get into all that, check out Table 13-3 for a summary of the personal pronouns.

Table 13-3   Object and Reflexive Pronouns

Subject Pronoun	Reflexive Pronoun	Direct Object Pronoun	Indirect Object Pronoun
je	me	me	me
tu	te	te	te
il	se	le	lui
elle	se	la	lui
nous	nous	nous	nous
vous	vous	vous	vous
ils, elles	se	les	leur

Here's the order:

REMEMBER

1. **Me, te, se, nous,** or **vous**

2. **Le, la,** or **les**

3. **Lui** or **leur**

4. **Y**

5. **En**

Of course, you can't have a bunch of these pronouns in the same sentence — two is the maximum. Check out the following examples of correctly placed pronouns:

> **Il m'a donné le livre.** (*He gave me the book.*) becomes **Il me l'a donné.** (*He gave it to me.*)
>
> **Elle nous en parle.** (*She's talking to us about it.*)
>
> **Je vais le lui montrer.** (*I'm going to show it to him.*)
>
> **Il y en a trois.** (*There are three [of them].*)

TIP

Me, te, nous, and **vous** are identical as direct, indirect, and reflexive pronouns, and they all come first when you have double pronouns.

If you have a sentence that contains more than two things that could potentially be replaced with these pronouns, you can just pick two to replace and leave the other(s) as-is. Take the sentence **J'ai acheté des vêtements pour vous à Paris.** (*I bought some clothes for you in Paris*).

This sentence has three phrases that you can replace with pronouns:

>> **des vêtements** (*some clothes*) can be replaced by the adverbial pronoun **en** (*some*)

>> **pour vous** (*for you*) can be replaced by the indirect pronoun **vous** (*you*)

>> **à Paris** (*in Paris*) can be replaced by the adverbial pronoun **y** (*there*)

So by choosing any two of the replacements, here are the three different ways to rewrite the sentence:

>> **Je vous y ai acheté des vêtements.** (*I bought you some clothes there.*)

>> **Je vous en ai acheté à Paris.** (*I bought you some in Paris.*)

>> **J'y en ai acheté pour vous.** (*I bought some for you there.*)

Using pronouns in commands

You use the word order discussed in the preceding section for all verb tenses, moods, and constructions, except the affirmative imperative (see Chapter 14 for more on commands). In the affirmative imperative, the pronouns follow the verb and are joined to it with hyphens; here's the slightly different double-pronoun order that applies to affirmative imperatives:

1. **Le, la,** or **les**

2. **Moi, toi, lui, nous, vous,** or **leur**

3. **Y**

4. **En**

Remember that the pronouns **me** and **te** change to **moi** and **toi** in affirmative commands (see Chapter 14).

The important difference between the affirmative imperative compared to the other verb constructions (see the preceding section) is that the direct objects **le, la,** and **les** now come first, rather than second.

> **Montrez-le-moi.** (*Show it to me.*)
>
> **Donnez-nous-en.** (*Give us some.*)
>
> **Va-t'en !** (*Go away!*)

PRACTICE

Answer these questions by using double pronouns. You can answer however you like; I provide possible responses in the Answer Key at the end of this chapter so that you can check your choice and placement of pronouns.

Q. Combien d'amis as-tu en France?

A. J'y en ai trois. (*I have three there.*)

51 Vas-tu t'habituer à la pluie ?

52 Peut-elle m'envoyer le paquet à mon bureau ?

53 Quand vont-ils montrer le film aux enfants ?

54 Pouvez-vous me donner les clés ?

55 Veux-tu prendre un verre chez moi ?

Answer Key to "Getting a Hold on Pronouns" Practice Questions

1. **Il les cherche.** (*He's looking for them.*)

2. **Nous la connaissons.** (*We are familiar with it.*)

3. **L'avez-vous ?** (*Do you have it?*)

4. **Je le finis.** (*I'm finishing it.*)

5. **Qui la connaît ?** (*Who knows her?*)

6. **Elle le veut.** (*She wants it.*)

7. **Nous les voyons.** (*We see them.*)

8. **La cherches-tu ?** (*Are you looking for it?*)

9. **Je la sais.** (*I know it.*)

10. **Ils les achètent.** (*They're buying them.*)

11. **Je peux vous voir.**

12. **Mes amis/amies ne me comprennent pas.**

13. **Regardez-moi.**

14. **Est-ce qu'elles nous écoutent ?/Nous écoutent-elles ?/Elles nous écoutent ?**

15. **Je les aime.**

16. **Nous l'avons/On l'a.**

17. **Ils vont la boire.**

18. **Je l'ai vu.**

19. **Est-ce que tu les veux ?/Les veux-tu ?/Tu les veux ?**

20. **Nous devons l'acheter.**

21. **Il lui téléphone.** (*He's calling him.*)

22. **Nous lui demandons de l'argent.** (*We are asking him for some money.*)

23. **Vas-tu m'acheter cette bicyclette ?** (*Are you going to buy me this bike?*)

24. **Parlez-leur.** (*Talk to them.*)

25. **Je lui ai emprunté un stylo.** (*I borrowed a pen from her.*)

26. **Il m'a dit de partir.**

27. **Il nous conseille.**

(28) **Ils nous ont volé de l'argent.**

(29) **Elle ne m'a pas parlé.**

(30) **Je vous demande d'aider.**

(31) **Il y travaille.** (*He works there.*)

(32) **J'y réfléchis.** (*I'm thinking about it.*)

(33) **Vas-tu y conduire tout seul ?** (*Are you going to drive there all alone?*)

(34) **J'y suis.** (*I'm there.*)

(35) **Je n'y suis jamais allé.** (*I've never been there.*)

(36) **Est-ce que vous y avez assisté ?/Y avez-vous assisté ?/Vous y avez assisté ?**

(37) **Il y est entré.**

(38) **Ils/Elles vont y répondre.**

(39) **Nous y pensons.**

(40) **J'y vais maintenant.**

(41) **Nous en connaissons beaucoup.** (*We know a lot [of them].*)

(42) **Elle en a pas mal.** (*She has quite a few [of them].*)

(43) **J'en ai besoin de six.** (*I need six [of them].*)

(44) **En avez-vous un ?** (*Do you have one?*)

(45) **Il en a bu.** (*He drank some.*)

(46) **Qu'en penses-tu ?** (*What do you think about it?*)

(47) **Je n'en ai pas.** (*I don't have any.*)

(48) **Elle en connaît quatre.** (*She knows four [of them].*)

(49) **Nous en cherchons.** (*We're looking for some.*)

(50) **Est-ce que tu en veux une ?** (*Do you want one?*)

(51) **Oui, je vais m'y habituer.** (*Yes, I'm going to get used to it.*)

Non, je ne vais pas m'y habituer. (*Yes, I'm going to get used to it.* (*No, I'm not going to get used to it.*)

(52) **Oui, elle peut t'y envoyer le paquet.** (*Yes, she can send you the package there.*)

Oui, elle peut te l'envoyer à ton bureau. (*Yes, she can send it to you at your office.*)

Non, elle ne peut pas t'y envoyer le paquet. (*No, she can't send you the package there.*)

Non, elle ne peut pas te l'envoyer à ton bureau. (*No, she can't send it to you at your office.*)

(53) **Ils vont le leur montrer demain.** (*They're going to show it to them tomorrow.*)

(54) **Oui, je peux vous les donner.** (*Yes, I can give them to you.*)

Non, je ne peux pas vous les donner. (*No, I can't give them to you.*)

(55) **Oui, je veux y en prendre un.** (*Yes, I want to have one there.*)

Non, je ne veux pas y en prendre un. (*No, I don't want to have one there.*)

4

Just Do It, and Now You've Done It: Commands and Past Tenses

Chapter **14**

I Command You: The Imperative

The *imperative* is the verb mood used for giving orders, making suggestions, and offering advice. It's the only personal French verb form that you don't use with a subject pronoun, but it's still *personal* because it has different forms for each of the three grammatical persons that you can give orders to: **tu** (*you*, singular and informal), **nous** (*we*), and **vous** (*you*, plural and/or formal).

The imperative is a *mood*, not a tense — it indicates something that you're telling someone to do, but because that person may or may not actually do it, you don't use the indicative. A *mood* is a verb form that indicates how the speaker feels about the action of the verb, whether it's a command (the imperative mood, explained in this chapter), real (the indicative mood), conditional (the conditional mood), or subjective (the subjunctive mood).

This chapter explains how to conjugate the imperative, covers the differences between affirmative and negative commands, and provides some ways to give commands without the imperative.

Conjugating the Imperative

There are only three imperative conjugations: **tu** (*you*, singular and informal), **nous** (*we*), and **vous** (*you*, plural and/or formal). With no subject pronoun to guide you, getting the imperative conjugations right is extra important because they're the only things that tell you who's being ordered to do something. The following sections show you how to conjugate the imperative of regular, irregular, and reflexive verbs.

Regular verbs

The imperative conjugations of many French verbs are exactly the same as the present tense — except that you don't use a subject pronoun with them. (Check out Chapter 6 for how to conjugate regular verbs in the present tense.)

Imperative of –er verbs

Regular **–er** verbs use their present tense conjugations for the **nous** and **vous** imperative. (Just drop **–er** from the infinitive, and then add **–ons** for the **nous** form or **–ez** for the **vous** form.) For the **tu** form, however, **–er** verbs use their present tense conjugation minus the final **s**.

See Table 14-1 for the present tense and imperative of **parler** (*to talk, to speak*) — the subject pronouns are in parentheses to remind you that you don't use them with the imperative.

Table 14-1   Imperative of Parler (to Talk, Speak), a Regular –er Verb

Present Tense	Translation	Imperative	Translation
tu parles	*you talk, you speak*	**(tu) parle**	*talk, speak*
nous parlons	*we talk, we speak*	**(nous) parlons**	*let's talk, let's speak*
vous parlez	*you talk, you speak*	**(vous) parlez**	*talk, speak*

PRACTICE

Provide all three imperative forms for each of these verbs.

Q. marcher

A. **marche, marchons, marchez** (*walk, let's walk, walk*)

1 travailler _____

2 étudier _____

3 danser _____

4 chanter _____

5 penser _____

6 compter _____

7 écouter _____

8 jouer _____

Imperative of –ir and –re verbs

Imperative conjugations for regular –ir and –re verbs are the same as the present tense in all three forms.

For –ir verbs, drop the –ir from the infinitive and add

> » –is for the tu form
>
> » –issons for the nous form
>
> » –issez for the vous form

Table 14-2 shows the conjugations of a regular –ir verb, choisir (*to choose*).

Table 14-2 Imperative of Choisir (to Choose), a Regular –ir Verb

Present Tense	Translation	Imperative	Translation
tu choisis	*you choose*	(tu) choisis	*choose*
nous choisissons	*we choose*	(nous) choisissons	*let's choose*
vous choisissez	*you choose*	(vous) choisissez	*choose*

For –re verbs, drop the –re and add

> » –s for the tu form
>
> » –ons for the nous form
>
> » –ez for the vous form

See Table 14-3 for the imperative forms of a regular –re verb, vendre (*to sell*).

Table 14-3 Imperative of Vendre (to Sell), a Regular –re Verb

Present Tense	Translation	Imperative	Translation
tu vends	*you sell*	(tu) vends	*sell*
nous vendons	*we sell*	(nous) vendons	*let's sell*
vous vendez	*you sell*	(vous) vendez	*sell*

Note: The tu imperative of –er verbs doesn't end in s, but the tu imperative of –ir and –re verbs does.

PRACTICE

Provide all three imperative forms for each of these verbs.

Q. obéir

A. obéis, obéissons, obéissez (*obey, let's obey, obey*)

⑨ finir _____

⑩ étendre _____

⑪ réussir _____

⑫ défendre _____

⑬ courir _____

⑭ attendre _____

⑮ répondre_____

⑯ agir _____

Irregular verbs

As long as you know how to conjugate irregular verbs in the present tense, you shouldn't have any trouble figuring out their imperative conjugations because most irregular verbs use the same conjugations for the present tense and the imperative. (Check out Chapter 6 to see how to conjugate irregular verbs in the present tense.) The following sections show you how to conjugate the various irregular verbs in the imperative.

Irregular –er verbs

Stem-changing and spelling-change verbs follow the same rules as regular –er verbs in the imperative (see the section "Imperative of –er verbs," earlier in this chapter): They use their present tense conjugations for the **nous** and **vous** imperative and the present tense minus the final **s** for the **tu** form. Table 14-4 and Table 14-5 show examples of these conjugations by using the stem-changing verb **acheter** (*to buy*) and the spelling-change verb **commencer** (*to begin*).

Table 14-4   Imperative of Acheter (to Buy), a Stem-Changing Verb

Present Tense	Translation	Imperative	Translation
tu achètes	*you buy*	(tu) achète	*buy*
nous achetons	*we buy*	(nous) achetons	*let's buy*
vous achetez	*you buy*	(vous) achetez	*buy*

Table 14-5   Imperative of Commencer (to Begin), a Spelling-Change Verb

Present Tense	Translation	Imperative	Translation
tu commences	*you begin*	(tu) commence	*begin*
nous commençons	*we begin*	(nous) commençons	*let's begin*
vous commencez	*you begin*	(vous) commencez	*begin*

Aller (*to go*), the only truly irregular **–er** verb, also follows this pattern. See Table 14-6.

Table 14-6   Imperative of the Irregular Verb Aller (to Go)

Present Tense	Translation	Imperative	Translation
tu vas	*you go*	**(tu) va**	*go*
nous allons	*we go*	**(nous) allons**	*let's go*
vous allez	*you go*	**(vous) allez**	*go*

Provide all three imperative forms for each of these verbs.

Q. commencer

A. **commence, commençons, commencez** (*begin, let's begin, begin*)

17   peser _____

18   manger _____

19   jeter _____

20   nettoyer _____

21   effacer _____

22   répéter_____

23   bouger _____

24   aller _____

Irregular –ir and –re verbs

The imperative of most irregular **–ir** and **–re** verbs is the same as the present tense (without the subject pronoun, of course). Take a look at Table 14-7 for the irregular **–ir** verb **partir** (*to leave*) and Table 14-8 for the irregular **–re** verb **mettre** (*to put*).

Table 14-7   Imperative of Partir (to Leave), an Irregular –ir Verb

Present Tense	Translation	Imperative	Translation
tu pars	*you leave*	**(tu) pars**	*leave*
nous partons	*we leave*	**(nous) partons**	*let's leave*
vous partez	*you leave*	**(vous) partez**	*leave*

The only **–ir** verbs that don't follow this pattern are verbs that end in **–frir** or **–vrir** such as **offrir** (*to offer*) and **ouvrir** (*to open*), and the verbs **avoir** (*to have*), **savoir** (*to know*), and **vouloir** (*to want*).

Table 14-8   Imperative of Mettre (to Put), an Irregular –re Verb

Present Tense	Translation	Imperative	Translation
tu mets	*you put*	**(tu) mets**	*put*
nous mettons	*we put*	**(nous) mettons**	*let's put*
vous mettez	*you put*	**(vous) mettez**	*put*

The only **–re** verb that doesn't follow this pattern is **être** (*to be*).

Ouvrir and other **–vrir** and **–frir** verbs that you conjugate in the same way in the present tense (flip back to Chapter 6 for more on the present tense) follow the same pattern as **–er** verbs in the imperative: You use the present tense **nous** and **vous** forms and the **tu** form minus **s**. See Table 14-9 for the imperatives of **ouvrir**.

Table 14-9   Imperative of Ouvrir (to open), Conjugated Like –er Verbs

Present Tense	Translation	Imperative	Translation
tu ouvres	*you open*	**(tu) ouvre**	*open*
nous ouvrons	*we open*	**(nous) ouvrons**	*let's open*
vous ouvrez	*you open*	**(vous) ouvrez**	*open*

Four French verbs — **avoir** (*to have*; Table 14-10), **être** (*to be*; Table 14-11), **savoir** (*to know*; Table 14-12), and **vouloir** (*to want*; Table 14-13) — have irregular imperative conjugations.

Table 14-10   Imperative of Avoir (to Have)

Present Tense	Translation	Imperative	Translation
tu as	*you have*	**(tu) aie**	*have*
nous avons	*we have*	**(nous) ayons**	*let's have*
vous avez	*you have*	**(vous) ayez**	*have*

Table 14-11   Imperative of Être (to Be)

Present Tense	Translation	Imperative	Translation
tu es	*you are*	**(tu) sois**	*be*
nous sommes	*we are*	**(nous) soyons**	*let's be*
vous êtes	*you are*	**(vous) soyez**	*be*

Table 14-12   Imperative of Savoir (to Know)

Present Tense	Translation	Imperative	Translation
tu sais	*you know*	**(tu) sache**	*know*
nous savons	*we know*	**(nous) sachons**	*let's know*
vous savez	*you know*	**(vous) sachez**	*know*

REMEMBER

Vouloir (*to want*) in the imperative isn't a command for someone to want something, but rather a way of making a very polite request: **Veuillez m'excuser** (*Please excuse me*). **Vouloir** has no **nous** imperative because it doesn't make sense to say, "Let's want!" or "Let's excuse ourselves!" See Table 14-13.

Table 14-13   Imperative of Vouloir (to Want)

Present Tense	Translation	Imperative	Translation
tu veux	*you want*	**(tu) veuille**	*please*
nous voulons	*we want*	(not applicable)	(not applicable)
vous voulez	*you want*	**(vous) veuillez**	*please*

PRACTICE

Provide all of the imperative forms for each of these verbs.

Q. prendre

A. **prends, prenons, prenez** (*take, let's take, take*)

25 dormir _____

26 avoir _____

27 écrire _____

28 savoir _____

29 faire _____

30 être _____

31 couvrir _____

32 venir _____

33 dire _____

34 vouloir _____

Pronominal verbs

To use pronominal verbs (see Chapter 7) in the imperative, you start by conjugating the verb itself according to whichever of the rules outlined in the preceding sections applies. Then you attach the correct form of the reflexive pronoun to the end of the verb with a hyphen, as Table 14-14 illustrates with **se coucher** (*to go to bed*) and Table 14-15 shows with **se taire** (*to be quiet*).

Table 14-14   Imperative of Se Coucher (to go to bed)

Present Tense	Translation	Imperative	Translation
tu te couches	*you go to bed*	**(tu) couche-toi**	*go to bed*
nous nous couchons	*we go to bed*	**(nous) couchons-nous**	*let's go to bed*
vous vous couchez	*you go to bed*	**(vous) couchez-vous**	*go to bed*

Table 14-15   Imperative of Se Taire (to be quiet)

Present Tense	Translation	Imperative	Translation
tu te tais	*you are being quiet*	**(tu) tais-toi**	*be quiet*
nous nous taisons	*we are being quiet*	**(nous) taisons-nous**	*let's be quiet*
vous vous taisez	*you are being quiet*	**(vous) taisez-vous**	*be quiet*

PRACTICE

Provide all three imperative forms for each of these pronominal verbs.

Q.   se coiffer

A.   **coiffe-toi, coiffons-nous, coiffez-vous** (*fix your hair, let's fix our hair, fix your hair*)

35   se raser _____

36   se doucher _____

37   se reposer _____

38   s'amuser _____

39   se lever _____

40   s'habiller _____

41   se marier _____

42   s'endormir _____

Giving Affirmative and Negative Commands

You can use affirmative commands to tell people to do something and negative commands to tell them not to do something. Other than the meaning, the only real difference between the affirmative and negative imperative is the word order you must use when the command includes reflexive, object, and/or adverbial pronouns (flip back to Chapter 13 for more on pronouns). The following sections help you keep everything straight.

Making a to-do list: Affirmative commands

Affirmative commands tell someone to do something. Remember that the sentence has no subject pronoun, so the verb conjugation alone tells you who's being ordered to do the action.

To create an affirmative command, just begin your statement with the verb in the imperative, and then add on anything else you need, such as an adverb or direct object.

> **Mange plus lentement.** (*Eat more slowly.*)
>
> **Fermez la porte.** (*Close the door.*)

The imperative doesn't always give commands; it can also offer suggestions or make requests, especially in the **nous** form.

> **Partons à midi.** (*Let's leave at noon.*)
>
> **Voyageons ensemble.** (*Let's travel together./Why don't we travel together?*)

The **vous** form of the imperative can also make a very polite request.

> **Veuillez m'excuser.** (*Please [be so kind as to] excuse me.*)
>
> **Ayez la bonté de fermer la porte.** (*Won't you please close the door?/Please be so kind as to close the door.*)

Any reflexive, direct object, indirect object, and adverbial pronouns have to follow the affirmative imperative, attached by hyphens. The affirmative imperative is the only type of sentence in which these pronouns follow the verb. In all other tenses and moods, including the negative imperative, these pronouns go before the verb. (See Chapter 13 for more info on these pronouns, including what order they go in when you have two in the same sentence.)

> **Parle-nous !** (*Talk to us!*)
>
> **Montre-le-moi !** (*Show it to me!*)

When the **tu** form of the imperative of an **–er** verb is followed by **y** or **en**, the verb reclaims the **s** from its present tense conjugation, to make pronunciation easier.

> **Manges-en !** (*Eat some!*)
>
> **Vas-y !** (*Go ahead!*)

PRACTICE

Translate these commands into French, in the conjugation for the pronoun in parentheses.

Q. Open the door. (tu)

A. Ouvre la porte.

43 Let's read the newspaper. (nous) _____

44 Look at this painting. (vous) _____

45 Buy some books. (tu) _____

46 Let's go to the bakery. (nous) _____

47 Please close the window. (vous) _____

48 Do your homework. (tu) _____

49 Let's leave at noon. (nous) _____

50 Eat! (vous) _____

Don't do it! Negative commands

When you tell someone not to do something in French, you use a negative command by putting **ne** in front of the verb and the second part of the negative structure — **pas** (*not*), **rien** (*nothing*), **jamais** (*never*), and so on — after the verb. (See Chapter 9 for info about making French verbs negative.) Here are some examples:

> **Ne parle pas comme ça.** (*Don't talk like that.*)

> **Ne revenons jamais ici.** (*Let's never come back here.*)

REMEMBER

If the verb requires a preposition, the word order depends on what kind of negation you're using. If you're using a negative adverb, the preposition goes after it, as in **Ne demandons pas à Pierre** (*Let's not ask Pierre*), but if it's a negative pronoun, the preposition goes before it, such as **N'aie peur de rien** (*Don't be afraid of anything*). See Chapter 9 to read about negation and Chapter 12 for information about verbs that have to be followed by a preposition.

Like with all verb tenses and moods (except affirmative commands, which you can read about in the previous section), when you're using the negative imperative, any reflexive, object, and adverbial pronouns always precede the verb. (Go to Chapter 13 to read about object and adverbial pronouns). Check out these example sentences:

> **Ne le dis pas.** (*Don't say it.*)

> **Ne nous mentez jamais !** (*Don't ever lie to us!*)

PRACTICE

Translate these negative commands into French in the conjugation for the pronoun in parentheses.

Q. Don't eat this cake. (vous)

A. **Ne mangez pas ce gâteau.**

51 Don't talk during the movie. (tu) _____

52 Let's not go out tonight. (nous) _____

53 Don't read my letter. (vous) _____

54 Don't work today. (tu) _____

55 Don't buy bread. (vous) _____

56 Let's not say hello. (nous) _____

57 Don't lie to me ! (tu) _____

58 Don't open the window. (vous) _____

Identifying Other Ways to Give Commands

The imperative is the most common way to give orders and make suggestions in French, but you have a few other options, as well. Here's a quick overview:

» **Suggesting with the present tense:** You can use the present tense (see Chapter 6) to give a softened command, such as to a child.

- **Tu vas au lit maintenant.** (*Go to bed now.*)
- **Vous faites vos devoirs avant de regarder la télé.** (*Do your homework before watching TV.*)

» **Commanding with the infinitive:** Use the infinitive for impersonal orders when you're giving instructions to an unknown audience, such as on posted signs and in instruction manuals.

- **Fermer la porte et les fenêtres en partant la nuit.** (*Close the door and windows when leaving at night.*)
- **Hacher les oignons et les ajouter à la soupe.** (*Chop the onions and add them to the soup.*)

Chapter 10 has more information about the French infinitive.

» **Forbidding with "défense de":** The expression **défense de** (literally: *prohibited from*) gives short, impersonal *do not do this* commands on posted signs. You probably won't use it yourself, unless you're in charge of making signs to display on doors and windows.

- **Défense d'entrer** (*Do not enter*)
- **Défense de fumer** (*No smoking*)

Rewrite each of these alternative commands by using the **vous** form of the imperative.

PRACTICE

Q. Défense d'entrer

A. N'entrez pas (*Do not enter.*)

59 Attacher la ceinture de sécurité. _____

60 Vous fermez la porte, s'il vous plaît. _____

61 Mélanger la sauce et ajouter du sel. _____

62 Vous faites le lit ce matin. _____

63 Nettoyer après usage. _____

64 Défense de fumer _____

65 Téléphoner avant 17 h 00. _____

66 Défense d'ouvrir _____

Answer Key to "I Command You: The Imperative" Practice Questions

1. **travaille, travaillons, travaillez** (*work, let's work, work*)

2. **étudie, étudions, étudiez** (*study, let's study, study*)

3. **danse, dansons, dansez** (*dance, let's dance, dance*)

4. **chante, chantons, chantez** (*sing, let's sing, sing*)

5. **pense, pensons, pensez** (*think, let's think, thing*)

6. **compte, comptons, comptez** (*count, let's count, count*)

7. **écoute, écoutons, écoutez** (*listen, let's listen, listen*)

8. **joue, jouons, jouez** (*play, let's play, play*)

9. **finis, finissons, finissez** (*finish, let's finish, finish*)

10. **étends, étendons, étendez** (*stretch, let's stretch, stretch*)

11. **réussis, réussissons, réussissez** (*succeed, let's succeed, succeed*)

12. **défends, défendons, défendez** (*defend, let's defend, defend*)

13. **cours, courons, courez** (*run, let's run, run*)

14. **attends, attendons, attendez** (*wait, let's wait, wait*)

15. **réponds, répondons, répondez** (*respond, let's respond, respond*)

16. **agis, agissons, agissez** (*act, let's act, act*)

17. **pèse, pesons, pesez** (*weigh, let's weigh, weigh*)

18. **mange, mangeons, mangez** (*eat, let's eat, eat*)

19. **jette, jetons, jetez** (*throw, let's throw, throw*)

20. **nettoie, nettoyons, nettoyez** (*clean, let's clean, clean*)

21. **efface, effaçons, effacez** (*erase, let's erase, erase*)

22. **répète, répétons, répétez** (*repeat, let's repeat, repeat*)

23. **bouge, bougeons, bougez** (*move, let's move, move*)

24. **va, allons, allez** (*go, let's go, go*)

25. **dors, dormons, dormez** (*sleep, let's sleep, sleep*)

26. **aie, ayons, ayez** (*have, let's have, have*)

(27) **écris, écrivons, écrivez** (*write, let's write, write*)

(28) **sache, sachons, sachez** (*know, let's know, know*)

(29) **fais, faisons, faites** (*do/make, let's do/make, do/make*)

(30) **sois, soyons, soyez** (*be, let's be, be*)

(31) **couvre, couvrons, couvrez** (*cover, let's cover, cover*)

(32) **viens, venons, venez** (*come, let's come, come*)

(33) **dis, disons, dites** (*say, let's say, say*)

(34) **veuille, —, veuillez** (*please, —, please*)

(35) **rase-toi, rasons-nous, rasez-vous** (*shave, let's shave, shave*)

(36) **douche-toi, douchons-nous, douchez-vous** (*shower, let's shower, shower*)

(37) **repose-toi, reposons-nous, reposez-vous** (*rest, let's rest, rest*)

(38) **amuse-toi, amusons-nous, amusez-vous** (*have fun, let's have fun, have fun*)

(39) **lève-toi, levons-nous, levez-vous** (*get up, let's get up, get up*)

(40) **habille-toi, habillons-nous, habillez-vous** (*get dressed, let's get dressed, get dressed*)

(41) **marie-toi, marions-nous, mariez-vous** (*get married, let's get married, get married*)

(42) **endors-toi, endormons-nous, endormez-vous** (*go to sleep, let's go to sleep, go to sleep*)

(43) **Lisons le journal.**

(44) **Regardez cette peinture./Regardez ce tableau.**

(45) **Achète des livres.**

(46) **Allons à la boulangerie.**

(47) **Veuillez fermer la fenêtre./Ayez la bonté de fermer la fenêtre.**

(48) **Fais tes devoirs.**

(49) **Partons à midi.**

(50) **Mangez !**

(51) **Ne parle pas pendant/durant le film.**

(52) **Ne sortons pas ce soir.**

(53) **Ne lisez pas ma lettre.**

(54) **Ne travaille pas aujourd'hui.**

(55) **N'achetez pas de pain.**

(56) **Ne disons pas bonjour.**

(57) **Ne me mens pas !**

(58) **N'ouvrez pas la fenêtre.**

(59) **Attachez votre ceinture de sécurité.** (*Fasten your seatbelt.*)

(60) **Fermez la porte s'il vous plaît.** (*Open the door please.*)

(61) **Mélangez la sauce et ajoutez du sel.** (*Stir the sauce and add some salt.*)

(62) **Faites le lit ce matin.** (*Make the bed this morning.*)

(63) **Nettoyez après usage.** (*Clean after using.*)

(64) **Ne fumez pas.** (*Do not smoke*)

(65) **Téléphonez avant 17 h 00.** (*Call before 5 pm.*)

(66) **N'ouvrez pas.** (*Do not open*)

Chapter **15**

It's All in the Past: Passé Composé

When you want to say what happened, you usually need the **passé composé** — a compound verb conjugation that's far from passé. The **passé composé** is actually the most common French past tense. You use it when you want to say that something happened or that something has happened.

The **passé composé** is a compound conjugation, meaning that it's conjugated with an *auxiliary* (or helping) verb, plus the past participle. This chapter explains all about auxiliary verbs; how to find the past participle of regular, stem-changing, spelling-change, and irregular verbs; agreement; and how to use the **passé composé**.

Creating the Passé Composé

The **passé composé** is the French equivalent of both the simple past (*I saw*) and the present perfect (*I have seen*). For the most part, you use the **passé composé** — **j'ai vu** in this example — when you'd use either of those tenses in English.

The **passé composé** is a compound verb tense, which means it has two parts:

>> An auxiliary verb, either **avoir** or **être**, which you conjugate in the present tense (see Chapter 6 for more about the present tense)

>> A past participle, see "Finding past participles" later in this chapter.

The following sections break down the two components of the **passé composé** so that you can conjugate this verb tense.

Choosing your helper: avoir or être

In order to conjugate verbs in the **passé composé**, you first need to know how to conjugate the two auxiliary verbs: **avoir** and **être** (you can find out how to do this conjugation in Chapter 6). After you conjugate the appropriate auxiliary verb in the present tense, you add the desired past participle — and voilà! The **passé composé**.

The auxiliary you need depends on the verb you're using it with. No need to worry, though. More than 99 percent of French verbs use **avoir**, leaving just a few intransitive verbs that require **être**. (*Intransitive* means the verb doesn't have a direct object. For example, *to go* is an intransitive verb.) The intransitive verbs in Table 15-1 are known as **être** verbs.

Table 15-1   **Verbs Conjugated with Être in the Passé Composé**

Verb	Translation	Verb	Translation
aller	to go	partir	to leave
arriver	to arrive	passer	to pass
descendre	to go down	rester	to stay
entrer	to enter	retourner	to return
monter	to go up	sortir	to go out
mourir	to die	tomber	to fall
naître	to be born	venir	to come

Furthermore, most of the derivatives of the above verbs need **être** in the **passé composé**, as well: **devenir** (*to become*), **rentrer** (*to return home*), and so on.

Decide which auxiliary verb you should use for these intransitive verbs, **avoir** or **être**.

Q. descendre

A. être

1   mourir _____

2   courir _____

3   arriver _____

4   devenir _____

(5) tomber _____

(6) finir _____

(7) marcher _____

(8) déménager _____

(9) naître _____

(10) aller _____

REMEMBER

In addition to the **être** verbs listed in Table 15-1, another group of verbs uses **être** as its auxiliary verb in the **passé composé**: Pronominal verbs (see Chapter 7 for more about those verbs). Every single pronominal verb is conjugated with **être** in the **passé composé**.

> **Je me suis levé tôt.** (*I got up early.*)

> **Est-ce que tu t'es douché ?** (*Did you take a shower?*)

TIP

Être verbs are usually *intransitive* (meaning they have no direct object). However, you can use some of these verbs *transitively* (with a direct object), meaning that they are either

» Followed directly by a noun, with no preposition (Chapter 12 goes into prepositions)

» Preceded by a direct object pronoun (see Chapter 13 for more about pronouns)

When you use **être** verbs transitively, you need to use the auxiliary **avoir**. Compare the following sentences.

> **Je suis descendu avec les cartons.** (*I went downstairs with the boxes.*)

> **J'ai descendu les cartons.** (*I took the boxes downstairs.*)

Table 15-2 shows which **être** verbs this intransitive/transitive rule affects and how their meanings differ according to usage.

Table 15-2   Using Être Verbs without and with Direct Objects

Verb	Intransitive Meaning (with être)	Transitive Meaning (with avoir)
descendre	*to go down*	*to take down*
entrer	*to enter, go in*	*to take/bring/put in*
monter	*to go up*	*to take up/to put together*
passer	*to pass (by, in front of, behind)*	*to spend time, to pass a place (no preposition)*
rentrer	*to return home*	*to take/bring in*
retourner	*to return (to/from a place)*	*to return (something)*
sortir	*to go out*	*to take out*

For example:

> **Je suis passé derrière la boulangerie.** (*I passed behind the bakery.*)

> **J'ai passé la boulangerie sans m'arrêter.** (*I passed the bakery without stopping.*)

Decide which auxiliary verb you need to use — either **avoir** or **être** — with these phrases in the **passé composé**.

PRACTICE

Q. sortir les valises (to take the suitcases out)

A. avoir

11. passer la journée ici (to spend the day here) _____

12. retourner en France (to return to France) _____

13. entrer dans la bibliothèque (to enter the library) _____

14. descendre l'escalier (to go down the stairs) _____

15. monter à minuit (to go up at midnight) _____

16. rentrer chez nous (to return home) _____

17. sortir avec des amis (to go out with friends) _____

18. passer devant l'école (to pass in front of the school) _____

19. entrer le mot de passe (to put in the password) _____

20. monter un plateau (to take a tray upstairs) _____

Finding past participles

The second part of the **passé composé**, after the auxiliary verb (see the preceding section), is the *past participle*. In English, most past participles end in *–ed* or *–en*: *walked, chosen, returned*. In French, the past participle usually ends in **–é**, **–i**, or **–u**, depending on what kind of verb it is: **marché, choisi, rendu**. The following sections show how to form the past participle of regular and irregular verbs.

TIP

The past participle isn't only for the **passé composé** and the other compound tenses. You can often use it as an adjective.

Je suis fatigué. (*I'm tired.*)

Nous sommes déçus. (*We are disappointed.*)

J'ai vu beaucoup de feuilles mortes. (*I saw a lot of dead leaves.*)

Past participles of regular verbs

Regular verbs have regular past participles. Each of the three categories of regular verbs has its own past participle formation. To find the past participle of any **–er** verb (including stem-changing and spelling change verbs), just replace the **–er** ending with **–é**. You pronounce the past participles of **–er** verbs exactly the same as the infinitives. Here are some examples:

>> **parler** (*to talk*) becomes **parlé**

>> **bouger** (*to move*) becomes **bougé**

>> **essayer** (*to try*) becomes **essayé**

To create the past participle for regular –**ir** verbs, replace –**ir** with –**i**:

>> **choisir** (*to choose*) becomes **choisi**

>> **réussir** (*to succeed*) becomes **réussi**

Regular verbs that end in –**re** drop the ending and add –**u**:

>> **entendre** (*to hear*) becomes **entendu**

>> **vendre** (*to sell*) becomes **vendu**

PRACTICE

Provide the past participle for each of these verbs.

Q. manger

A. **mangé** (*eaten*)

21 travailler _____

22 rendre _____

23 finir _____

24 commencer _____

25 perdre _____

26 déménager _____

27 grossir _____

28 attendre _____

29 préférer _____

30 confondre _____

Past participles of irregular verbs

Some irregular verbs follow the same rules as regular verbs, some have patterns, and some are completely irregular. You just have to memorize the different rules; with practice, you can master them in no time. Table 15-3 shows you which patterns to look for.

See Appendix A for lists of verbs that follow each conjugation pattern.

Table 15-3   Past Participle Irregular Verb Patterns

Verb Type	Change	Examples
Irregular –er verbs		
Stem-changing and spelling-change verbs, as well as **aller**	Replace –**er** with –**é** (same as regular –**er** verbs)	**appeler** (*to call*) becomes **appelé**
		commencer (*to begin*) becomes **commencé**
		aller (*to go*) becomes **allé**

(continued)

Table 15-3 *(continued)*

Verb Type	Change	Examples
Irregular –ir verbs		
Verbs conjugated like **partir** (see Chapter 6)	Change **–ir** to **–i** (same as regular **–ir** verbs)	**partir** (*to leave*) becomes **parti**
		sortir (*to go out*) becomes **sorti**
		dormir (*to sleep*) becomes **dormi**
Verbs that end in -frir or -vrir	Drop **–rir** and add **–ert**	**ouvrir** (*to open*) becomes **ouvert**
		offrir (*to offer*) becomes **offert**
		souffrir (*to suffer*) becomes **souffert**
Venir, tenir, and all their derivatives	Replace **–ir** with **–u**	**venir** (*to come*) becomes **venu**
		devenir (*to become*) becomes **devenu**
		tenir (*to hold*) becomes **tenu**
		obtenir (*to obtain*) becomes **obtenu**
Verbs that end in **–cevoir**	Change **–cevoir** to **–çu**	**apercevoir** (*to glimpse*) becomes **aperçu**
		décevoir (*to disappoint*) becomes **déçu**
		recevoir (*to receive*) becomes **reçu**
Irregular –re verbs		
Mettre (*to put*) and its derivatives	Past participle of **mettre** is **mis**	**admettre** (*to admit*) becomes **admis**
		permettre (*to permit*) becomes **permis**
		promettre (*to promise*) becomes **promis**
Prendre (*to take*) and its derivatives	Past participle of **prendre** is **pris**	**apprendre** (*to learn*) becomes **appris**
		comprendre (*to understand*) becomes **compris**
		surprendre (*to surprise*) becomes **surpris**
Verbs ending in **–aître** (except **naître**)	Drop **–aître** and replace it with **–u**	**connaître** (*to know*) becomes **connu**
		paraître (*to seem*) becomes **paru**
		apparaître (*to appear*) becomes **apparu**
Verbs that end in **–aindre**, **–eindre**, or **–oindre**	Drop **–dre** in favor of **–t**	**craindre** (*to fear*) becomes **craint**
		joindre (*to join*) becomes **joint**
		peindre (*to paint*) becomes **peint**
Verbs that end in **–uire**	Drop **–re** and and add **–t**	**conduire** (*to drive*) becomes **conduit**
		construire (*to build*) becomes **construit**

Determine the past participle for these irregular verbs.

PRACTICE

Q. recevoir

A. reçu (*received*)

(31) aller _____		(36) mettre _____	
(32) prendre _____		(37) introduire _____	
(33) apparaître _____		(38) sortir _____	
(34) couvrir _____		(39) adjoindre _____	
(35) craindre _____		(40) ouvrir _____	

Table 15-4 shows irregular verbs that choose to do their own thing with the past participle.

Table 15-4 Irregular Verbs That Have Uniquely Irregular Past Participles

Irregular –ir Verbs	Past Participle	Irregular –re Verbs	Past Participle
asseoir (*to seat*)	**assis**	**avoir** (*to have*)	**eu**
boire (*to drink*)	**bu**	**courir** (*to run*)	**couru**
croire (*to believe*)	**cru**	**devoir** (*to have to*)	**dû**
dire (*to say*)	**dit**	**écrire** (*to write*)	**écrit**
être (*to be*)	**été**	**faire** (*to do, to make*)	**fait**
falloir (*to be necessary*)	**fallu**	**lire** (*to read*)	**lu**
mourir (*to die*)	**mort**	**naître** (*to be born*)	**né**
pleuvoir (*to rain*)	**plu**	**pouvoir** (*to be able*)	**pu**
rire (*to laugh*)	**ri**	**savoir** (*to know*)	**su**
suivre (*to follow*)	**suivi**	**vivre** (*to live*)	**vécu**
voir (*to see*)	**vu**	**vouloir** (*to want*)	**voulu**

PRACTICE

Write the past participle for each of these irregular verbs.

Q. pleuvoir

A. plu (*rained*)

(41) savoir _____		(46) croire _____	
(42) faire _____		(47) pouvoir _____	
(43) vivre _____		(48) avoir _____	
(44) courir _____		(49) lire _____	
(45) voir _____		(50) être _____	

Keeping Grammatical Agreement in Mind

In addition to the auxiliary verb and past participle (which you can read about in the section "Creating the Passé Composé," earlier in this chapter), you need to consider a third element when using the **passé composé**, particularly in writing: grammatical agreement. *Agreement* is the addition or changing of certain letters to make one French part of speech agree with another. Just as French adjectives take on different forms to agree with their nouns (Chapter 11 goes over adjectives), past participles sometimes have to agree with their subjects.

Agreement with être verbs

When you use a verb that's conjugated with the auxiliary **être** in the **passé composé** (head back to the section "Choosing your helper: avoir or être," earlier in this chapter), the past participle has to agree with the subject in gender and number. This agreement is similar to the agreement of adjectives explained in Chapter 11, but past participles have no irregular agreements. Here are the basics for past participle agreement. When the subject is

>> **Masculine:** Use the default past participle.

   Philippe est allé au cinéma. (*Philippe went to the movies.*)

>> **Feminine:** Add an **–e**.

   Analise est allée au musée. (*Analise went to the museum.*)

>> **Masculine and plural:** add an **–s**.

   Ils sont allés au théâtre. (*They went to the theater.*)

>> **Feminine and plural:** Add **–es**.

   Geneviève et Denise sont allées au marché. (*Geneviève and Denise went to the market.*)

When the subject is a pronoun, such as **je** (*I*) or **tu** (*you*), you need to think about the gender of the person that the pronoun represents. I, Laura, have to write **je suis allée** (*I went*), but my husband writes **je suis allé**.

Don't forget that when you have two or more people or things, if at least one of those people or things is masculine, the agreement is masculine plural. For instance, consider **Mes sœurs et mon frère sont allés au cinéma hier soir** (*My sisters and brother went to the movies yesterday*). Even though more sisters went than brothers, the past participle is masculine plural.

WARNING

When the subject is **vous**, any of the four forms of the past participle might be correct — you must determine the gender and number of the person(s) **vous** refers to in order to know which form to use.

   Monsieur, quand êtes-vous arrivé ? (*Sir, when did you arrive?*)

   Madame, pourquoi êtes-vous rentrée ? (*Ma'am, why did you return home?*)

   Messieurs, où êtes-vous allés ? (*Gentlemen, where did you go?*)

   Mesdames, comment êtes-vous tombées ? (*Ladies, how did you fall?*)

Agreement with pronominal verbs

All pronominal verbs require that you use **être** as your auxiliary verb when forming the **passé composé**. (See the section "Choosing your helper: avoir or être," earlier in this chapter, for more on these helpful verbs.) In addition, pronominal verbs require agreement with the reflexive pronoun (see Chapter 7 for more on reflexive, reciprocal, and idiomatic pronominal verbs).

> **Elle s'est habillée.** (*She got dressed.*) The past participle **habillée** is feminine to agree with **elle se**.

> **Ils se sont levés très tôt.** (*They got up really early.*) The past participle **levés** is plural to agree with **ils se**.

However, if the sentence contains a direct object, you don't have any agreement of the past participle.

> **Elle s'est lavé les mains.** (*She washed her hands.*) **Mains** is the direct object, so the past participle **lavé** remains in the default (masculine singular) form.

> **Nous nous sommes acheté de la glace.** (*We bought ourselves some ice cream.*) **Glace** is the direct object, so the past participle **acheté** remains in the default form.

Remember that many French verbs require prepositions, which means they take indirect objects; however, sometimes the English translations of those verbs take direct objects. For example, **téléphoner à** takes an indirect object in French, but *to call* takes a direct object in English. I go into all things preposition-related in Chapter 12.

Write the correct form of the past participle for the subjects provided, assuming that the verb is used intransitively.

Q. elle (aller)

A. **allée** (*went*)

51 ils (venir) _____

52 la fille (sortir) _____

53 nous (descendre) _____

54 il (naître) _____

55 vous (partir) _____

56 elles (monter) _____

57 je (tomber) _____

58 les étudiants (arriver) _____

59 le chien (mourir) _____

60 tu (entrer) _____

Putting It All Together: Conjugating the Passé Composé

After you know which auxiliary verb to use (covered in the section "Choosing your helper: avoir or être," earlier in this chapter), the past participle of your verb (which I go over in the section "Finding past participles," earlier in this chapter), and whether you need agreement (check out the section "Keeping Grammatical Agreement in Mind," earlier in this chapter), you can conjugate the **passé composé**. (Finally, amirite?) Just use the present tense of the auxiliary verb, either **avoir** or **être**, followed by the past participle. Take a look at the following table, which shows **parler** (*to speak*) in the **passé composé**; it doesn't require agreement.

parler (to speak)

j'ai parlé	nous avons parlé
tu as parlé	vous avez parlé
il/elle/on a parlé	ils/elles ont parlé

Marie a parlé avec mon frère hier. (*Marie spoke with my brother yesterday.*)

REMEMBER

The **être** verbs require agreement, which I indicate in parentheses in this **aller** (*to go*) table.

aller (to go)

je suis allé(e)	nous sommes allé(e)s
tu es allé(e)	vous êtes allé(e)(s)
il est allé	ils sont allés
elle est allée	elles sont allées
on est allé(e)(s)	

Elle est allée en France il y a deux ans. (*She went to France two years ago.*)

Pronominal verbs — such as **se lever** (*to get up*) also need agreement — you can read more about these types of verbs in Chapter 7.

se lever (to get up)

je me suis levé(e)	nous nous sommes levé(e)s
tu t'es levé(e)	vous vous êtes levé(e)(s)
il s'est levé	ils se sont levés
elle s'est levée	elles se sont levées
on s'est levé(e)(s)	

Nous nous sommes levés très tôt. (*We got up very early.*)

PRACTICE

Conjugate each of these verbs into the **passé composé** for the grammatical person in parentheses.

Q. finir (je)

A. **j'ai fini** (*I finished*)

61 se coucher (tu) _____

62 rentrer (il) _____

63 venir (nous) _____

64 lire (vous) _____

65 s'habiller (elles) _____

66 voyager (je) _____

67 écrire (tu) _____

68 avoir (elle) _____

69 vendre (nous) _____

70 sortir (ils) _____

Using the Passé Composé

To properly use the **passé composé** in a normal sentence, just follow this simple formula:

> subject + auxiliary verb + past participle **J'ai pleuré.** *(I cried.)*
>
> **Ils sont partis.** *(They left.)*

Of course, writing and speaking include much more than just simple sentences. You use the **passé composé** to refer to one of three things:

- Something that was entirely completed once in the past.
  - **Je suis allé à la banque hier.** *(I went to the bank yesterday.)*
  - **Est-il arrivé avant la fête ?** *(Did he arrive before the party?)*
- Something that happened a certain number of times in the past.
  - **J'ai visité la tour Eiffel trois fois.** *(I've visited the Eiffel Tower three times.)*
  - **Combien de fois as-tu téléphoné ?** *(How many times did you call?)*
- A series of actions that occurred one after another in the past.
  - **Je me suis levé, j'ai déjeuné et je suis parti avant 7 h 00.** *(I got up, had breakfast, and left before 7 a.m.)*
  - **Quand nous avons entendu les cris, nous avons téléphoné à la police.** *(When we heard the screams, we called the police.)*

You often use the **passé composé** in conjunction with the imperfect. You can read about the imperfect tense in Chapter 16.

The following example sentences show you how to use the **passé composé** in other constructions, such as negative sentences and questions. When you negate the **passé composé**, ne goes in front of the auxiliary verb, and the second part of the negative structure goes after it. (You can read about negation in Chapter 9 and questions in chapter 8.)

> **Je n'ai pas pleuré.** *(I didn't cry.)*
>
> **Il n'est jamais arrivé.** *(He never arrived.)*

The only exception is **personne**, which goes after the past participle, instead of after the auxiliary verb.

> **Je n'ai vu personne.** *(I didn't see anyone.)*
>
> **Il n'a parlé à personne.** *(He didn't talk to anyone.)*

When you ask a question by using inversion (Chapter 8 can answer any questions you have about inversion), you invert just the subject and auxiliary verb, and then put the past participle after that.

As-tu mangé ? (*Have you eaten?*)

À qui a-t-il parlé ? (*Whom did he talk to?*)

Any object, adverbial, and reflexive pronouns (which you can read about in Chapter 13) precede the auxiliary verb, whether **avoir** or **être**.

Je l'ai déjà fait. (*I already did it.*)

Il me l'a donné. (*He gave it to me.*)

When you have negation and pronouns, the pronouns go directly in front of the auxiliary verb, and **ne** precedes them.

Je ne l'ai pas fait. (*I didn't do it.*)

Tu ne nous l'a pas montré. (*You didn't show it to us.*)

PRACTICE

You're in France, writing a postcard to your best friend. Translate these sentences into French, using the **passé composé** to describe what you did and didn't do.

Q. This morning, I got up at 8 a.m.

A. Ce matin, je me suis levé(e) à 8 h 00.

Carte Postale

[5]

Salut Charles,

71. I had breakfast and then went to Montmartre. _____

72. I saw a lot of artists and bought this postcard. _____

73. They told me to visit Notre Dame. _____

74. I asked for directions twice and I didn't get lost. _____

75. I found an interesting restaurant and ate there several times. _____

Charles Degrate
2b Leevina Trail
New York, NY 12345
USA

Answer Key to "It's All in the Past: Passé Composé" Practice Questions

(1) **être**

(2) **avoir**

(3) **être**

(4) **être**

(5) **être**

(6) **avoir**

(7) **avoir**

(8) **avoir**

(9) **être**

(10) **être**

(11) **avoir**

(12) **être**

(13) **être**

(14) **avoir**

(15) **être**

(16) **être**

(17) **être**

(18) **être**

(19) **avoir**

(20) **avoir**

(21) **travaillé** (*worked*)

(22) **rendu** (*returned*)

(23) **fini** (*finished*)

(24) **commencé** (*started*)

(25) **perdu** (*lost*)

(26) **déménagé** (*moved*)

(27) **grossi** (*fattened*)

(28) **attendu** (*waited*)

(29) **préféré** (*preferred*)

(30) **confondu** (*confused*)

(31) **allé** (*gone*)

(32) **pris** (*taken*)

(33) **apparu** (*appeared*)

(34) **couvert** (*covered*)

(35) **craint** (*feared*)

(36) **mis** (*put*)

(37) **introduit** (*introduced*)

(38) **sorti** (*gone out*)

(39) **adjoint** (*appointed*)

(40) **ouvert** (*opened*)

(41) **su** (*known*)

(42) **fait** (*done, made*)

(43) **vécu** (*lived*)

(44) **couru** (*ran*)

(45) **vu** (*seen*)

(46) **cru** (*believed*)

(47) **pu** (*was able*)

(48) **eu** (*had*)

(49) **lu** (*read*)

(50) **été** (*been*)

(51) **venus**

(52) **sortie**

(53) **descendus/descendues**

(54) **né**

(55) **parti/partie/partis/parties**

(56) **montées**

(57) **tombé/tombée**

(58) **arrivés**

(59) **mort**

(60) **entré/entrée**

(61) **tu t'es couché(e)** (*you went to bed*)

(62) **il est rentré** (*he returned home*)

(63) **nous sommes venu(e)s** (*we came*)

(64) **vous avez lu** (*you read*)

(65) **elles se sont habillées** (*they got dressed*)

(66) **j'ai voyagé** (*I traveled*)

(67) **tu as écrit** (*you wrote*)

(68) **elle a eu** (*she had*)

(69) **nous avons vendu** (*we sold*)

(70) **ils sont sortis** (*they went out*)

(71) **J'ai déjeuné/J'ai pris le petit-déjeuner./J'ai pris mon petit-déjeuner et puis je suis allé(e) à Montmartre.**

(72) **J'ai vu beaucoup d'artistes et j'ai acheté cette carte postale.**

(73) **Ils m'ont dit de visiter Notre-Dame.**

(74) **J'ai demandé le chemin/la route deux fois et je ne me suis pas perdu(e).**

(75) **J'ai trouvé un restaurant intéressant et j'y ai mangé plusieurs fois.**

IN THIS CHAPTER

» **Conjugating the imparfait**

» **Getting better acquainted with the imparfait tense**

» **Deciding between the imparfait and the passé composé**

» **Discovering the recent past**

Chapter **16**

When the Past Isn't Perfect: The Imparfait Tense

T he **imparfait** (*imperfect*) tense isn't flawed — just unfinished. Grammatically speaking, *perfect* means complete, and the **imparfait** tells you that an action wasn't completed — it was an ongoing state of being (*it was hot, I was hungry*) — or that it happened repeatedly (*I used to go to the beach every weekend*). You often use the **imparfait** in conjunction with the **passé composé** to describe some action (**imparfait**) that got interrupted by some other action (**passé composé**), as in *I was eating when you called*. (Check out Chapter 15 for more info about the **passé composé**.) You often translate the **imparfait** as *was/were doing* or *used to do* in English.

This chapter explains how and when to use the **imparfait**, how to conjugate regular and irregular verbs in the **imparfait**, the difference between the **imparfait** and **passé composé**, and how to use them together. It also introduces the *recent past*, the third and final past tense that is essential for beginning French learners.

Conjugating the Imparfait

The **imparfait** is the easiest of all the French tenses to conjugate because you conjugate virtually all verbs exactly the same way. You take the present tense **nous** form of the verb (see Chapter 6), drop **–ons**, and add the **imparfait** endings, as shown in the following table.

Person	Singular	Plural
First	–ais	–ions
Second	–ais	–iez
Third	–ait	–aient

These endings are the same for all verbs in the **imparfait**. The following sections show you how to conjugate all the different verbs — regular, stem-changing, spelling-change, and irregular (all of which you can read more about in Chapter 6) — to show you how easy this tense is.

TIP

Despite the different endings, the singular conjugations and third-person plural conjugation all sound identical, so the subject pronoun lets you know who was talking.

Regular –er verbs

You use the method described in the preceding section to conjugate all verbs. For example, the **nous** present tense form of the regular **–er** verb **parler** (*to speak*) is **parlons**, so the imperfect stem is **parl–**, and the conjugations for all regular **–er** verbs look like this.

parler (to speak, to talk)

je parlais	nous parlions
tu parlais	vous parliez
il/elle/on parlait	ils/elles parlaient

Il parlait trop vite. (*He was speaking too quickly.*)

Verbs that end in **–ier**, such as **étudier** (see the following table), can look a little strange in some of the **imparfait** conjugations. When you drop **–ons** from the **nous** present tense form **étudions**, you find a stem than ends in i: **étudi–**. Because the **nous** and **vous imparfait** endings begin with i, you end up with a double i in those conjugations.

étudier (to study)

j'étudiais	nous étudiions
tu étudiais	vous étudiiez
il/elle/on étudiait	ils/elles étudiaient

Nous étudiions hier soir. (*We were studying yesterday evening.*)

TIP

The **nous** and **vous** forms of the **imparfait** end in **–ions** and **–iez** for all verbs.

> **Nous parlions.** (*We were talking.*)
>
> **Vous fermiez.** (*You were closing.*)

But verbs that end in **–ier** also end in **–ions** and **–iez** in the present tense.

> **Nous étudions.** (*We study.*)

> **Vous skiez.** (*You ski.*)

Therefore, the double **i** is what tells you that **–ier** verbs are in the **imparfait**.

> **Nous étudiions.** (*We were studying.*)

> **Vous skiiez.** (*You were skiing.*)

PRACTICE

Conjugate these regular **–er** verbs in the **imparfait** for the subject in parentheses.

Q. danser (je)

A. **je dansais** (*I was dancing*)

1. chanter (tu) _____

2. monter (il) _____

3. crier (nous) _____

4. travailler (vous) _____

5. gagner (elle) _____

6. étudier (je) _____

7. fumer (tu) _____

8. écouter (on) _____

9. habiter (nous) _____

10. copier (vous) _____

Regular –ir and –re verbs

The **nous** present tense form of the regular **–ir** verb **finir** is **finissons**, so the root for all the **imparfait** conjugations is **finiss–**. Check out this table.

finir (to finish)

je finissais	nous finissions
tu finissais	vous finissiez
il/elle/on finissait	ils/elles finissaient

Elles finissaient leurs études au Canada. (*They were finishing their studies in Canada.*)

Vendons is the **nous** present tense form of the regular **–re** verb **vendre**, so the root is **vend–**. (See the following table.)

vendre (to sell)

je vendais	nous vendions
tu vendais	vous vendiez
il/elle/on vendait	ils/elles vendaient

Je vendais ma voiture. (*I was selling my car.*)

Conjugate these regular **–ir** and **–re** verbs in the **imparfait** for the subject in parentheses.

Q. vendre (je)

A. **je vendais** (*I was selling*)

11 choisir (tu) _____

12 rendre (il) _____

13 dépendre (vous) _____

14 choisir (nous) _____

15 perdre (elles) _____

16 agir (je) _____

17 confondre (tu) _____

18 remplir (on) _____

19 attendre (nous) _____

20 rougir (vous) _____

Stem-changing verbs

The **nous** form of stem-changing verbs doesn't have a stem change in the present, so the **imparfait** doesn't, either. The **nous** form of **payer** is **payons**, so the stem is **pay–**, and the **nous** form of **acheter** is **achetons**, so the stem is **achet–**. The following tables show you the conjugations for these verbs. (I introduce stem-changing verbs in Chapter 6.)

payer (to pay)

je payais	nous payions
tu payais	vous payiez
il/elle/on payait	ils/elles payaient

Vous payiez trop. (*You were paying too much.*)

acheter (to buy)

j'achetais	nous achetions
tu achetais	vous achetiez
il/elle/on achetait	ils/elles achetaient

Tu achetais beaucoup de pain. (*You were buying/used to buy a lot of bread.*)

Spelling-change verbs

The **nous** form of spelling-change verbs has a spelling change, so you keep that for most of the **imparfait** conjugations. The **nous** form of **commencer** is **commençons**, giving you the stem **commenç–**, and the **nous** form of **manger** is **mangeons**, so the stem is **mange–**. (See the following tables.)

However, note that the **nous** and **vous imparfait** endings begin with the soft vowel **i**, so you don't need the spelling change (from **c** to **ç** with **commencer** and **g** to **ge** with **manger**) in those conjugations. See Chapter 6 for more information about spelling-change verbs.

commencer (to start, to begin)

je commençais	nous commencions
tu commençais	vous commenciez
il/elle/on commençait	ils/elles commençaient

Il commençait à lire. (*He was beginning to read.*)

manger (to eat)

je mangeais	nous mangions
tu mangeais	vous mangiez
il/elle/on mangeait	ils/elles mangeaient

Nous mangions ensemble. (*We were eating/used to eat together.*)

PRACTICE

Conjugate these stem-changing and spelling-change verbs in the **imparfait**.

Q. commencer (je)

A. **je commençais** (*I was starting*)

21 essayer (tu) _____

22 lancer (il) _____

23 appeler (nous) _____

24 mener (vous) _____

25 rejeter (elles) _____

26 nager (je) _____

27 prétendre (tu) _____

28 lever (on) _____

29 pincer (nous) _____

30 bouger (vous) _____

Irregular verbs

What's the only irregularity of irregular verbs in the **imparfait**? Well, they're not irregular —
you conjugate them just like regular verbs, with the present-tense **nous** form, minus the **–ons**.
Then, you add the imperfect endings.

aller (to go)

j'allais	nous allions
tu allais	vous alliez
il/elle/on allait	ils/elles allaient

Ils allaient au parc. (*They were going to the park.*)

venir (to come)

je venais	nous venions
tu venais	vous veniez
il/elle/on venait	ils/elles venaient

Tu venais seul. (*You were coming alone.*)

écrire (to write)

j'écrivais	nous écrivions
tu écrivais	vous écriviez
il/elle/on écrivait	ils/elles écrivaient

Elle écrivait une longue lettre. (*She was writing a long letter.*)

French has just one single irregular verb that remains irregular in the imperfect: **être**. The
present-tense **nous** form of **être** is **sommes** — it doesn't have an **–ons** to drop. Instead, you
use the irregular stem **ét–** and add the **imparfait** endings to that.

être (to be)

j'étais	nous étions
tu étais	vous étiez
il/elle/on était	ils/elles étaient

Vous étiez en retard. (*You were late.*)

PRACTICE

Conjugate these irregular verbs in the **imparfait** for the subject in parentheses.

Q. aller (je)

A. j'allais (*I was going*)

31 avoir (tu) _____

32 être (il) _____

33 faire (nous) _____

34 devoir (vous) _____

35 aller (elles) _____

36 savoir (je) _____

37 tenir (tu) _____

38 lire (on) _____

39 vouloir (nous) _____

40 être (vous) _____

Taking a Closer Look at the Imparfait

REMEMBER

You can use the **imparfait** to express a number of things that happened or existed in the past. Here's what to express with the **imparfait**:

>> Something that happened an unknown number of times, especially habitual actions:

  • **Je visitais le Louvre tous les jours.** (*I visited/used to visit the Louvre every day.*)

  • **L'année dernière, il lisait régulièrement.** (*Last year, he read/used to read regularly.*)

>> States of being and descriptions:

  • **Quand j'étais petit, j'aimais danser.** (*When I was little, I liked dancing/I used to like to dance.*)

  • **La voiture faisait du bruit.** (*The car was making noise./The car used to make noise.*)

>> Actions or states of being that have no specific beginning or end:

  • **Je regardais la télé pendant le petit déjeuner.** (*I watched/was watching TV during breakfast.*)

  • **Nous avions besoin de tomates.** (*We needed tomatoes.*)

>> Two things that were happening at the same time:

  • **Il travaillait et j'étudiais.** (*He was working, and I was studying.*)

  • **Je lisais pendant que mon frère jouait au tennis.** (*I read while my brother played tennis.*)

>> Background information and actions/states of being that got interrupted:

- **Travaillais-tu quand je t'ai téléphoné ?** (*Were you working when I called you?*)

- **J'avais faim, donc j'ai acheté un sandwich.** (*I was hungry, so I bought a sandwich.*)

Note that the interruption is expressed with the **passé composé**. See the section "Deciding Whether to Use Imparfait or Passé Composé," later in this chapter, for more information on when to use which tense.

>> Wishes, suggestions, and conditions after **si** (*if*):

- **Si seulement elle venait avec nous.** (*If only she were coming with us.*)

- **Et si on allait au ciné ce soir ?** (*How about going to the movies tonight?*)

>> Time, date, and age:

- **C'était lundi quand . . .** (*It was Monday when . . .*)

- **Tu étais trop jeune.** (*You were too young.*)

- **Il était une fois . . .** (*Once upon a time . . .*)

 Translate these sentences into French using the **imparfait**.

PRACTICE

Q. Were they ready?

A. Étaient-ils prêts ?

(41) We used to live together. _____

(42) It was hot yesterday. _____

(43) Antoine was singing. _____

(44) Paul and Michel watched a movie every week. _____

(45) If only you had the key. _____

(46) I was sleeping. _____

(47) She was very pretty. _____

(48) How about if I help you? _____

(49) He was scared. _____

(50) I wanted to travel. _____

Deciding Whether to Use the Imparfait or Passé Composé

The **imparfait** and the **passé composé** express the past differently, so only by working together can they fully express what happened in the past. In order for you to use the right one at the right time, you need to know what each tense describes. Table 16-1 spells out their differences. (You can read more about the **passé composé** in Chapter 15.)

Table 16-1 Functions of the Imparfait and Passé Composé

Uses of the Imparfait	Uses of the Passé Composé
What was going on with no indication of when it started or ended	Things that happened with a definite beginning and/or end
Habitual or repeated actions	Single events
Simultaneous actions	Sequential actions
Something that got interrupted	Actions that interrupted something
Background information	Changes in physical or mental states
General descriptions	

In a nutshell, the **imparfait** usually describes the background state of being, and the **passé composé** explains the foreground actions and events. Between the two of them, you get a complete picture of what happened in the past.

The following sections break down the different situations in which you have to choose between the **imparfait** and the **passé composé**; you can also find some hints to help you make that decision.

When relying on context clues

TIP

Certain terms can help you decide whether to use the **imparfait** or **passé composé**. The following terms are usually used with the **imparfait**:

>> **chaque semaine/mois/année** (*every week/month/year*)

>> **de temps en temps** (*from time to time*)

>> **d'habitude/normalement** (*usually*)

>> **en général** (*in general*)

>> **généralement** (*generally*)

>> **le lundi, le mardi** . . . (*on Mondays, on Tuesdays . . .*)

>> **le matin** (*in the mornings*)

>> **le soir** (*in the evenings*)

>> **le week-end** (*on the weekends*)

>> **parfois/quelquefois** (*sometimes*)

>> **souvent** (*often*)

>> **tous les jours** (*every day*)

>> **toutes les semaines** (*every week*)

TIP

These terms tell you that you probably should use the **passé composé**:

>> **lundi, mardi** . . . (*on Monday, on Tuesday* . . .)

>> **plusieurs fois** (*several times*)

>> **soudain/soudainement** (*suddenly*)

>> **tout à coup** (*all of a sudden*)

>> **un jour** (*one day*)

>> **un week-end** (*one weekend*)

>> **une fois, deux fois, trois fois** . . . (*once, twice, three times* . . .)

PRACTICE

Carefully consider the lists in the previous section to determine whether the term provided calls for the **imparfait** or **passé compose** in this exercise.

Q. toutes les semaines

A. imparfait

51 un jour _____

52 de temps en temps _____

53 quatre fois _____

54 le matin _____

55 normalement _____

56 soudain _____

57 jeudi _____

58 tout à coup _____

59 généralement _____

60 chaque semaine _____

When describing actions that have no end in sight

When you use the **imparfait** to describe an action, you're saying that it had no precise beginning or end.

> **J'écrivais une lettre.** (*I was writing a letter.*)

> **Il me regardait.** (*He was looking at me.*)

These actions are incomplete, so you use the **imparfait**. You know that, at some point, I was in the process of writing a letter, but you don't know whether I ever finished it or when I started or stopped. Likewise, someone was looking at me for an unspecified amount of time.

In contrast, the **passé composé** says that an action did have a specific start and/or end. Compare the preceding examples to the following sentences.

> **J'ai écrit une lettre.** (*I wrote a letter.*)

> **Il m'a regardé.** (*He looked at me.*)

The first example sentence has a definite ending — the letter is written. The second sentence indicates that for some reason, this guy turned to look at me. These actions are complete, so you use the **passé composé**.

When making a habit of repeating an action

When something was habitual or repeated, use the **imparfait**.

> **J'allais au café le samedi et j'écrivais des lettres.** (*I used to go to the café on Saturdays and write letters.*)

Here, you don't know how many times I went to the café and wrote letters. Because this was something I habitually did on Saturdays, I use the **imparfait**.

Compare the preceding example sentence to something that happened a specific number of times, in which case, you need the **passé composé**.

> **Je suis allé au café samedi et j'ai écrit des lettres.** (*I went to the café on Saturday and wrote letters.*)

The actions in this example sentence are complete, so you use the **passé composé**. On Saturday, I went to the café, sat down, and wrote letters. It's done.

When describing the general state of being

The **imparfait** describes the general state of being of a person or thing.

> **Étienne avait faim.** (*Étienne was hungry.*)

This is just the way Étienne felt — he was hungry. In this instance, you use the **imparfait**. Compare the preceding example to the following sentence, which indicates a change in a state of being.

Quand il a vu la pizza, Étienne a eu faim. (*When he saw the pizza, Étienne got/became hungry.*)

Here, Étienne hadn't been hungry, but then he saw that delicious-looking pizza and suddenly was hungry. You indicate this change in his feeling by using the **passé composé**.

When taking two (or more) actions at a time

When you have two or more actions, the tense you use depends on whether the actions are simultaneous or sequential:

>> **Simultaneous:** You use the **imparfait** to express two or more things that were happening at the same time.

Henriette conduisait pendant que Thierry chantait. (*Henriette drove while Thierry sang.*)

The driving and singing were happening at the same time, so you use the **imparfait**.

>> **Sequential:** You need the **passé composé** for things that happened one after the other.

Ils sont partis, et puis Viviane a commencé à pleurer. (*They left, and then Viviane started to cry.*)

They left first, and then after they left, Viviane started to cry. Because these actions are sequential, you use the **passé composé**.

When getting interrupted – how rude!

The **imparfait** and **passé composé** work together to express something that interrupted something else. The **imparfait** gives you the background info — what was happening when something else (expressed with the **passé composé**) occurred.

Je lisais quand quelqu'un a frappé à la porte. (*I was reading when someone knocked on the door.*)

Quand nous sommes arrivés, tout le monde mangeait. (*When we arrived, everyone was eating.*)

Il se promenait quand il a trouvé le chien. (*He was walking when he found the dog.*)

The verbs in the **imparfait** in the preceding three examples tell you what was happening, and the verbs in the **passé composé** tell you what interrupted them.

Your boss needs to you write up a report about this morning's meeting. Conjugate the verbs in parentheses into the French **imparfait** or **passé composé**, as required.

PRACTICE

Q. La réunion _____ (commencer) à 8 h 00.

A. La réunion a commencé à 8 h 00. (*The meeting began at 8 a.m.*)

XYZ, Cie.
11, rue de Dai
Paris

Élisabeth (61) _____ (prendre) des notes pendant que Juliette

(62) _____ (faire) son exposé. Elle (63) _____ (demander) s'il y

(64) _____ (avoir) des questions. Thomas (65) _____ (dire) oui —

il (66) _____ (vouloir) plus de détails. Juliette (67) _____ (expliquer)

quelque chose de très compliqué quand Marc (68) _____ (arriver).

Il (69) _____ (porter) des pizzas, et soudainement tout le monde

(70) _____ (avoir) faim.

Understanding the Recent Past

To talk about something that *just happened*, you can use **le passé récent** — *the recent past*. This construction means "to have just done something" and is the opposite of the near future (discussed in Chapter 10, meaning "to be going to do something"). The recent past is the third and final past tense (after the **passé compose**, see Chapter 15) and the **imparfait** (explained previously in this chapter) that beginners need to understand in order to communicate in French.

The recent past has three parts:

>> The verb **venir** (*to come*) conjugated into the present tense (see Chapter 6 for the details on conjugating **venir**)

>> The preposition **de** (Chapter 12 tells you all about prepositions)

>> The infinitive of the main verb (see Chapter 10 to brush up on infinitives)

Here are a few examples.

Je viens de manger. (*I just ate.*)

Il vient d'arriver. (*He just arrived.*)

Nous venons de finir le projet. (*We just finished the project.*)

With pronominal verbs (see Chapter 7), the reflexive pronoun stays right in front of the infinitive.

Tu viens de te doucher. (*You just took a shower.*)

Elle vient de s'habiller. (*She just got dressed.*)

To talk about something that *had just happened* (not right now, but considering it from a point in the past), you use the recent past construction (as in the preceding example sentences), but this time, conjugate **venir** into the **imparfait**.

Je venais de manger. (*I had just eaten.*)

Il venait d'arriver. (*He had just arrived.*)

Tu venais de te doucher. (*You had just taken a shower.*)

Elle venait de s'habiller. (*She had just gotten dressed.*)

PRACTICE

Translate these sentences into French, using the recent past.

Q. I just started.

A. Je viens de commencer.

71 We just finished. _____

72 You (tu) just came downstairs. _____

73 She just left. _____

74 They (ils) had just spoken. _____

75 You (vous) just opened the door. _____

76 I had just gone out. _____

77 We had just woken up. _____

78 They (elles) just went to bed. _____

79 He had just called. _____

80 Did you just fall? _____

Answer Key to "The Imparfait Tense" Practice Questions

(1) **tu chantais** (*you were singing*)

(2) **il montait** (*he was going upstairs*)

(3) **nous criions** (*we were screaming*)

(4) **vous travailliez** (*you were working*)

(5) **elles gagnaient** (*they were winning*)

(6) **j'étudiais** (*I was studying*)

(7) **tu fumais** (*you were smoking*)

(8) **on écoutait** (*we were listening*)

(9) **nous habitions** (*we were living*)

(10) **vous copiiez** (*you were copying*)

(11) **tu choisissais** (*you were choosing*)

(12) **il rendait** (*he was returning*)

(13) **vous dépendiez** (*you were depending*)

(14) **nous choisissions** (*we were choosing*)

(15) **elles perdaient** (*they were losing*)

(16) **j'agissais** (*I was acting*)

(17) **tu confondais** (*you were confusing*)

(18) **on remplissait** (*we were filling*)

(19) **nous attendions** (*we were waiting*)

(20) **vous rougissiez** (*you were blushing*)

(21) **tu essayais** (*you were trying*)

(22) **il lançait** (*he was throwing*)

(23) **nous appelions** (*we were calling*)

(24) **vous meniez** (*you were leading*)

(25) **elles rejetaient** (*they were rejecting*)

(26) **je nageais** (*I was swimming*)

(27) **tu prétendais** (*you were claiming*)

(28) **on levait** (*someone was lifting/we were lifting*)

(29) **nous pincions** (*we were pinching*)

(30) **vous bougiez** (*you were moving*)

(31) **tu avais** (*you had*)

(32) **il était** (*he was*)

(33) **nous faisions** (*we were doing/making*)

(34) **vous deviez** (*you had to*)

(35) **elles allaient** (*they were going*)

(36) **je savais** (*I knew*)

(37) **tu tenais** (*you were holding*)

(38) **on lisait** (*we were reading*)

(39) **nous voulions** (*we wanted*)

(40) **vous étiez** (*you were*)

(41) **Nous habitions/vivions ensemble; On habitait/vivait ensemble.**

(42) **Il faisait chaud hier.**

(43) **Antoine chantait.**

(44) **Paul et Michel regardaient un film chaque semaine./Paul et Michel regardaient un film toutes les semaines.**

(45) **Si seulement tu avais la clé./Si seulement vous aviez la clé.**

(46) **Je dormais.**

(47) **Elle était très jolie.**

(48) **Et si je t'aidais ?/Et si je vous aidais ?**

(49) **Il avait peur.**

(50) **Je voulais voyager.**

(51) **passé composé**

(52) **imparfait**

(53) **passé composé**

(54) **imparfait**

55. imparfait

56. passé composé

57. passé composé

58. passé composé

59. imparfait

60. imparfait

61. prenait

62. faisait

63. a demandé

64. avait

65. a dit

66. voulait

67. expliquait

68. est arrivé

69. portait

70. a eu

71. Nous venons de finir./On vient de finir.

72. Tu viens de descendre (les escaliers).

73. Elle vient de partir.

74. Ils venaient de parler.

75. Vous venez d'ouvrir la porte.

76. Je venais de sortir.

77. Nous venions de nous réveiller./On venait de se réveiller.

78. Elles viennent de se coucher./Elles viennent d'aller au lit.

79. Il venait d'appeler.

80. Est-ce que tu viens de tomber ?/Viens-tu de tomber ?/Tu viens de tomber ?

5
The Part of Tens

Chapter **17**

Ten (or so) Essential French Phrases

I n addition to nouns, verbs, and all of the other parts of speech, a whole world of little phrases make up a huge part of any communication. You're likely to pick up on these things while you learn more French, but you can supercharge your conversational skills by just taking a moment to see how to use them.

Here are ten (or so) essential phrases to help you communicate in French every day.

C'est

These four letters are actually two words: **ce** (*this/that*) + **est** (*is*, from **être**, *to be*), which contract just like all other two-letter-words-ending-in-e + word-starting-with-a-vowel (like **le** in Chapter 3, **ne** in Chapter 9, and so on).

So **c'est** means *this/that is* or *it is*; and you'll use it every time you speak French:

» For talking about days and dates:

- **C'est lundi.** (*It's Monday.*)
- **C'est le 5 mai.** (*It's May 5.*)

See Chapter 5 for more about the calendar in French.

>> Pair **c'est** with adjectives that describe something already mentioned, such as **J'ai lu ce livre, c'est incroyable !** (*I've read that book, it's incredible!*)

>> Follow **c'est** with singular nouns. For example:

  ● **C'est une bonne idée.** (*That's a good idea.*)

  ● **C'est une fille !** (*It's a girl!*)

REMEMBER

>> When introducing plural nouns, **c'est** becomes **ce sont** (*these/those are*): **Ce sont mes enfants.** (*These are my kids.*)

The verb can also be conjugated into other tenses, such as the imperfect (see Chapter 16): **C'était incroyable !** (*It was incredible!*)

Il y a

Another essential, everyday expression is **il y a**, which means *there is* or *there are*. This phrase is made up of three words:

>> **il:** Masculine singular subject pronoun (see Chapter 1)

>> **y:** Adverbial pronoun that generally means *there* (see Chapter 13)

>> **a:** Third-person singular conjugation of **avoir** (*to have*)

So **il y a** literally means "*it has there,*" but the idiomatic equivalents are *there is* or *there are*:

Il y a un problème. (*There's a problem.*)

Est-ce qu'il y a quelque chose à manger ? (*Is there anything to eat?*)

WARNING

The verb is always third-person singular, even with plural nouns:

Il y a beaucoup de problèmes ! (*There are lots of problems!*)

Est-ce qu'il y a des pommes ? (*Are there any apples?*)

The verb can be conjugated into other tenses, such as the imperfect (see Chapter 16):

Il y avait un problème. (*There was a problem.*)

Il y avait beaucoup de problèmes ! (*There were lots of problems!*)

Que veut dire . . . ? and Comment dit-on . . . ?

When you read or hear something in French that you don't understand, the expression **Que veut dire . . . ?** (*What does . . . mean?*) is your friend: **Que veut dire « écureuil » ?** (*What does "écureuil" mean?*)

The counterpoint to the above is **Comment dit-on . . . ?** (*How do you say . . . ?*), which you use when trying to figure out how to say something in French: **Comment dit-on « squirrel » en français ?** (*How do you say "squirrel" in French?*)

C'est-à-dire

Want to offer clarification or further information? Then master the expression **c'est-à-dire** (*that is, i.e.;* or literally, *that is to say*).

> **Je vais partir après le déjeuner, c'est-à-dire vers 14 h 00.** (*I'm going to leave after lunch; that is, around 2 p.m.*)
>
> **Laura, c'est-à-dire l'auteur de ce bouquin, est géniale !** (*Laura, i.e., the author of this book, is awesome!*)

Au cas où

Keep the French expression **au cas où** (*[just] in case*) at the ready when you need to express a precaution you're taking, such as bringing an umbrella in case of rain or buying extra bread so that you don't run out.

> **Je pense qu'il va pleuvoir, j'apporte un parapluie, au cas où.** (*I think it's going to rain, I'm bringing an umbrella, just in case.*)
>
> **Rachète du pain, au cas où.** (*Buy some more bread, just in case.*)

À mon avis

If you need to express an opinion, **à mon avis** (*in my opinion*) is the phrase to use: **À mon avis, c'est une expression essentielle.** (*In my opinion, it's an essential expression.*)

TIP

The word **mon** is a possessive adjective (see Chapter 4 for the rundown of possessive adjectives) which means that you can change it out for other possessive adjectives in order to talk about others' opinions:

- » **à ton avis** (*in your opinion*)
- » **à son avis** (*in his/her opinion*)
- » **à notre avis** (*in our opinion*)

- » **à votre avis** (*in your opinion*)
- » **à leur avis** (*in their opinion*)

Ah bon (?)

The French expression **ah bon** looks like it means *oh good*, but it doesn't. It simply acknowledges what someone just said, whether positive or negative.

> – **J'ai perdu mon emploi.** (*I lost my job.*)
>
> – **Ah bon.** (*Oh, I see.*)

REMEMBER

By raising your pitch at the end, you can turn it into a gentle request for confirmation or further information.

> – **Nous avons pris une grande décision.** (*We've made a big decision.*)
>
> – **Ah bon ?** (*Really? What is it?*)

J'arrive

The simple phrase **j'arrive** literally means *I'm arriving*: **J'arrive de Rome à 18 h 00.** (*I'm arriving from Rome at 6 pm.*)

But it's often used more like *I'm on my way, I'll be right there*, such as when talking on the phone or an intercom system.

> **Dis à Christine que j'arrive.** (*Tell Christine I'll be right there.*)
>
> **J'arrive !** (*I'm on my way! I'll be right down!*)

You can even use it when you're actually with the other person and need to leave for a moment:

> **Oups, j'ai oublié mon portefeuille. J'arrive.** (*Oops, I forgot my wallet. I'll be right back.*)

TIP

Conjugate **arriver** for another subject to express the same sort of meaning for them.

> **Bonjour Christine, Laura arrive.** (*Hello Christine, Laura is on her way.*)
>
> **Attendez-nous, on arrive !** (*Wait for us, we're on our way!*)

Avoir besoin de/Avoir envie de

These two essential French expressions have single-word English equivalents. **Avoir besoin de** (*to need*) literally means *to have need of*. It can be used in front of nouns.

> **J'ai besoin de ton assistance.** (*I need your help.*)
>
> **Il a besoin d'un ordinateur.** (*He needs a computer.*)

You can also put it in front of verbs.

> **Elle a besoin de partir tôt.** (*She needs to leave early.*)

> **Nous avons besoin de parler.** (*We need to talk.*)

Avoir envie de (*to want, to feel like*) literally means *to have want of*. It too can be used with both nouns and verbs.

> **Il a envie d'un vélo.** (*He wants a bike.*)

> **J'ai envie de lire le journal.** (I feel like reading the newspaper.)

Avoir = "to be"

(This Part of Tens has ten parts of its own. Wow, that's so meta!)

It's generally true that "to be" is être in French, but not always. Many of English's essential "to be" expressions have French equivalents with avoir.

REMEMBER

In these expressions, **avoir** (which normally means *to have*) means *to be*:

>> **avoir (5 / 50 / 500 . . .) ans** (*to be [5 / 50 / 500 . . .] years old*)

>> **avoir chaud** (*to be hot*)

>> **avoir de la chance** (*to be lucky*)

>> **avoir faim** (*to be hungry*)

>> **avoir froid** (*to be cold*)

>> **avoir honte** (*to be ashamed*)

>> **avoir peur** (*to be afraid*)

>> **avoir raison** (*to be right*)

>> **avoir soif** (*to be thirsty*)

>> **avoir tort** (*to be wrong*)

IN THIS CHAPTER

» Celebrating holidays in French

» Offering congratulations and good wishes

» Wishing everyone good luck

» Expressing French pride

Chapter **18**

Ten Celebratory French Expressions

O ne of the best parts of learning French is getting to celebrate holidays, birthdays, and other special occasions with your new French-speaking friends. Here are ten celebratory French expressions and good wishes for all kinds of occasions throughout the year.

Bonne Année !

Everyone likes the start of a new year, right? To wish someone a *Happy New Year!*, say, «**Bonne Année !**»

DIFFERENCES In the U.S. you might wish someone a "Happy New Year!" toward the end of December if you know that you're not going to see each other before January. It's also common to offer this good wish to strangers, such as cashiers and other customers during your end-of-year shopping. In contrast, the French never say «**Bonne Année**» until it's actually the new year. Instead, in December you can say «**Bonnes fêtes**» (*Happy holidays*), which covers Christmas, Hanukkah, and the new year.

Meilleurs vœux !

Write **meilleurs vœux** at the end of a letter to offer someone your *best wishes*. You can also use it to wish someone well after illness or injury.

If you say it during the end-of-year holidays, **Meilleurs vœux** means *Season's greetings*. Other non-denominational holiday wishes include **Joyeuses fêtes !** (*Happy holidays!*) and **Bonnes fêtes !**

Or you can be specific. For example:

> **Joyeux Noël !** (*Merry Christmas!*)
>
> **Joyeux Hanoucca !** (*Happy Hanukkah!*)

Joyeux anniversaire !

To wish someone a *Happy birthday!*, you can say **Joyeux anniversaire !** or **Bon anniversaire !**

TIP

The French version of the birthday song is sung to the same tune as in English:

> **Joyeux anniversaire !**
>
> **Joyeux anniversaire !**
>
> **Joyeux an – ni – ver – sai – re . . . !**
>
> **Joyeux anniversaire !**

It's a fun challenge to quickly sing the birthday person's name at the end of the third line.

The word **anniversaire** means both *birthday* and, as you might have guessed, *anniversary*. So you can also use **Joyeux anniversaire !** to wish someone a *happy anniversary*.

Bonne chance !

When you want to offer your hopes that someone's dream comes true, you can wish them *Good luck!* with the expression **Bonne chance !**

Use this expression for events that are truly based on luck, when the recipient of your wish has no control over whether it comes true or not, such as winning the lottery or catching all the green lights during their work commute.

Bon courage !

Use this expression when there's no luck involved, just a lot of hard work.

In English, this expression is still equivalent to *Good luck!*, but **Bon courage** ! indicates that you support the efforts of the person you're speaking to and are sure they'll succeed — for example, in passing a test or acing an interview.

You can also use **Bon courage** ! to encourage someone — whether friend, foe, or stranger — who's performing a grueling task, such as climbing a mountain or trying to get a bunch of kids at a sleepover to settle down.

You can put the adjective **bon** (*good*) in front of many other nouns to wish someone well or express your hopes that they have a good time.

> **Bon appétit** ! *(Have good meal! Enjoy your meal!)*

> **Bon match** ! *(Have a good game! Enjoy your game!)*

> **Bon voyage** ! *(Have a good trip! Enjoy your trip!)*

If the noun is feminine, the adjective must be, too.

> **Bonne baignade** ! *(Have a nice swim! Enjoy your swim!)*

> **Bonne promenade** ! *(Have a nice walk! Enjoy your walk!)*

Félicitations !

To say *Congratulations!*, use the French exclamation **Félicitations** ! If you want to specify what you're congratulating them for, you can use the preposition **pour**.

> **Félicitations pour ta nomination** ! *(Congratulations for your nomination, for getting nominated!)*

> **Félicitations pour ton nouveau travail** ! *(Congratulations on the new job!)*

Rather than an exclamation, you can talk about congratulating someone by using **félicitations** as a noun in the expression **offrir ses félicitations à quelqu'un (pour quelque chose)** (*to congratulate someone [for something]*).

> **Je veux offrir mes félicitations à Aline pour son livre.** (*I want to congratulate Aline for her book.*)

The exclamation also has a related verb: **féliciter** (*to congratulate*).

> **Je te félicite** ! (*I congratulate you!*)

À votre santé !

When someone proposes a toast, **À votre santé** ! is the closest equivalent to *Cheers!* It literally means *To your health!* (formal and/or plural, see Chapter 1).

Of course, there's also an informal/singular variation: **À ta santé !** (*To your health!*) And there's also a more playful one: **À notre santé !** (*To our health!*)

À la vôtre !

À la vôtre ! is a contracted form of **À votre santé !** (from the preceding section). This expression literally means *To yours!* (formal and/or plural). It has the same variations: **À la tienne !** (*To yours!*) (informal/singular) and **À la nôtre !** (*To ours!*)

TIP

The final word in each of these expressions is the possessive pronoun, which you can read about in Chapter 4. The possessive pronoun used is feminine because it replaces the feminine noun **santé** (*health*).

Vive la France !

This patriotic expression means *Long live France!* and is a celebration of French culture and history.

English-speaking Francophiles often use it on its own, but for the French, it's really the second half of a two-part expression used by politicians and officials.

> **Vive la République et vive la France !** (*Long live the Republic and long live France!*)

Bonne fête !

When you don't know or don't have a specific term for a particular holiday or event, you can use the generic **Bonne fête !** to wish someone a *Happy celebration!*

You may find this phrase particularly useful on Bastille Day, the French national holiday. The French don't have an equivalent to "Happy Bastille Day!" So if you want to wish them well this day, say, «**Bonne fête !**»

Bonne fête also means "*happy name day*" and, in French-speaking Canada, "*happy birthday.*"

6

Appendixes

Appendix **A**

Verb Charts

U se these verb charts as a quick-reference guide to conjugations for regular, spelling-change, stem-changing, and irregular verbs. (Chapter 6 shows verbs conjugated in the present tense according to each pattern.)

Note: In this appendix, I list the conjugations in order of the pronouns, from first- to third-person singular and then first- to third-person plural: **je, tu, il/elle/on, nous, vous, ils/elles** (or for the imperative [commands], **tu, nous, vous**).

Regular Verbs

You conjugate regular verbs by taking the verb stem (infinitive minus **–er/–ir/–re**) and adding the appropriate ending from Table A-1 (regular **–er** verbs), A-2 (regular **–ir** verbs), or A-3 (regular **–re** verbs):

>> **Present:** Infinitive minus **–er, –ir,** or **–re** ending

>> **Imperfect:** Present-tense indicative **nous** form minus **–ons**

Table A-1 Regular –er verbs

Subject	Present	Imperfect
je	–e	–ais
tu	–es	–ais
il/elle/on	–e	–ait
nous	–ons	–ions
vous	–ez	–iez
ils/elles	–ont	–aient

For example: **parler** (*to talk, speak*)

> **Present Participle:** parlant
>
> **Past Participle:** parlé; **Auxiliary Verb:** avoir
>
> **Imperative:** parle, parlons, parlez
>
> **Present:** parle, parles, parle, parlons, parlez, parlent
>
> **Imperfect:** parlais, parlais, parlait, parlions, parliez, parlaient

Table A-2 Regular –ir verbs

Subject	Present	Imperfect
je	–is	–ais
tu	–is	–ais
il/elle/on	–it	–ait
nous	–issons	–ions
vous	–issez	–iez
ils/elles	–issent	–aient

For example: **finir** (*to finish*)

> **Present Participle:** finissant
>
> **Past Participle:** fini; **Auxiliary Verb:** avoir
>
> **Imperative:** finis, finissons, finissez
>
> **Present:** finis, finis, finit, finissons, finissez, finissent
>
> **Imperfect:** finissais, finissais, finissait, finissions, finissiez, finissaient

Table A-3   Regular –re verbs

Subject	Present	Imperfect
je	–s	–ais
tu	–s	–ais
il/elle/on	-----	–ait
nous	–ons	–ions
vous	–ez	–iez
ils/elles	–ent	–aient

For example: **vendre** (*to sell*)

Present Participle: vendant

Past Participle: vendu; **Auxiliary Verb:** avoir

Imperative: vends, vendons, vendez

Present: vends, vends, vend, vendons, vendez, vendent

Imperfect: vendais, vendais, vendait, vendions, vendiez, vendaient

Spelling-Change Verbs

–cer Verbs

commencer (to begin)

Present Participle: commençant

Past Participle: commencé; **Auxiliary Verb:** avoir

Imperative: commence, commençons, commencez

Present: commence, commences, commence, commençons, commencez, commencent

Imperfect: commençais, commençais, commençait, commencions, commenciez, commençaient

Verbs conjugated like **commencer** — which changes the **c** to **ç** in some conjugations — include **agacer** (*to annoy*), **annoncer** (*to announce*), **avancer** (*to advance*), **effacer** (*to erase*), **lancer** (*to throw*), and **menacer** (*to threaten*).

–ger Verbs

manger (to eat)

Present Participle: mangeant

Past Participle: mangé; **Auxiliary Verb:** avoir

Imperative: mange, mangeons, mangez

Present: mange, manges, mange, mangeons, mangez, mangent

Imperfect: mangeais, mangeais, mangeait, mangions, mangiez, mangeaient

Similar verbs that sometimes need to put an **e** after the **g** include **bouger** (*to move*), **corriger** (*to correct*), **déménager** (*to move house*), **déranger** (*to disturb*), **diriger** (*to direct*), **exiger** (*to demand*), **juger** (*to judge*), **mélanger** (*to mix*), **nager** (*to swim*), and **voyager** (*to travel*).

Stem-Changing Verbs

–eler Verbs

appeler (to call)

Present Participle: appelant

Past Participle: appelé; **Auxiliary Verb:** avoir

Imperative: appelle, appelons, appelez

Present: appelle, appelles, appelle, appelons, appelez, appellent

Imperfect: appelais, appelais, appelait, appelions, appeliez, appelaient

Similar verbs that sometimes double the **l** include **épeler** (*to spell*), **rappeler** (*to call back, recall*), and **renouveler** (*to renew*).

–eter Verbs

jeter (to throw)

Present Participle: jetant

Past Participle: jeté; **Auxiliary Verb:** avoir

Imperative: jette, jetons, jetez

Present: jette, jettes, jette, jetons, jetez, jettent

Imperfect: jetais, jetais, jetait, jetions, jetiez, jetaient

Hoqueter (*to hiccup*), **projeter** (*to project*), and **rejeter** (*to reject*) are conjugated the same way, doubling the **t** in some conjugations.

–e*er Verb

lever (to lift)

>**Present participle:** levant
>
>**Past Participle:** levé; **Auxiliary Verb:** avoir
>
>**Imperative:** lève, levons, levez
>
>**Present:** lève, lèves, lève, levons, levez, lèvent
>
>**Imperfect:** levais, levais, levait, levions, leviez, levaient

Similar verbs that add a grave accent (**è**) in some conjugations include **acheter** (*to buy*), **amener** (*to take*), **enlever** (*to remove*), **mener** (*to lead*), and **promener** (*to walk*).

–é*er Verbs

gérer (to manage)

>**Present participle:** gérant
>
>**Past Participle:** géré; **Auxiliary Verb:** avoir
>
>**Imperative:** gère, gérons, gérez
>
>**Present:** gère, gères, gère, gérons, gérez, gèrent
>
>**Imperfect:** gérais, gérais, gérait, gérions, gériez, géraient

Other verbs that change the acute accent (**é**) to a grave accent (**è**) in some conjugations are **célébrer** (*to celebrate*), **compléter** (*to complete*), **espérer** (*to hope*), and **répéter** (*to repeat*).

–yer Verbs

nettoyer (to clean)

>**Present participle:** nettoyant
>
>**Past Participle:** nettoyé; **Auxiliary Verb:** avoir
>
>**Imperative:** nettoie, nettoyons, nettoyez
>
>**Present:** nettoie, nettoies, nettoie, nettoyons, nettoyez, nettoient
>
>**Imperfect:** nettoyais, nettoyais, nettoyait, nettoyions, nettoyiez, nettoyaient

Employer (*to use*), **ennuyer** (*to bore*), **noyer** (*to drown*), and **payer** (*to pay*) likewise change the **y** to **i** in some conjugations.

Irregular Verbs

aller (to go)

Present Participle: allant

Past Participle: allé; **Auxiliary Verb:** être

Imperative: va, allons, allez

Present: vais, vas, va, allons, allez, vont

Imperfect: allais, allais, allait, allions, alliez, allaient

avoir (to have)

Present Participle: ayant

Past Participle: eu; **Auxiliary Verb:** avoir

Imperative: aie, ayons, ayez

Present: ai, as, a, avons, avez, ont

Imperfect: avais, avais, avait, avions, aviez, avaient

boire (to drink)

Present Participle: buvant

Past Participle: bu; **Auxiliary Verb:** avoir

Imperative: bois, boyons, boyez

Present: bois, bois, boit, buvons, buvez, boivent

Imperfect: buvais, buvais, buvait, buvions, buviez, buvaient

connaître (to know)

Present Participle: connaissant

Past Participle: connu; **Auxiliary Verb:** avoir

Imperative: connais, connaissons, connaissez

Present: connais, connais, connaît, connaissons, connaissez, connaissent

Imperfect: connaissais, connaissais, connaissait, connaissions, connaissiez, connaissaient

Other verbs conjugated like **connaître** include **disparaître** (*to disappear*), **méconnaître** (*to be unaware of*), **paraître** (*to seem*), and **reconnaître** (*to recognize*).

devoir (must, to have to)

Present Participle: devant

Past Participle: dû; **Auxiliary Verb:** avoir

Imperative: dois, devons, devez

Present: dois, dois, doit, devons, devez, doivent

Imperfect: devais, devais, devait, devions, deviez, devaient

dire (to say, tell)

Present Participle: disant

Past Participle: dit; **Auxiliary Verb:** avoir

Imperative: dis, disons, dites

Present: dis, dis, dit, disons, dites, disent

Imperfect: disais, disais, disait, disions, disiez, disaient

This conjugation pattern is the same for **redire** (*to repeat, to say again*).

être (to be)

Present Participle: étant

Past Participle: été; **Auxiliary Verb:** avoir

Imperative: sois, soyons, soyez

Present: suis, es, est, sommes, êtes, sont

Imperfect: étais, étais, était, étions, étiez, étaient

faire (to do, make)

Present Participle: faisant

Past Participle: fait; **Auxiliary Verb:** avoir

Imperative: fais, faisons, faites

Present: fais, fais, fait, faisons, faites, font

Imperfect: faisais, faisais, faisait, faisions, faisiez, faisaient

Défaire (*to undo, dismantle*), **refaire** (*to do/make again*), and **satisfaire** (*to satisfy*) follow the same pattern.

mettre (to put, to place)

Present Participle: mettant

Past Participle: mis; **Auxiliary Verb:** avoir

Imperative: mets, mettons, mettez

Present: mets, mets, met, mettons, mettez, mettent

Imperfect: mettais, mettais, mettait, mettions, mettiez, mettaient

Verbs like **mettre** include **admettre** (*to admit*), **commettre** (*to commit*), **permettre** (*to permit*), **promettre** (*to promise*), and **soumettre** (*to submit*).

offrir (to offer)

Present Participle: offrant

Past Participle: offert; **Auxiliary Verb:** avoir

Imperative: offre, offrons, offrez

Present: offre, offres, offre, offrons, offrez, offrent

Imperfect: offrais, offrais, offrait, offrions, offriez, offraient

Verbs conjugated like **offrir** include **couvrir** (*to cover*), **découvrir** (*to discover*), **ouvrir** (*to open*), **recouvrir** (*to re-cover, conceal*), and **souffrir** (*to suffer*).

partir (to leave)

Present Participle: partant

Past Participle: parti; **Auxiliary Verb:** être

Imperative: pars, partons, partez

Present: pars, pars, part, partons, partez, partent

Imperfect: partais, partais, partait, partions, partiez, partaient

Other verbs like **partir** are **repartir** (*to restart, set off again*), **dormir** (*to sleep*), **sentir** (*to feel*), and **sortir** (*to go out*).

pouvoir (can, to be able to)

Present Participle: pouvant

Past Participle: pu; **Auxiliary Verb:** avoir

Present: peux, peux, peut, pouvons, pouvez, peuvent

Imperfect: pouvais, pouvais, pouvait, pouvions, pouviez, pouvaient

prendre (to take)

Present Participle: prenant

Past Participle: pris; **Auxiliary Verb:** avoir

Imperative: prends, prenons, prenez

Present: prends, prends, prend, prenons, prenez, prennent

Imperfect: prenais, prenais, prenait, prenions, preniez, prenaient

Other verbs like **prendre** include **apprendre** (*to learn*), **comprendre** (*to understand*), and **surprendre** (*to surprise*).

savoir (to know)

Present Participle: sachant

Past Participle: su; **Auxiliary Verb:** avoir

Imperative: sache, sachons, sachez

Present: sais, sais, sait, savons, savez, savent

Imperfect: savais, savais, savait, savions, saviez, savaient

venir (to come)

Present Participle: venant

Past Participle: venu; **Auxiliary Verb:** être

Imperative: viens, venons, venez

Present: viens, viens, vient, venons, venez, viennent

Imperfect: venais, venais, venait, venions, veniez, venaient

Verbs conjugated like **venir** include **devenir** (*to become*), **parvenir** (*to reach, achieve*), **revenir** (*to come back*), and **se souvenir** (*to remember*).

voir (to see)

Present Participle: voyant

Past Participle: vu; **Auxiliary Verb:** avoir

Imperative: vois, voyons, voyez

Present: vois, vois, voit, voyons, voyez, voient

Imperfect: voyais, voyais, voyait, voyions, voyiez, voyaient

Revoir (*to see again*) is conjugated the same.

vouloir (to want)

Present Participle: voulant

Past Participle: voulu; **Auxiliary Verb:** avoir

Imperative: veuille, N/A, veuillez

Present: veux, veux, veut, voulons, voulez, veulent

Imperfect: voulais, voulais, voulait, voulions, vouliez, voulaient

Appendix **B**

Verbs with Prepositions

Many French verbs need a preposition when they're followed by an object or an infinitive. English has some verbs that need prepositions, called *phrasal verbs*, but they're not at all the same thing as in French. Phrasal verbs require different prepositions depending on meaning, such as *to move on* and *to move in*.

French has a few verbs that have different meanings depending on which preposition follows, but most verbs just require a certain preposition that, confusingly, often has no English translation or has a meaning that doesn't correspond to the general meaning of the preposition. This appendix points out some of the more common verbs and the prepositions that go with them.

Table B-1 Verbs That Require à

Verb + à	Translation	Verb + à	Translation
aider à + infinitive	to help to do something	**s'intéresser à** + noun	to be interested in something
s'amuser à + infinitive	to have fun doing	**inviter** (someone) **à** + noun	to invite (someone) to something
arriver à + infinitive	to manage to do/succeed in doing	**se mettre à** + infinitive	to start, set about doing
assister à + noun	to attend something	**persister à** + infinitive	to persist in doing
s'attendre à +infinitive	to expect to do	**plaire à** + person	to please/be pleasing to someone
chercher à + infinitive	to attempt to do/to look to do	**se préparer à** + infinitive	to prepare oneself to/to get ready to do
conseiller à + person	to advise someone	**réfléchir à** + noun	to think about something
consentir à +infinitive	to consent to doing	**renoncer à** + infinitive	to give up doing
se décider à + infinitive	to decide to do, make up one's mind to do	**répondre à** + person or noun	to answer someone/something
demander à + person	to ask someone	**résister à** + infinitive/noun	to resist doing/to stand up to something
dire à + person	to tell someone	**réussir à** + infinitive	to manage to do/succeed in doing
emprunter à + person	to borrow from someone	**serrer la main à** + person	to shake someone's hand
encourager à + infinitive	to encourage to do	**servir à** + infinitive	to be used for doing/serve to do
faire attention à +noun	to pay attention to/watch out for something	**tarder à** + infinitive	to delay/be late in doing
s'habituer à + noun or infinitive	to get used to something/doing	**téléphoner à** + person	to call someone
hésiter à +infinitive	to hesitate to do	**voler à** + person	to steal from someone

Table B-2 Verbs Followed by de

Verb + de	Translation	Verb + de	Translation
accepter de + infinitive	to accept, agree to do	**finir de** + infinitive	to finish doing
s'agir de + infinitive/noun	to be a question of doing/something	**se méfier de** + infinitive	to beware of
avoir besoin de + noun	to need	**mériter de** + infinitive	to deserve to do
avoir envie de + infinitive/noun	to want, to feel like doing/something	**se moquer de** + noun	to make fun of
avoir peur de + infinitive/noun	to be afraid of doing/something	**offrir de** + infinitive	to offer to do
cesser de + infinitive	to stop, cease doing	**oublier de** + infinitive	to forget to do
choisir de + infinitive	to choose to do	**persuader de** + infinitive	to persuade to do
conseiller de + infinitive	to advise to do	**se plaindre de** + noun	to complain about something
craindre de + infinitive	to fear doing	**prier de** + infinitive	to beg to do
décider de + infinitive	to decide to do	**promettre de** + infinitive	to promise to do
défendre à quelqu'un de + infinitive	to forbid (someone) to do	**proposer de** + infinitive	to suggest doing

Verb + de	Translation	Verb + de	Translation
demander à quelqu'un de + infinitive	*to ask (someone) to do*	**refuser de** + infinitive	*to refuse to do*
se dépêcher de + infinitive	*to hurry to do*	**regretter de** + infinitive	*to regret doing*
dire à quelqu'un de + infinitive	*to tell (someone) to do something*	**remercier de** + infinitive	*to thank for doing*
empêcher de + infinitive	*to prevent, keep from doing*	**risquer de** + infinitive	*to risk doing*
essayer de + infinitive	*to try to do*	**se souvenir de** + infinitive/noun	*to remember doing/something*
s'excuser de + infinitive	*to apologize for doing*	**venir de** + infinitive	*to have just done something*
féliciter de + infinitive	*to congratulate for doing*		

Table B-3   Verbs That Need Other Prepositions

Verb	Translation	Verb	Translation
Verbs with contre			
s'asseoir contre + noun/person	*to sit leaning against something/someone*	**échanger** + noun	*to exchange something for something else*
se battre contre + noun/person	*to fight (against) something/someone*	**se fâcher contre** + person	*to get mad at someone*
Verbs with dans			
boire quelque chose dans + noun	*to drink something out of something*	**lire dans** + noun	*to read in (a publication)*
courir dans + noun	*to run through/around something*	**manger dans** + noun	*to eat out/off of*
coûter dans les + plural amount	*to cost about*	**prendre quelque chose dans** + noun	*to take something from something*
entrer dans + noun	*to enter somewhere*	**regarder dans** + noun	*to look in something*
fouiller dans + noun	*to look through something*	**vivre dans** + noun	*to live in something*
Verbs with en			
agir en + noun	*to act like something*	**écrire en** + language	*to write in a language*
casser en + noun/number	*to break (something) in(to) something or a number of pieces*	**se vendre en** + noun	*to be sold in (bottles, packs)*
couper en + number	*to cut (something) in(to) a number of pieces*	**se changer en** + noun	*to change/turn into something*
croire en + noun	*to believe in something*	**transformer en** + noun	*to change something into something else*
Verbs with par			
commencer par + infinitive	*to begin/start by doing something*	**jurer par** + noun	*to swear by*
finir par + infinitive	*to end up doing/to finally do*	**sortir par** + noun	*to leave via*
Verbs with pour			
être pour + noun	*to be in favor of*	**payer pour** + person	*to pay for someone*
parler pour + person	*to speak on behalf of*	**signer pour** + person	*to sign on behalf of someone*
Verbs with sur			
acheter + noun + **sur le marché**	*to buy (something) at the market*	**s'étendre sur** + noun	*to spread (oneself) out over/to elaborate on something*

Verb	Translation	Verb	Translation
appuyer sur + noun	*to press something*	**interroger** (someone) **sur** (something)	*to question someone about something*
compter sur + noun/person	*to count on something/someone*	**se jeter sur** + person	*to throw oneself upon someone*
se concentrer sur + noun	*to concentrate/focus on something*	**prendre modèle sur** + person	*to model oneself on someone*
copier sur + person	*to copy from someone*	**réfléchir sur** + noun	*to study, to examine something*
s'endormir sur + noun	*to fall asleep over something*	**revenir sur** + noun	*to go back over something*
Verbs with **vers**			
se diriger vers + noun	*to move toward/make/head for*	**tourner vers** + noun	*to turn toward something*
regarder vers + noun	*to face/look toward something*		

Table B-4   Verbs with Prepositions in English but Not in French

Verb	Translation	Verb	Translation
aller + infinitive	*to be going to do something*	**être censé** + infinitive	*to be supposed to do something*
approuver + noun	*to approve of something*	**habiter** + noun	*to live in some place*
attendre + noun	*to wait for something*	**ignorer** + noun	*to be unaware of something*
chercher + noun	*to look for something*	**mettre** + noun	*to put something on*
demander + noun	*to ask for something*	**payer** + noun	*to pay for something*
devoir + infinitive	*to have to, be obliged to do something*	**pouvoir** + infinitive	*to be able to to do something*
écouter + noun	*to listen to something*	**regarder** + noun	*to look at something*
envoyer chercher + noun	*to send for something*	**sentir** + noun	*to smell of something*
essayer + noun	*to try something on*	**soigner** + person	*to take care of someone (health)*

Appendix C
English-French Dictionary

H ere's some of the French vocabulary used throughout this book, arranged alphabetically by the English translation, to help you when speaking or writing French.

a, an, one: **un (m.)/une (f.)**
about, of, from: **de**
above: **au-dessus (de)**
accomplice: **un/une complice**
to act: **agir**
to advance: **avancer**
advice: **des conseils**
to be afraid: **avoir peur**
after: **après**
again: **encore**
against: **contre**
allowed: **permis**
alone: **seul**
already: **déjà**
although: **bien que**
always: **toujours**
and: **et**
and/or: **et/ou**

anniversary: **un anniversaire**
to announce: **annoncer**
to annoy: **ennuyer**
annoying: **agaçant**
to answer: **répondre**
to appear: **apparaître**
to appoint, attach: **adjoindre**
April: **avril**
around: **autour (de)**
to arrange: **arranger**
to arrive: **arriver**
as much/many: **autant (de)**
as soon as: **aussitôt que**
to be ashamed: **avoir honte**
to ask: **demander**
asparagus: **des asperges**
at, to, in: **à**
athlete: **un/une athlète**

August: **août**
avocado: **un avocat**
backpack: **un sac à dos**
badly: **mal**
baker: **un boulanger/une boulangère**
to bathe: **se baigner**
to be: **être**
to be ___ years old: **avoir ____ ans**
because: **parce que**
beer: **la bière**
before: **avant**
to begin: **commencer**
behind: **derrière**
to believe: **croire**
below: **en-dessous (de)**
best wishes: **meilleurs vœux**
better: **mieux**
big, fat: **gros**
bike: **le vélo**
birthday: **un anniversaire**
to blush: **rougir**
boat: **un bateau**
boldly: **hardiment**
to bore: **ennuyer**
to borrow: **emprunter**
to be born: **naître**
both . . . and: **et . . . et**
boules: **la pétanque**
boy: **un garçon**
to bring up, raise: **élever**
broccoli: **des brocolis**
broken: **cassé**
brother: **le frère**
to build: **bâtir**
but: **mais**
to buy: **acheter**
by: **par**
café: **le café**
to call: **appeler**
to call back, recall: **rappeler**
to call: **téléphoner**
can, to be able to: **pouvoir**
carefully: **soigneusement**
cat: **un chat**
to celebrate: **célébrer, fêter**
cellphone: **un portable/mobile**
certainly: **certainement**
chair: **une chaise**
to change: **changer**
chess: **les échecs**

child: **un/une enfant**
Chinese: **chinois**
to choose: **choisir**
city: **la ville**
to claim: **prétendre**
to clean: **nettoyer**
clearly: **clairement**
to climb: **monter**
clothing: **les vêtements**
coach: **un entraîneur**
coat: **un manteau**
coffee: **le café**
to be cold: **avoir froid**
to come: **venir**
to complete: **compléter**
to confuse: **confondre**
to congratulate: **féliciter**
congratulations: **félicitations**
to consider: **considérer**
continually: **continuellement**
to copy: **copier**
to correct: **corriger**
to count: **compter**
to cover: **couvrir**
to cry: **pleurer**
currently: **actuellement**
cute: **mignon**
day: **un jour**
the day after tomorrow: **après-demain**
the day before yesterday: **avant-hier**
December: **décembre**
to deceive: **tromper**
to decide: **décider**
to defend: **défendre**
to demand: **exiger**
to denounce: **dénoncer**
to depend: **dépendre**
to descend: **descendre**
desk: **un bureau**
to die: **mourir**
difficult: **difficile**
dilemma: **un dilemme**
to direct: **diriger**
disappointed: **déçu**
discouraged: **déconseillé**
to dispatch: **dépêcher**
to divorce: **divorcer**
to do: **faire**
dog: **un chien**
door: **une porte**

down: **en bas**
to dress: **habiller**
to drink: **boire**
to drive: **conduire**
early: **en avance, tôt**
to earn: **gagner**
to eat: **manger**
eighty: **quatre-vingt(s)**
either . . . or: **ou . . . ou/soit . . . soit**
elevator: **un ascenseur**
to employ: **employer**
employee: **un employé/une employée**
English: **anglaise**
enormously: **énormément**
enough: **assez (de)**
to enter: **entrer**
equality: **égalité** (f.)
equals: **égal**
to erase: **effacer**
to establish: **établir**
everywhere: **partout**
expensive: **cher**
eyes: **les yeux** (m.)
fair: **équitable/juste**
to fall: **tomber**
to fall asleep: **s'endormir**
famous: **célèbre**
far: **loin**
father: **le père**
favorite: **préféré**
to fear: **craindre**
February: **février**
fifty: **cinquante**
to fill: **remplir**
finally: **enfin**
to find: **trouver**
to finish: **finir**
fire: **le feu**
fish: **un poisson**
flight: **un vol**
floor: **un étage**
fluently: **couramment**
folding: **pliant**
for: **pour**
for a long time: **longtemps**
forbidden: **interdit**
formal: **formel**
formerly: **autrefois**
fortunately: **heureusement**
forty: **quarante**

freedom: **la liberté**
to freeze: **geler**
French: **français**
fresh: **frais**
Friday: **vendredi**
friend: **un ami/une amie**
to frighten: **effrayer**
from, about, of: **de**
from/about the: **des** (pl.)/**du** (sing. m.)
funny: **drôle/rigolo/amusant**
furniture: **les meubles** (m.)
to get big(ger), fat(ter): **grossir**
to get dressed: **s'habiller**
to get married: **se marier**
girl: **une fille**
to give: **donner**
to give back, return (something): **rendre**
gladly: **volontiers**
to go: **aller**
to go out: **sortir**
to grow: **grandir**
good: **bon**
good luck: **bonne chance**
good luck, keep up the good work: **bon courage**
grapefruit: **le pamplemousse**
Greek: **grec**
guitar: **une guitare**
hair: **les cheveux**
happy: **heureux**
happy (holiday): **bonne fête**
Happy birthday!: **Bon/Joyeux anniversaire !**
happy holidays: **meilleurs vœux/bonnes fêtes**
Happy New Year!: **Bonne Année !**
hard: **dur**
hat: **un chapeau**
to hate: **détester**
haunted: **hanté**
to have: **avoir**
to have just (done): **venir de**
he, it: **il**
headphones: **les écouteurs** (m.)
helicopter: **un hélicoptère**
to hear: **entendre**
here: **ici**
to hesitate: **hésiter**
to hiccup: **hoqueter**
his, her, its (adj.): **sa** (f.)/**son** (m.)/**ses** (pl.)
his, hers, its (pron.): **le sien** (m. sing.), **la sienne**
    (f. sing.), **les siens** (m.pl.), **les siennes** (f. pl.)
to hold: **tenir**

holiday: **la fête**
homework: **les devoirs** (m.)
hope: **un espoir**
to hope: **espérer**
horse: **un cheval**
hot (appearance): **sexy**
hot (temperature): **chaud**
to be hot: **avoir chaud**
how: **comment**
how do you say . . .?: **comment dit-on . . .?**
how much/many: **combien (de)**
to be hungry: **avoir faim**
husband: **le mari**
I: **je**
I see: **ah bon**
idea: **une idée**
ideal: **idéal**
immediately: **immédiatement**
in front of: **devant**
in, to (a country): **en**
in my opinion: **à mon avis**
to influence: **influencer**
inside: **dedans**
to install: **installer**
intelligently: **intelligemment**
interesting: **intéressant**
to introduce: **introduire**
it is, this is: **c'est**
Italian: **italien**
itinerary: **un itinéraire**
January: **janvier**
July: **juillet**
June: **juin**
just as, so as: **ainsi que**
just in case: **au cas où**
kettle of fish: **une poissonnière**
key: **une clé**
kind: **gentil**
kindly: **gentiment**
to know: **savoir, connaître**
lastly: **dernièrement**
late: **tard, en retard**
laundry: **la lessive**
lawyer: **un avocat, une avocate**
lazy: **paresseux**
to lead: **mener**
leader: **un dirigeant/une dirigeante**
leaf: **la feuille**
to leaf through: **feuilleter**
to leave: **partir**

less: **moins**
to lie: **mentir**
to lift, raise: **lever**
to like, to love: **aimer**
to listen (to): **écouter**
a little: **un peu de**
to live [somewhere]: **habiter, vivre**
lively: **vif**
to lodge: **loger**
long live France: **vive la France**
to look for: **chercher**
to lose: **perdre**
a lot: **beaucoup**
to be lucky: **avoir de la chance**
ma'am: **madame**
majority, most of: **la plupart de**
man: **un homme**
to manage: **gérer**
March: **mars**
marijuana: **la mari**
May: **mai**
mean: **méchant**
meanly: **méchamment**
meat: **la viande**
to meet: **rencontrer**
to meet: **se réunir**
meeting: **la réunion**
to melt: **fondre**
midnight: **minuit** (m.)
mild: **doux**
mine: **le mien** (m. sing.), **la mienne** (f. sing.),
    les miens (m. pl.), **les miennes** (f. pl.)
minus: **moins**
miss: **mademoiselle**
to moderate: **modérer**
Monday: **lundi**
mother: **la mère**
to move: **bouger**
to move (in): **emménager**
to move house: **déménager**
Mr.: **monsieur**
Mrs.: **madame**
museum: **un musée**
must, to have to: **devoir**
my: **mon** (m. object)/**ma** (f. object)/**mes** (pl. object)
near: **près**
to need: **avoir besoin de**
neighbor: **un voisin/une voisine**
neither. . . nor: **ne . . . ni . . . ni**
never: **ne . . . jamais**

new: **neuf, nouveau**
newly: **nouvellement**
newspaper: **un journal**
newsstand: **un kiosque**
next: **ensuite**
nice: **sympa**
ninety: **quatre-vingt-dix**
no: **non**
no one: **ne . . . personne**
noisy: **bruyant**
none: **ne . . . aucun, ne . . . nul**
noon: **midi**
not: **ne . . . pas**
not always: **ne . . . pas toujours**
not anymore, no more: **ne . . . plus**
not at all: **ne . . . pas du tout**
not yet: **ne . . . pas encore**
November: **novembre**
now: **maintenant**
nowhere: **ne . . . nulle part**
nurse: **un infirmier/une infirmière**
October: **octobre**
of, from, about: **de**
office: **un bureau**
often: **souvent**
oh really: **ah bon**
on: **sur**
on foot, walking: **à pied**
on purpose: **exprès**
one, we, they: **on**
one hundred: **cent**
one thousand: **mille**
only: **ne . . . que**
to open: **ouvrir**
or: **ou**
or else: **ou bien**
our: **notre (sing.)/nos (pl.)**
to our health: **à notre santé**
ours: **le nôtre (m. sing.), la nôtre (f. sing.),**
    les nôtres (pl.)
to ours: **à la nôtre**
outside: **dehors**
paint, painting: **la peinture**
to pant: **haleter**
paper: **le papier**
park: **le parc**
participant: **un participant/une participante**
party: **la fête**
to pass: **passer**
pasta: **les pâtes**

to pay: **payer**
perfect: **parfait**
perfectly: **parfaitement**
pharmacy: **une pharmacie**
piece: **un morceau**
to pinch: **pincer**
plan: **un projet**
plate: **une assiette**
to play: **jouer**
politely: **poliment**
to possess: **posséder**
postcard: **la carte postale**
to prefer: **préférer**
present (gift): **le cadeau**
present (tense): **le présent**
to present: **présenter**
pretty: **joli**
progress: **les progrès**
project: **un projet**
to project: **projeter**
to pronounce: **prononcer**
provided that: **pourvu que**
puppy: **un chiot**
to put: **mettre**
to put to sleep: **endormir**
quickly: **vite**
quite a bit: **pas mal de**
quite a few: **bien des**
to rain: **pleuvoir**
rarely: **rarement**
to react: **réagir**
ready: **prêt**
to receive: **recevoir**
recently: **récemment**
to reflect: **réfléchir**
to reject: **rejeter**
to remove: **enlever**
to renew: **renouveler**
rent: **le loyer**
to repeat: **répéter**
to replace: **remplacer**
required: **requis**
response: **une réponse**
to return [somewhere]: **retourner**
to be right: **avoir raison**
to run: **courir**
sad: **triste**
sadly: **tristement**
Saturday: **samedi**
saucer: **une soucoupe**

to say: **dire**
to scream: **crier**
to seat: **asseoir**
to see: **voir**
to sell: **vendre**
to send: **dépêcher**
to send: **envoyer**
September: **septembre**
serious: **grave**
seventy: **soixante-dix**
she, it: **elle**
shrimp: **les crevettes** (f.)
similar: **pareil**
since: **depuis**
since, as: **puisque**
sir: **monsieur**
sixty: **soixante**
to ski: **skier**
to sleep: **dormir**
slow: **lent**
slowly: **lentement**
small: **petit**
to smoke: **fumer**
so: **donc**
so that: **afin que, pour que**
soccer: **le football/le foot**
some: **du** (m.)/**de la** (f.)/**des** (pl.)/**de l'** (vowel/mute h)
sometimes: **parfois, quelquefois**
somewhere: **quelque part**
soon: **bientôt**
Spanish: **espagnol**
to spell: **épeler**
to spend (time): **passer**
spicy: **épicé**
spinach: **les épinards** (m.)
spring: **le printemps**
stage: **un étage**
to stay: **rester**
store: **un magasin**
strawberry: **la fraise**
to stretch: **étendre**
to succeed: **réussir**
sufficiently: **suffisamment**
to suggest: **suggérer**
summer: **été**
Sunday: **dimanche**
supposed to: **censé**
survivor: **un survivant/une survivante**
sweater: **un pull**
to sweep: **balayer**

to take: **prendre**
to talk, to speak: **parler**
tall: **grand**
tea: **le thé**
ten: **dix**
that: **ce** (m.)/**cette** (f.)/**cet** (m. before vowel or mute *h*)
that is: **c'est-à-dire**
the: **le** (m.)/**la** (f.)/**les** (pl.)
their: **leur** (sing. object)/**leurs** (pl. object)
theirs: **le leur** (m. sing.), **la leur** (f. sing.), **les leurs** (pl.)
then: **puis, ensuite**
there: **là**
there is/are: **il y a**
these: **ces**
they: **ils** (m.)/**elles** (f.)
thin: **mince**
to think: **penser**
to be thirsty: **avoir soif**
thirty: **trente**
this: **ce** (m.)/**cette** (f.)/**cet** (m. before vowel or mute *h*)
those: **ces**
to throw: **jeter, lancer**
Thursday: **jeudi**
today: **aujourd'hui**
together: **ensemble**
totally: **carrément**
tourist: **un/une touriste**
town: **la ville**
toy: **un jouet**
translator: **un traducteur, une traductrice**
to travel: **voyager**
to try: **essayer**
to, at, in: **à**
to/at/in the: **au** (m. sing.)/**aux** (pl.)
too much/many: **trop** (de)
toward: **vers**
truly/really: **vraiment**
Tuesday: **mardi**
Tunisian: **tunisien**
twenty: **vingt**
twisted: **tordu**
ugly: **moche**
unfortunate: **malheureux**
unhappy: **malheureux**
unless: **à moins que**
to untangle: **débrouiller**
up: **en haut**
to use: **utilise**
to use (tu): **tutoyer** (inf.)

to use (**vous**): **vouvoyer** (form.)
vacation: **les vacances** (f.)
very: **très**
to wait (for): **attendre**
waiter: **un serveur**
waitress: **une serveuse**
to wake up: **se réveiller**
to walk: **marcher**
to walk [something]: **promener**
wallet: **un portefeuille**
to want: **avoir envie de**
to want: **vouloir**
to warn: **avertir**
to watch, to look at: **regarder**
water: **eau** (f.)
we: **nous**
Wednesday: **mercredi**
to weigh: **peser**
well: **bien**
what: **quoi**
what does . . . mean?: **que veut dire . . .?**
What time is it?: **Quelle heure est-il ?**
whatever, no matter what: **quoi que**
What's the date?: **Quelle est la date ?**
when: **quand, lorsque**
where: **où**
whereas, while: **tandis que**
which: **quel** (m. sing.), **quelle** (f. sing.), **quels** (m. pl.), **quelles** (f. pl.)

which one: **lequel** (m. sing.), **laquelle** (f. sing.), **lesquels** (m. pl.), **lesquelles** (f. pl.)
while: **pendant que**
while, whereas: **alors que**
who: **qui**
why: **pourquoi**
wife: **une femme**
to win: **gagner**
window: **la fenêtre**
winter: **hiver**
with: **avec**
without: **sans**
woman: **une femme**
to work, function: **marcher**
to work: **travailler**
worse: **pire**
to be worth: **valoir**
to be wrong: **avoir tort**
yes: **oui**
yes (in response to a negation): **si**
yesterday: **hier**
you: **tu** (sing. inf.)/**vous** (pl. and/or form.)
your (**tu**): **ton** (m. object)/**ta** (f. object)/ **tes** (pl. object)
your (**vous**): **votre** (sing. object)/**vos** (pl. object)
to your health: **à ta santé**
to your health: **à votre santé**
yours: **le tien** (sing., inf.)/**le vôtre** (form. and/or pl.)
to yours: **à la tienne** (inf.)/**à la vôtre** (form.)

Appendix D

French-English Dictionary

Here's some of the vocabulary used throughout this book, arranged alphabetically by the French term, to help you when listening to or reading French.

à: *to, at, in*
à la nôtre: *to ours*
à la tienne: *to yours*
à la vôtre: *to yours*
à notre santé: *to our health*
à ta santé: *to your health*
à votre santé: *to your health*
à moins que: *unless*
un abricot: *apricot*
acheter: *to buy*
actuellement: *currently*
adjoindre: *to appoint, to attach*
afin que: *so that*
agaçant: *annoying*
agir: *to act*
ah bon: *oh really, I see*
aimer: *to like, to love*
ainsi que: *just as, so as*
aller: *to go*
alors que: *while, whereas*
amener: *to bring*
un ami/une amie: *friend*
un ananas: *pineapple*

anglais: *English*
un anniversaire: *birthday, anniversary*
annoncer: *to announce*
un anorak: *windbreaker*
août: *August*
apparaître: *to appear*
un appartement: *apartment*
appeler: *to call*
après: *after*
après que: *after, when*
après-demain: *the day after tomorrow*
un arbre: *tree*
argent (m.): *money*
arranger: *to arrange*
arriver: *to arrive*
un artichaut: *artichoke*
un ascenseur: *elevator*
des asperges (f.): *asparagus*
asseoir: *to seat (someone else)*
s'asseoir: *to sit*
assez: *enough*
une assiette: *plate*
un/une athlète: *athlete*

attendre: *to wait (for)*
au (m. sing.): *to, at, in the*
une aubergine: *eggplant*
aujourd'hui: *today*
aussitôt: *as soon as*
autant (de): *as much/many*
un auteur: *author*
automne (m.): *autumn/fall*
autour (de): *around*
autrefois: *formerly*
aux (pl.): *to/at/in the*
avancer: *to advance*
avant (que): *before*
avant-hier: *the day before yesterday*
avec: *with*
avertir: *to warn*
un avion: *plane*
un avocat/une avocate: *lawyer*
avoir: *to have*
avoir . . . ans: *to be . . . years old*
avoir besoin de: *to need*
avoir chaud: *to be hot*
avoir de la chance: *to be lucky*
avoir envie de: *to want/feel like*
avoir faim: *to be hungry*
avoir froid: *to be cold*
avoir honte: *to be ashamed*
avoir peur: *to be afraid*
avoir raison: *to be right*
avoir soif: *to be thirsty*
avoir tort: *to be wrong*
avril: *April*
balayer: *to sweep*
une banane: *banana*
un bateau: *boat*
bâtir: *to build*
beaucoup: *a lot*
une bicyclette: *bike*
bien: *well*
bien des: *quite a few*
bien que: *although*
bientôt: *soon*
une bière: *beer*
boire: *to drink*
une boisson: *drink*
bon: *good*
Bonne Année !: *Happy New Year!*
Bon anniversaire !: *Happy birthday!/Happy anniversary!*
bonne chance: *good luck*
bon courage: *good luck, keep up the good work*

bonne fête: *happy (holiday)*
bouger: *to move*
un boulanger/une boulangère: *baker*
une boulangerie: *bakery*
des brocolis (m.): *broccoli*
une brute: *boor, lout*
bruyant: *noisy*
un bureau: *office, desk*
le cadeau: *present, gift*
le café: *coffee, café*
un caissier/une caissière: *cashier*
carrément: *squarely*
la carte postale: *postcard*
au cas où: *just in case*
cassé: *broken*
ce (m.): *this, that*
célèbre: *famous*
célébrer: *to celebrate*
censé: *supposed to*
cent: *one hundred*
une cerise: *cherry*
certainement: *certainly*
ces: *these, those*
c'est: *it is, this is*
c'est-à-dire: *that is*
cet (m., in front of vowel): *this, that*
cette (f.): *this, that*
une chaise: *chair*
la chambre: *bedroom*
changer: *to change*
un charpentier: *carpenter*
un chat: *cat*
chaud: *hot (temperature)*
une chaussette: *sock*
une chaussure: *shoe*
cher: *expensive*
chercher: *to look for*
un cheval: *horse*
les cheveux (m.): *hair*
un chien: *dog*
chinois: *Chinese*
un chiot: *puppy*
le chocolat: *chocolate*
choisir: *to choose*
le ciel: *sky*
cinquante: *fifty*
un citron: *lemon*
clairement: *clearly*
un clavier: *keyboard*
une clé: *key*

combien (de): *how much/how many*
commencer: *to begin*
comment: *how*
comment dit-on . . .?: *how do you say . . .?*
compléter: *to complete*
un/une complice: *accomplice*
compter: *to count*
conduire: *to drive*
confondre: *to confuse*
une connaissance: *acquaintance*
connaître: *to know, be familiar with*
les conseils (m.): *advice*
considérer: *to consider*
continuellement: *continually*
contre: *against*
copier: *to copy*
corriger: *to correct*
couramment: *fluently*
courir: *to run*
couvrir: *to cover*
craindre: *to fear*
une crémerie: *dairy shop*
des crevettes (f.): *shrimp*
crier: *to scream*
croire: *to believe*
de: *of, from, about*
de la (f. sing.): *some*
débrouiller: *to untangle*
décembre: *December*
décider: *to decide*
déconseillé: *discouraged*
déçu: *disappointed*
dedans: *inside*
défendre: *to defend*
dehors: *outside*
déjà: *already*
demain: *tomorrow*
demander: *to ask*
déménager: *to move house*
dénoncer: *to denounce*
dépêcher: *to send, to dispatch*
dépendre: *to depend*
depuis: *since*
dernièrement: *lastly/lately*
derrière: *behind*
des (pl.): *some; from/about the*
descendre: *to descend*
en dessous (de): *below*
au-dessus (de): *above*
détester: *to hate*

devant: *in front of*
devoir: *must, to have to*
les devoirs (m.): *homework*
difficile: *difficult*
un dilemme: *dilemma*
dimanche: *Sunday*
dire: *to say*
un dirigeant/une dirigeante: *leader*
diriger: *to direct*
divorcer: *to divorce*
dix: *ten*
donc: *so*
donner: *to give*
dormir: *to sleep*
un doudou: *blankie*
doux: *mild, soft*
drôle: *funny*
du (m. sing.): *some*
du (m. sing.): *from/about the*
une dupe: *dupe, sucker*
dur: *hard*
eau (f.): *water*
une écharpe: *scarf*
les échecs (m.): *chess*
une école: *school*
écouter: *to listen (to)*
un écouteur: *earbud*
les écouteurs (m.): *headphones*
un écrivain: *writer*
effacer: *to erase*
effrayer: *to frighten*
égal: *equals*
un électricien/une électricienne: *electrician*
élever: *to bring up, raise*
elle: *she, it*
elles (f.): *they*
une émission: *TV show*
emménager: *to move (in)*
un employé/une employée: *employee*
employer: *to employ*
emprunter: *to borrow*
en: *in, to (a country)*
en avance: *early*
en bas: *down*
en haut: *up*
en retard: *late*
encore: *again*
endormir: *to put to sleep*
un/une enfant: *child*
enfin: *finally*

enlever: *to remove*
ennuyer: *to bore, to annoy*
énormément: *enormously*
ensemble: *together*
ensuite: *next*
entendre: *to hear*
un entraîneur/une entraîneuse: *coach*
entrer: *to enter*
envoyer: *to send*
épeler: *to spell*
épicé: *spicy*
une épicerie: *grocery store*
les épinards (m.): *spinach*
équitable: *fair*
espagnol: *Spanish*
espérer: *to hope*
un espoir: *hope*
essayer: *to try*
et: *and*
et . . . et: *both . . . and*
et/ou: *and/or*
établir: *to establish*
un étage: *stage, floor*
été (m.): *summer*
étendre: *to stretch*
être: *to be*
un étudiant/une étudiante: *student*
exiger: *to demand*
exprès: *on purpose*
faire: *to do, to make*
félicitations (f.): *congratulations*
féliciter: *to congratulate*
une femme: *woman, wife*
une fenêtre: *window*
la fête: *party, holiday*
fêter: *to celebrate*
le feu: *fire*
la feuille: *leaf*
feuilleter: *to leaf through*
février: *February*
une fille: *girl*
finir: *to finish*
fondre: *to melt*
le foot/le football: *soccer*
formel: *formal*
un fouillis: *mess, tangle*
frais: *fresh, cool*
une fraise: *strawberry*
français: *French*

un frère: *brother*
une frite: *fry*
le fromage: *cheese*
fumer: *to smoke*
gagner: *to win, to earn*
un gant: *glove*
un garçon: *boy*
le gâteau: *cake*
geler: *to freeze*
gentil: *kind*
gentiment: *kindly*
gérer: *to manage*
la glace: *ice cream*
un gouverneur: *governor*
grand: *tall*
grandir: *to grow*
gras: *fat, fatty*
grave: *serious*
grec: *Greek*
gros: *big, fat*
grossir: *to get big(ger), fat(ter)*
une guitare: *guitar*
habiller: *to dress*
habiter: *to live*
une habitude: *habit*
haleter: *to pant*
hanté: *haunted*
hardiment: *boldly*
le haricot: *bean*
le hasard: *luck, chance*
la hauteur: *height*
un hébergement: *lodging*
l'hébreu (m.): *Hebrew*
un hélicoptère: *helicopter*
l'hélium (m.): *helium*
l'herbe (f.): *grass*
le héros: *hero*
hésiter: *to hesitate*
heureusement: *fortunately*
heureux: *happy*
le hibou: *owl*
hier: *yesterday*
une histoire: *story*
hiver (m.): *winter*
le hockey: *hockey*
le homard: *lobster*
un homme: *man*
hoqueter: *to hiccup*
le hublot: *porthole*

une huître: *oyster*
une humeur: *mood*
ici: *here*
idéal: *ideal*
une idée: *idea*
une idole: *idol*
il: *he, it*
il y a: *there is/there are*
ils (m.): *they*
immédiatement: *immediately*
un infirmier/une infirmière: *nurse*
influencer: *to influence*
un ingénieur/une ingénieure: *engineer*
installer: *to install*
intelligemment: *intelligently*
interdit: *forbidden*
intéressant: *interesting*
introduire: *to introduce*
italien: *Italian*
un itinéraire: *itinerary*
jamais: *never, ever*
janvier: *January*
je: *I*
jeter: *to throw*
le jeu: *game*
jeudi: *Thursday*
joli: *pretty*
jouer: *to play*
un jouet: *toy*
un jour: *day*
un journal: *newspaper*
un joyau: *jewel/gem*
Joyeux anniversaire !: *Happy birthday!/Happy anniversary!*
juillet: *July*
juin: *June*
jusqu'à (ce que): *until*
un kiosque (à journaux): *newsstand*
la (f.): *the*
là: *there*
une lampe: *lamp*
lancer: *to throw*
le (m.): *the*
lent: *slow*
lentement: *slowly*
lequel: *which one*
les (pl.): *the*
la lessive: *laundry*
leur (sing.): *their*
le leur: *theirs*
leurs (pl.): *their*

lever: *to lift, raise*
le lit: *bed*
un livre: *book*
loger: *to lodge*
loin: *far*
longtemps: *for a long time*
lorsque: *when*
le loyer: *rent*
lundi: *Monday*
ma (f.): *my*
madame: *ma'am, Mrs.*
mademoiselle: *miss*
un magasin: *store*
mai: *May*
maintenant: *now*
un maire: *mayor*
mais: *but*
une maison: *house*
mal: *badly*
malheureux: *unhappy, unfortunate*
manger: *to eat*
marcher: *to walk, to work*
mardi: *Tuesday*
la mari: *marijuana*
le mari: *husband*
mars: *March*
méchamment: *meanly*
méchant: *mean*
un médecin: *doctor*
meilleurs vœux: *best wishes, happy holidays*
mener: *to lead*
mentir: *to lie*
mercredi: *Wednesday*
une mère: *mother*
mes (pl.): *my*
mettre: *to put*
les meubles (m.): *furniture*
midi: *noon*
le mien: *mine*
mieux: *better*
mignon: *cute*
mille: *one thousand*
mince: *thin*
un/une ministre: *minister*
minuit: *midnight*
un mobile: *cellphone*
un portable: *cellphone*
moche: *ugly*
modérer: *to moderate*
moins: *less, minus*

le mois: *month*
mon (m.): *my*
à mon avis: *in my opinion*
monsieur: *sir, Mr.*
monter: *to climb*
un morceau: *piece*
mourir: *to die*
la moutarde: *mustard*
un musée: *museum*
la musique: *music*
naître: *to be born*
ne . . . aucun: *none*
ne . . . jamais: *never*
ne . . . ni . . . ni: *neither . . . nor*
ne . . . nul: *none*
ne . . . nulle part: *nowhere*
ne . . . pas: *not*
ne . . . pas du tout: *not at all*
ne . . . pas encore: *not yet*
ne . . . pas toujours: *not always*
ne . . . personne: *no one*
ne . . . plus: *not anymore, no more*
ne . . . que: *only*
nettoyer: *to clean*
neuf, neuve: *new*
le nez: *nose*
non: *no*
nos (pl.): *our*
notre (sing.): *our*
la nôtre: *ours (f. sing)*
le nôtre: *ours (m. sing)*
nous: *we*
nouveau: *new*
nouvellement: *newly*
novembre: *November*
octobre: *October*
un œil: *eye*
un oignon: *onion*
un oiseau: *bird*
on: *one, we, they*
un ordinateur: *computer*
un oreiller: *pillow*
ou: *or*
où: *where*
ou bien: *or else*
ou . . . ou: *either . . . or*
oui: *yes*
ouvrir: *to open*
le pain: *bread*
le pamplemousse: *grapefruit*

le papier: *paper*
par: *by*
le parc: *park*
parce que: *because*
pareil: *similar*
paresseux: *lazy*
parfait: *perfect*
parfaitement: *perfectly*
parfois: *sometimes*
parler: *to talk, to speak*
partir: *to leave*
un participant/une participante: *participant*
partout: *everywhere*
pas mal de: *quite a bit*
passer: *to spend (time), to pass*
les pâtes (f.): *pasta*
un patron/une patronne: *boss*
payer: *to pay*
un peintre: *painter*
la peinture (f.): *paint, painting*
le pelage: *fur*
pendant que: *while*
penser: *to think*
perdre: *to lose*
un père: *father*
permis: *allowed*
une personne: *person*
peser: *to weigh*
la pétanque: *boules*
petit: *small*
un peu de: *a little bit*
une pharmacie: *pharmacy*
un pharmacien/une pharmacienne: *pharmacist*
à pied: *on foot, walking*
pincer: *to pinch*
pire: *worse*
un plat: *dish*
pleurer: *to cry*
pleuvoir: *to rain*
pliant: *folding*
un plombier: *plumber*
la plupart de: *the majority*
plus de: *more than*
un poète: *poet*
un poisson: *fish*
une poissonnière: *fish kettle*
poliment: *politely*
un pompier: *firefighter*
un portable: *laptop*
une porte: *door*

un portefeuille: *wallet*
posséder: *to possess*
pour: *for/in order to*
pour que: *so that*
pourquoi: *why*
pourvu que: *provided that*
pouvoir: *can, to be able to*
préféré: *favorite*
préférer: *to prefer*
premier: *first*
prendre: *to take*
près (de): *near*
le présent: *present (gift, tense)*
présenter: *to present*
prêt: *ready*
prétendre: *to claim*
le printemps: *spring*
le prix: *price*
un professeur: *teacher*
les progrès (m.): *progress*
un projet: *project, plan*
projeter: *to project/plan*
promener: *to walk*
prononcer: *to pronounce*
puis: *then*
puisque: *since, as*
un pull: *sweater*
quand: *when*
quarante: *forty*
quatre-vingt-dix: *ninety*
quatre-vingt(s): *eighty*
que veut dire . . .?: *what does . . . mean?*
quel: *which*
Quelle est la date ?: *What's the date?*
Quelle heure est-il ?: *What time is it?*
quelque part: *somewhere*
quelquefois: *sometimes*
qui: *who*
quoi: *what*
quoi que: *whatever, no matter what*
quoique: *even though*
rappeler: *to call back, recall*
rarement: *rarely*
réagir: *to react*
récemment: *recently*
recevoir: *to receive*
réfléchir: *to reflect*
regarder: *to watch, to look at*
rejeter: *to reject*
remplacer: *to replace*

remplir: *to fill*
rencontrer: *to meet*
rendre: *to give back, return (something)*
renouveler: *to renew*
répéter: *to repeat*
répondre: *to answer*
une réponse: *response*
requis: *required*
rester: *to stay*
retourner: *to return*
une réunion: *meeting*
se réunir: *to meet, gather*
réussir: *to succeed*
une robe: *dress*
rougir: *to blush*
s'endormir: *to fall asleep*
s'habiller: *to get dressed*
sa (f.): *his, her, its*
un sac à dos: *backpack*
samedi: *Saturday*
sans: *without*
savoir: *to know*
un sculpteur: *sculptor*
se baigner: *to bathe, swim*
se marier: *to get married*
se réveiller: *to wake up*
secret: *secret*
septembre: *September*
une série: *series*
ses (pl.): *his, her, its*
seul: *alone*
sexy: *hot (appearance)*
si: *yes (in response to a negation)*
le sien: *his, hers, its*
skier: *to ski*
une sœur: *sister*
soigneusement: *carefully*
soit . . . soit: *either . . . or*
soixante: *sixty*
soixante-dix: *seventy*
son (m.): *his, her, its*
sortir: *to go out*
une soucoupe: *saucer*
souvent: *often*
un stylo: *pen*
suffisamment: *sufficiently*
suggérer: *to suggest*
sur: *on*
un survivant/une survivante: *survivor*
sympa: *nice*

ta (f.): *your*
tandis que: *while, whereas*
tard: *late*
téléphoner à: *to call*
un témoin: *witness*
tenir: *to hold*
une tente: *tent*
tes (pl.): *your*
le thé: *tea*
le tien: *yours*
tomber: *to fall*
ton (m.): *your*
tordu: *twisted*
tôt: *early*
toujours: *always*
un/une touriste: *tourist*
un traducteur/une traductrice: *translator*
le travail: *work*
travailler: *to work*
trente: *thirty*
très: *very*
triste: *sad*
tristement: *sadly*
tromper: *to deceive*
trop (de): *too much/many*
trouver: *to find*
tu (sing. and inf.): *you*
tunisien: *Tunisian*
tutoyer: *to use tu*
un (m.): *a, an, one*
une (f.): *a, an, one*
une université: *college, university*
une valise: *suitcase*
utiliser: *to use*
les vacances (f.): *vacation*
valoir: *to be worth*

une vedette: *movie star*
le vélo: *bike*
un vendeur/une vendeuse: *seller*
vendre: *to sell*
vendredi: *Friday*
venir: *to come*
venir de: *to have just* (done)
un verre: *glass*
vers: *toward*
les vêtements (m.): *clothing*
la viande: *meat*
une victime: *victim*
vif: *lively/bright (color)*
la ville: *city, town*
le vin: *wine*
vingt: *twenty*
vite: *quickly*
vive la France: *long live France*
vivre: *to live*
un voisin/une voisine: *neighbor*
voir: *to see*
une voiture: *car*
le vol: *flight*
volontiers: *gladly*
vos (pl.): *your*
votre (sing.): *your*
la vôtre: *yours* (f. sing.)
le vôtre: *yours* (m. sing.)
vouloir: *to want*
vous (pl. and/or form.): *you*
vouvoyer: *to use vous*
voyager: *to travel*
vraiment: *truly/really*
le yaourt: *yogurt*
les yeux (m.): *eyes*

Index

About the Author

Laura K. Lawless is a French fanatic. From the day she learned her first French words (the numbers one through ten at age 10), she has been obsessed with the language of love. Her first trip to France, at 15, further convinced her that French would always be an essential part of her life. Laura has a BA in International Studies from the Monterey Institute of International Studies, and she has done graduate work in French and Spanish translation, interpretation, linguistics, and literature. She also studied French at Institut de formation internationale in Mont-St-Aignan, France, and at the Alliance française in Toulouse, France. In 1999, after a year of teaching French and Spanish to adults, Laura began teaching French online, and to this day continues to create lessons, quizzes, listening exercises, and cool tools for students and teachers around the world. Her fascination with all things language guarantees that she'll never run out of ideas for her sites (www.lawlessfrench.com and www.lawlesslanguages.com) or books. Laura has traveled to 25 countries (and counting) and lived in Morocco and Costa Rica. After scheming and dreaming for more than half her life, she and her husband moved to the south of France in 2008, then to the French-Caribbean island of Guadeloupe five years later.

Dedication

For all the French students. I know it's hard sometimes, but it's worth it all the time. **Bon courage !**

Publisher's Acknowledgments

Executive Editor: Lindsay Lefevere

Senior Managing Editor: Kristie Pyles

Project Editor: Alissa Schwipps

Copy Editor: Laura Miller

Technical Editor: Aurélie Drouard

Production Editor: Mohammed Zafar Ali

Cover Image: © zigres/Adobe Stock Photos